WITHOUT GLORY IN ARABIA

So we left without glory but without disaster
Sir Humphrey Trevelyan,
Last High Commissioner, Federation
of South Arabia,
(Middle East in Revolution,
Macmillan, 1970)

WITHOUT GLORY
IN ARABIA
The British Retreat from Aden

**Peter Hinchcliffe, John T. Ducker
and Maria Holt**

I.B. TAURIS
LONDON · NEW YORK

Published in 2006 by I.B.Tauris & Co Ltd

6 Salem Road, London W2 4BU
175 Fifth Avenue, New York NY 10010

www.ibtauris.com

In the United States of America and Canada distributed by
Palgrave Macmillan a division of St. Martin's Press
175 Fifth Avenue, New York NY 10010

International Library of Colonial History 5

ISBN 10: 1 84511 140 0
ISBN 13: 978 1 84511 140 3

A full CIP record for this book is available from the British Library
A full CIP record is available from the Library of Congress

Library of Congress Catalog Card Number: available

Typeset in Melior by Keystroke, Jacaranda Lodge, Wolverhampton
Printed and bound in Great Britain by TJ International Ltd, Padstow, Cornwall

To the people of Yemen and the British
who worked amongst them

CONTENTS

Introduction   1

PETER HINCHCLIFFE AND MARIA HOLT

*Independence without ceremony – Britain's last seven years
in Aden – the wider context – new official and private source
material – oral history methodology*

1   Historical and constitutional background   8

JOHN T. DUCKER

*British Colonial policy – Aden policy debates – the strategic
imperative – the Federation of South Arabia – Aden Colony
joins the Federation – constitutional complexities, the search
for a solution – the impact of Yemen – the impact of the 1964
Labour government – the various parties and fronts – the
Eastern Aden Protectorate remains aloof – the handling of
Aden within the British government – the impact of the
United Nations – the denouement*

CONTENTS

ILLUSTRATIONS

PHOTOGRAPHS

MAPS

ADEN

I

Late sun restores the hills' contorted form
That midday bleached of colour, depth and line.
Sharp tongues of light
Now curl about the tomb whose lime-washed dome,
Bright half ellipse amid small fields of green,
Has stood for a millennium or two
To celebrate an ancient saint or sage,
A priest-king of an unremembered age.
Once he controlled a thriving incense trade
From towered cities at the desert's edge,
Where caravans of myrrh
Were halted, measured and assessed for tolls,
Till anarchy regained its old estate
And hungry nomads scoured the tumbled stones
In hope of gold the ruins might reveal,
Or some fine agate carved into a seal.
But surely he enjoyed the evening breeze
While sitting, as did I, among good friends,
Lean, dark men sinewed like taut springs,
Quick moving, nervous, garrulous as birds,
With bubbling laughter welling up within

At all our own absurdities.
Did he not love the evening light that fills
With reds and blues and saffrons, those stark hills?

II

September, overburdened with the heat,
Makes moving of a limb an act of will.
Now patience cracks, the storms
Of blinding temper and the sand
Obliterate both landscape and the mind;
Exposure flays, the darkest recess fills
With dust and anger till pursuing rain
Restores men's reason and the land again.
But even blessings here have darker sides,
The land gives nothing but it claims its fee;
For life renewing floods
Revive vendettas that have run decades
And spill fresh blood to mingle with the old
In feuds of ownership of barren fields.
Neither your spells, old king, nor my vain threats
Could stop the killing that this land begets.
Old images persist. The snake-like files
Of hill men, armed, dark stained with indigo,
Those twisting lines of blue,
Converging from surrounding mountainsides
To hector, parley or perhaps to pledge
A doubtful loyalty to their amir:
Their chanted rhymes of tribal escapades
Crescendo with the shouts, the fusillades.
The fear, the waiting for the raids, do you
Remember that? Seeing the work of years,
A small prosperity,
Built hand on hand, dissolving in the flames?
Yet those old battles had their recompense,
Intensity, an exultation, just to be alive;
The reputation and the pride it gave.
Old king, it must be quiet in the grave.

III

Yet did we wish to change those wilder ways,
The pride that soared with kite and lammergeyer
In knife-edged days,
When young men sought to etch an honoured name
Upon recited epics of the tribe?
We tried to force on anarchy a form,
To press amorphous dust into a mould,
Half hoping that the pattern would not hold.
Though one apart, I also loved this land
With passion just as potent as your own,
Wept for dead friends, your heirs,
And was consoled by brothers of your tribe.
Now what remains? Some fading photographs,
Curled sepia memories of past beliefs,
Whose truths are tangled into fairy tales
And turn to myths as recollection fails.

James Nash

ACKNOWLEDGEMENTS

The authors gratefully acknowledge the help of so many people in the preparation of this book. The numerous individual contributors, British and Yemeni, who, some in writing and others orally, gave so generously of their time reviving memories which many may have found painful. We are particularly grateful to the family of the late Robin Young CMG, one time British Agent and Deputy High Commissioner (Federation of South Arabia) who allowed us unimpeded access to his dairies. The chapter based on them is a memorial to a great colonial civil servant whose service in the Sudan and in South Arabia was in the best traditions of Her Majesty's Overseas Civil Service in the twilight of Empire.

We would also like to thank John Shipman for his painstaking and skilled editing of some of the material, his well-informed comments on the draft and his contribution to the chapter on the Eastern Aden Protectorate. We also owe a debt of gratitude to the Council for the Advancement of Arab–British Understanding, under whose auspices the Aden oral history project began, Chris Morton for his help and enthusiasm in gathering oral history narratives in Britain, Helen Balkwill-Clark for her tireless work in transcribing the oral history interviews, Mustafa Rajamanar, British Vice Consul in Aden, for his kind assistance with the interviews in Aden, and the CAABU Trust, the MBC Heritage of Islam Trust and the British Yemeni Society for their generous donations which helped the oral history project reach fruition.

ACKNOWLEDGEMENTS

The authors gratefully acknowledge the skilled assistance, courtesy and efficiency of the staff of the National Archives at Kew and the Oriental Room of the British Library who assisted greatly in the search for material and in copying various papers. Among those other individuals who helped particularly in regard to the Eastern Aden Protectorate chapter were Sultan Ghalib bin Awadh al Qua'iti, Joanna Ellis, John Harding, Stewart Hawkins and John Weakley. We also are grateful to Michael Crouch for his encouragement to make use of recollections contained in his book *An Element of Luck*. In regard to the chapter on the international context, we are grateful for the assistance of Sir John Wilton KCMG and Mr Frank Benchley CMG. M. Antonin Besse spent a considerable time reflecting on the Aden situation as he remembered it and especially that faced by commercial enterprises in the colony.

Finally our heartfelt thanks to our spouses, who were so unfailingly encouraging and optimistically supportive over the too many years that it took this book to see the light of day.

ABBREVIATIONS AND ACRONYMS

AA	Assistant Adviser (often referred to as Political Officer)
AAR	Assistant Adviser, Residency
ADC	Aide de camp
ANM	Arab Nationalist Movement
APL	Aden Protectorate Levies (became the Federal Regular Army)
ARAMCO	Arabian American Oil Company
ASP	Arab Socialist Party
ATUC	Aden Trades Union Congress
BA & AHC	British Agent and Assistant High Commissioner (official responsible for WAP and later the Federation outside Aden Colony/State)
CD&W	Colonial Development and Welfare Scheme (the British government's funding agency for colonial development)
CIGS	Chief of the Imperial General Staff
CONFISA	Command National Forces in South Arabia
DFID	Department for International Development
DG	Desert Guards
DO	District Officer
DOP	Defence and Overseas Policy Committee (of the British Cabinet)
DOP(O)	Defence and Overseas Policy (official) Committee (officials only)

EAP	Eastern Aden Protectorate
EIS	Egyptian Intelligence Service
EOKA	Ethniki Organosis Kyprion Agoniston (Greek Cypriot nationalist organisation)
ExCo	Executive Council (in Aden)
Feds	Federalists
FG	Federal Guard
FG 2	Federal Guard 2
FIO	Field (later Federal) Intelligence Officer
FLOSY	Front for the Liberation of Occupied South Yemen
FNG	Federal National Guard (alternative title to Federal Guard)
FNG 2	Federal National Guard 2 (Federal Guard 2 also used)
FOPC	Federal Operations Planning Committee
FPS	Famine Prevention Scheme (in the Eastern Protectorate)
FRA	Federal Regular Army (became the South Arabian Army)
FSF	Famine Services Fund (in the Eastern Protectorate)
GG	Government Guard
HBL	Hadhrami Bedouin Legion
HMG	Her Majesty's Government
HMOCS	Her Majesty's Overseas Civil Service (successor to Colonial Service)
HPS	Hadhramaut Pump Scheme
JAA	Junior Assistant Adviser
JIC	Joint Intelligence Committee
KAC	Kathiri Armed Constabulary
KOSB	King's Own Scottish Borderers
LegCo	Legislative Council (in Aden)
MECOM	Middle East Command (HQ British Forces in Aden)
MMG	Mission to Mediterranean Garrisons
MRA	Mukalla Regular Army
MTC	Mahra Tribal Council
NLF	National Liberation Front
ODA	Overseas Development Administration
OLOS	Organisation for the Liberation of the Occupied South
PCC	People's Constitutional Congress

PDRY	People's Democratic Republic of Yemen
PDU	Popular Democratic Union
PORF	Popular Organisation of Revolutionary Forces
PS	Permanent Secretary
PSP	People's Socialist Party
PWO	Prince of Wales' Own Regiment
QAC	Quaiti Armed Constabulary
RA	Resident Advisor (Mukalla responsible for EAP)
RABA	Resident Adviser and British Agent
RAOC	Royal Army Ordnance Corps
SAA	South Arabian Army
SA(E)	Senior Adviser (East) (Senior Political Officer responsible for half the Federation/WAP)
SA(W)	Senior Adviser (West) (Senior Political Officer responsible for the other half)
SAL	Southern Arabian League
SIS	Secret Intelligence Service (also referred to as MI6)
SPS	Sudan Political Service
UNF	United National Front
UNP	United National Party
WAP	Western Aden Protectorate
WRAC	Women's Royal Army Corps
YAR	Yemen Arab Republic

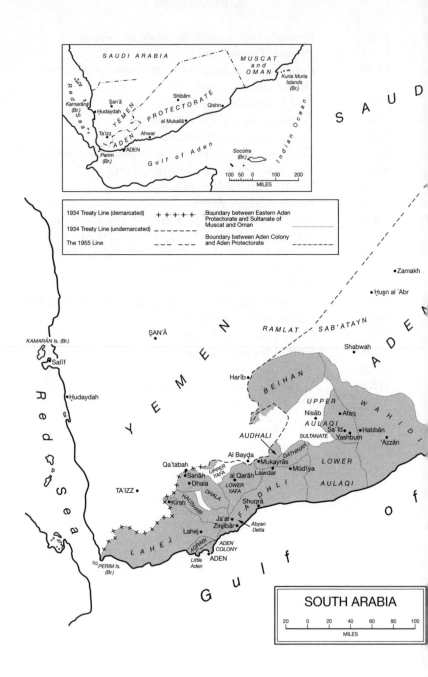

Map 1 Aden

INTRODUCTION

SETTING THE SCENE: PETER HINCHCLIFFE

Our period of occupation did the country little permanent good, for all the selfless work of many devoted Englishmen and so many good intentions. Whatever the rights and wrongs of the way we left, whatever was to come after us, the time for us to be there was over. And if we were to go, it was better not to linger on.

(Sir Humphrey Trevelyan.
Last words in *The Middle East in Revolution*)

On 29 November 1967 nearly 130 years of British rule over Aden came to an abrupt and inglorious conclusion. Not since the scuttle from Mandate in Palestine in 1948 had a British attempt at measured and deliberate decolonisation ended so abjectly and so unceremoniously. Unique in the post-Second World War British experience of shedding an Empire there was no designated successor regime to receive the symbols of independent statehood. There was no indigenous prime minister or president-in-waiting to haul up the newly designed national flag; no royal personage in attendance to mark Britain's relinquishment of responsibility and to welcome the latest member of the Commonwealth of nations. There was no exchange of national anthems nor any other, however minimal, reciprocal formalities. Just a bleak pause was all that occurred in the dying moments of a large operation of military withdrawal, allowing the outgoing High Commissioner to salute the Union Flag as it made its last descent at a heavily guarded Royal Air Force airfield. A moment marked by the band of the Royal Marines not with the National Anthem nor even 'Land of Hope and Glory' but, appropriately enough, 'Things ain't what they used to be'; a tune from a contemporary musical. Then Sir Humphrey Trevelyan, the last in a long line of Colonial potentates, accompanied by the rump of his staff, boarded a helicopter to fly to the flagship of one of the largest Royal Naval taskforces assembled since the Suez operation of 1956. The evacuation of Aden was complete. In Sir Humphrey's words in *The Middle East in Revolution:* 'We left without glory but without disaster'.

The purpose of this book is to look at the final stages of British rule in the last of its colonies in the Middle East and North Africa. (Bahrain and the other 'Trucial States' of the Gulf not fully independent until 1971 were protectorates in a treaty relationship with Britain and never colonial possessions. Oman had a special quasi-colonial relationship.) The period 1960 to 1967 has been chosen for our focus for a number of reasons. First it more or less coincides with the period of service in the former colony and protectorate by two of the three co-authors. Second the bulk of material recorded as part of an oral history archive by the other co-author falls within these seven years. Nevertheless for the sake of background we have looked at the significance of some of the events in the 1950s as well. Nearly 40 years has elapsed since the ill-fated Federation of South Arabia metamorphosed into the People's Democratic Republic of the Yemen (PDRY) but there are still many 'survivors' of this period, British and Yemeni, whose memories have enriched our researches. Sadly, many other key players are no longer with us, but some of them have contributed to this study through their memoirs, diaries and other documents.

One of the most striking primary sources for this period are the voluminous diaries kept by the late Robin Young CMG. He was a political officer in the Western Aden Protectorate (WAP) in the late 1950s, then a senior staff member of the British Agency – the office responsible for UK's interests in WAP – and ending up as British Agent and Deputy High Commissioner (Federation), making him the most important official of the Aden administration outside Aden Colony. Every evening he would try to find the time to retreat to his study and type out one or two A4 pages recording exactly what he had learned and done that day. The diary provides

vivid, highly detailed and accurate insights on what was h
ing at a day-to-day working level on the ground in the Prote
and also within the higher echelons of government, both in the
Colony in Aden and within the new Federal capital at Al
Ittihad. It is also a fascinating insight into the mind of a
senior colonial official who, disillusioned and dismayed with Her
Majesty's Government (HMG)'s policy after the arrival of a
Labour government in 1964, actively, at times, worked against
the implementation of a policy which he strongly believed was
detrimental to British interests in the Middle East and a betrayal
of Britain's friends in South Arabia. We are very grateful to Robin's
family for letting us make use of this unique resource; particularly
so, as is described in Chapter 5, he and I were instrumental in
destroying a large amount of official papers rescued from our office
at Al Ittihad, to stop them falling into the hands of the National
Liberation Front.

Quite apart from the quantity, quality and variety of our
documentary archive (including transcribed oral contributions, of
which more below) is the fascinating story of the last six or seven
years of British rule in Aden – 'rule' itself became progressively
misleading as an accurate description of the deteriorating situation
in both the hinterland and colony. At the start of 1960, and indeed
up to as late as the end of 1963, there seemed to be a reasonable
prospect of Britain achieving a respectable solution to the dilemma
of how to decolonise in South Arabia. There was then no apparent
lessening in the British commitment to maintaining a major
base in Aden. In 1962, the then Conservative government headed
by Harold Macmillan, in its Defence White Paper, justified the long-
term retention of our base there as part of the concept of strategic
mobility East of Suez, this despite the loss of many of our Imperial
responsibilities in the East; most notably India. Macmillan's
famous 'Wind of Change' seemed to be excluded from the Middle
East as the British beat an orderly retreat from empire elsewhere.

With the benefit of hindsight the odds of a peaceful transfer of
power to a future friendly successor regime were not entirely
propitious. Following the Suez fiasco, and especially the evidence
of Anglo-French collusion with Israel, Britain faced an uphill
struggle to regain any credibility, never mind influence, in the
wider Arab world. The year 1958 saw the overthrow of the once
British client regime of Hashemite Iraq. But for British intervention

King Hussein of Jordan might well have gone the same way. His position was to be under threat from internal and external threats for many years. The cold war involved increasing Soviet influence with 'progressive' regimes such as Syria and a newly stridently anti-western Iraq. Egypt, however, was the main problem for the UK as well as the protection of British interests in the Middle East. By 1960 President Nasser was at the apogee of his power and influence. Arab Nationalism and Nasserism were the two sides of the same coin. Nasser was determined to rid the Middle East of a colonial and/or neo-colonial presence on Arab soil and to strengthen his position as the voice of Arabism and the Arab super power and the most influential leader of the non-aligned group of nations in the region. His main enemy was Israel but he worked hard against both British and French influences. Accordingly the British in Aden and especially the military base was a primary target; his intervention in the Yemen and his subsequent virtual occupation of that country was as much aimed at getting the British out of South Arabia as maintaining a shaky republican regime in Sana'a. Arab nationalism, stridently articulated by Gamal Abdul Nasser and carried into every household in the Arab world via the new and ubiquitous transistor radio was a heady and inspirational message which few escaped and which few did not wholeheartedly embrace. The counter message, the presentation of British virtues and the explanation of its policies went largely unheard with the poor reception enjoyed by the BBC World Service – and where it did get through it was largely discounted as the last dying croaks of a once major and now discredited Imperial power. From the outset the general pan-Arab view, in the 'street' at least, was that the Federation was a neo-colonial device to maintain a British base protected by a client reactionary state and doomed to fail in the teeth of popular resistance.

The Yemen was Nasser's Vietnam. The campaign there and the humiliations of the 1967 war exposed the hollowness of his military machine, but by then the damage had been done and the Federation had lost the battle for survival in the aftermath of the British decision to cut its losses in most of the Arab world and regroup in the Gulf.

All this, however, was not foreseen with the adoption of a policy of 'strategic mobility' based in Aden and involving a primarily amphibious but land-based joint service task force. Three functions were envisaged: a staging post, an acclimatisation and storage point half way to the Far East (where Singapore was the principal base); as a toe-hold from which to keep an eye on our increasing oil interests, especially in the Arabian Gulf; and as a springboard from which to fulfill pledges to Arab rulers and other allies. Troops from Aden had played a major part in confronting a perceived Iraqi threat against Kuwait in 1961, a precursor of later conflicts. Earlier they had been part of a force which took on insurgents in Oman. As late as 1964 a Commando force flown in from Aden put down military mutinies in newly independent Tanganyika (about to become Tanzania), Kenya and Uganda at the somewhat embarrassed request of Presidents Nyerere, Kenyatta and Obote who had thought that they had said a final good bye to their former colonial master. In short, Aden was seen as an essential component in the maintenance of a British global strategy.

Aden as an old-style Imperial base, like its counterpart in Singapore, should also be seen as an aspect of Anglo/American strategy for the containment of communism in the cold war confrontation with the Soviet Union. The 'special' relationship between Britain and the United States was regarded as one of the keystones of British post-Second World War policy. It had recovered from the fierce disagreements on Suez. Although American global influence had increased mainly at British expense, especially in the Middle East since Suez, Washington appreciated an alliance with a power with remaining worldwide responsibilities as a cold war partner. The Gulf, Anglophone Africa and many parts of the East were still accepted as primarily a British sphere of influence. Our bases at Aden and Singapore were recognised as key elements in pursuing this partnership. The 'special' relationship was less one-sided in those days than today.

It is against this background that Chapters 1 and 7 by John Ducker should be read, chronicling as they do, the internal and external factors and developments which brought the British-created Federation of South Arabia into being and eventually to its knees. His chapter 4 is the story of the very different (from the rest of British 'protected' Arabia) Eastern Aden Protectorate (EAP) where he spent most of his seven years. Though one of its component sultanates entered the Federation, the most important elements of the EAP, the Sultanates of Quaiti and Kathiri, kept aloof from their troubled neighbours to the west, however in the end they succumbed to the same forces which brought the Federation down.

A number of British and Yemenis, who were John's and my contemporaries during this period, contribute much to the rest of this book. The majority are British voices: service people, civil servants serving either in the Colony – later Aden State – or in the Protectorates, or civilians working, almost exclusively, in Aden itself. Some of my former colleagues, all officials, have, sadly declined to be involved. They feel strongly that Britain's abrupt abandonment of the Federation which it created, was a shameful retreat from solemn undertakings made to its friends who had isolated themselves in hostile waters to serve our interests and then been unceremoniously dumped. One of them would like this book to be called the 'Great Betrayal'. He and others do not want to revisit painful memories. I can only respect their silence.

The Yemenis come from a variety of walks of life, some of them were strong opponents of the former colonial power, others have a nostalgic view of British times, comparing us favourably with the successor indigenous regimes some of which behaved with great brutality to many of their own people. Whatever their back-ground, however, they are part of a living history of that time – some with walk-on parts, others who influenced events and all with something interesting to say. We thank them for their help to Maria Holt – without it this book would have lacked an important dimension. I should mention at this point that some of Maria's material gathered as a result of the project she describes has found its way into Chapter 6 on the military and is identified as such in the end notes. Maria now takes up her introduction to her part of the oral history component of our book.

INTRODUCING THE ADEN ORAL HISTORY PROJECT:
MARIA HOLT

Following a brief visit to Aden in 1996, I became intrigued by the ghost of British colonialism; although Britain had left southern Arabia almost 30 years earlier, its presence still hovered in the air. Unlike Peter Hinchcliffe and John Ducker I had no personal experience of living and working in the region at that time and had no contemporaries or former colleagues to call on for recollections from that period. I started to wonder what life must have been like during the British colonial period in that area. As I had already met a number of people, both in Britain and in Yemen, who remembered British rule, it occurred to me that the period and its eyewitnesses could become the subjects of an oral history project. The idea was to glean the recollections of as wide a range of people as possible, both those who were deemed 'important' at the time and the many others whose names are not remembered by history, on both the Yemeni and the British sides. The 'Aden oral history project', which began in earnest at the end of 1999, grew out of a fascination with Aden and its history and was able to reach fruition thanks to the efforts of a disparate array of narrators to bring alive – through their memories and their words – a largely forgotten period of British history.

At first, the process of conducting oral history research seems deceptively simple. There are, however, difficulties and techniques, especially for the researcher who herself comes to the subject with no relevant personal background and unlike the other authors has no contemporary 'memory benchmark' for the investigations. It is not just a question of sitting someone down, turning on the microphone and inviting him or her to talk about the past. The reality is more complex. Rather than go through the complexities in this introduction I have outlined my methodology in Appendix 4. I also give some additional pointers as to how I went about my task during a very short but intensive visit to Yemen in late 2004, in introducing my chapters on the civilians in Aden and the revolution in Aden viewed primarily from a contemporary Yemeni viewpoint.

My lasting impression, especially from my time in Yemen and talking to Arabs in this country, is the extraordinary amount of interest in the project. Very many individuals from all walks of life, and I include many British civilians, seemed to welcome the opportunity to put into words their deeply felt but perhaps not adequately articulated feelings about British rule and the abrupt decision of Britain to pull out of Aden in 1967. For more about the Aden oral history project, please see Appendix 4.

CHAPTER ONE

HISTORICAL AND CONSTITUTIONAL BACKGROUND

John T. Ducker

To make some sense of the passion and violence, which engulfed Aden in the mid-1960s, some knowledge of the evolution of events in the preceding decade is essential. In the 1940s, the British government adopted the objective of bringing all its dependencies to independence and in every British colony and protectorate the authorities were engaged in a process of constitutional reform, political, social and economic development and the strengthening of government, with independence as the ultimate aim. There were no timetables and the forms of government evolving had many differences, but they were all based on the premise that there would be a degree of consent and that the state involved would have to be viable, implying both reasonably competent government and economic viability at an attainable level. In many places this was by no means easy or assured. Consent implied electoral systems, with an agreed franchise, then almost totally absent, and normally implied the transfer of power from traditional rulers or authorities to elected ones, which was bound to be disputatious. Competent government implied a level and depth of education, which was not present in most colonies, despite considerable advances. Economic viability gave rise to questions and answers, which differed from territory to territory according to the resources of each. Some economies were primitive, including, it has to be said, much of the Aden Protectorate.

Aden comprised the Crown Colony of Aden, with British forms of government and the Protectorate, with some 25 small states run

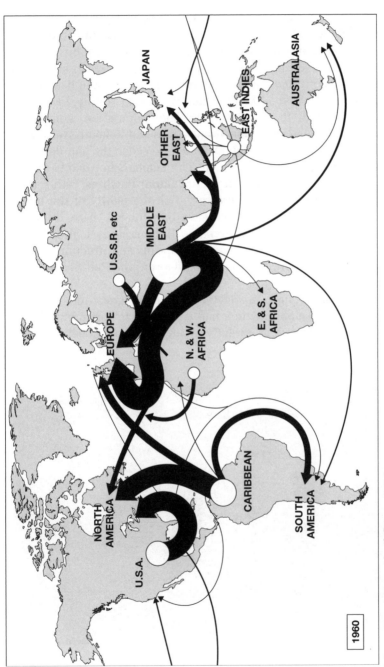

Map 2 International oil flows, 1960

on traditional lines by sultans or sheikhs in treaty relationship with Britain. Aden Colony was fully integrated into the international economy, the port being the second or third busiest port in the world, selling bunker oil and other supplies to ships and handling a considerable entrepôt trade. In 1955, Aden itself had a population of about 140,000, which was rising rapidly; by 1960 it was estimated to be 220,000. The population comprised principally Adeni and Protectorate Arabs and Yemeni Arabs, who numbered an estimated 90,000, which exceeded the population of Sana'a, the capital city of Yemen. The Yemenis in Aden belonged predominantly to the Shafai sect of Sunni muslims, rather than the Zaidi branch of the Shia, to which the family of the Imam of Yemen and many of the Yemenis belonged. Also living in cosmopolitan Aden were Somalis, Indians and smaller populations of Northern Arabs, Jews, Europeans and itinerant traders and sailors from around the Indian Ocean, the Red Sea and the Persian Gulf.

Aden colony had an elected municipal government and a Legislative Assembly, which had an elected majority from 1958. The native Adenis had a relatively high level of education and a

Figure 1.1 Shipping: the raison d'être for Aden Colony.

Figure 1.2 The BP refinery: Little Aden.

number of them held high-level positions in government, the police, business and the law. However, an increasing proportion of those living in Aden had not been born there or even in the Protectorate; many of them were illiterate Yemenis and Somalis, and the question already presented itself as to what part, if any, they should be permitted to play in the body politic. This was to become an acute problem in relation to the electoral franchise and democratic institutions. Nevertheless, in 1960 there was no reason to be pessimistic; there was a quite reasonable prospect that within a few years, the Colony, with its busy harbour and oil refinery, could be self-governing like Singapore, even if sovereignty remained with Britain. The urban and mercantile society of Aden was, however, far removed in nature from the society of the highly tribalised states in the Protectorate.

The Protectorate states extended from the Quaiti state in the east with a population of about 230,000 to minor sheikhdoms with only a handful of inhabitants. The total population of the protected states was about 700,000. The status of the rulers had been enhanced by British recognition and subsidies, but in some cases they were little more than a prominent family. Until the late 1930s, Britain had left the states to their own devices, and political, social and economic development was minimal. From 1937 onwards, however, most of them had entered into a new relationship with Britain, whereby Britain provided advice on all matters of public policy, except religion and the Sharia courts, and began to provide technical and financial assistance. By 1960, many of the rulers had an advisory council with a nominated membership, but at least half of the states were ruled more or less autocratically by the sheikh or sultan. By themselves, none of these states were 'viable' in any accepted meaning of the word. Their domestic economies were simple and always exposed to drought. In most of the Protectorate, tribesmen carried personal weapons, typically the Lee-Enfield rifle and a 'jambiya', a form of dagger. The town-dwellers distrusted the tribesmen, who had made a practice over the years of holding transit trade to ransom and were inclined to settle disputes violently.

In the Eastern Aden Protectorate (EAP), the far-sighted Sultan Saleh al Quaiti and a public-spirited Hadhrami, Sayyid Bubakr bin Sheikh al Kaf, supported by the British resident, Harold Ingrams, had in the 1930s negotiated a truce between the tribes which dramatically improved security and made possible substantial improvements in government and the economy. Tribesmen were forbidden to take their weapons into the settled areas and towns. The Quaiti state had six governors (Naib) responsible for maintaining law and order and implementing government policies, together with lower-level administrative units run by a Qaim. Mukalla had a municipal council. The Quaiti state levied import duties which provided it with a degree of financial independence. Remittances from Indonesia and the Far East declined drastically during the Second World War, but by the 1960s remittances from Saudi Arabia and the Gulf states were substantial and rising. By the early 1960s, they were estimated to be about £3 million per annum. The Kathiri state was much smaller and compact, and the sultan effectively ran the state with the state council and two governors. Thus these states were on the whole orderly and peaceful. Britain provided some financial and technical assistance, but otherwise did not intervene very actively.

The western frontier of the EAP was defined internally by more-or-less recognised state boundaries and externally by an agreement concluded in 1914 between Britain and the Ottoman Empire – the so-called Violet Line, which extended North Eastward at an angle of 45 degrees from near Harib. However, Yemen and Saudi Arabia never formally recognised this Line. The northern frontier of the EAP was also never agreed with Saudi Arabia, though in 1955 HMG announced that it planned to observe the 'modified Riyadh line' which more or less coincided with the southern edge of the Rub al Khali, the sand sea of southern Arabia. The eastern frontier of the EAP with Oman was un-demarcated but in practice was defined by a line drawn north from Ras Darbat Ali to 19 deg N 52 deg E.

The Mahra state was in large measure un-administered. The titular and reclusive ruler, Sultan Isa, lived on the island of Socotra off the coast of Africa; most of the Mahra lived on the mainland, where they occupied a considerable area of land between the Quaiti state and Oman. They recognised the Sultan's suzerainty, provided he did not attempt to interfere in their affairs. Not until late 1963, when a modest British presence was established on mainland Mahra territory, did the area see the creation of a tribal council as the beginning of a formal administration, making it possible for an oil concession negotiated with an American oil company to be acted upon.

The Western Aden Protectorate (WAP), comprising some 20 small states, was sandwiched between the Yemen and the sea, with Aden Colony the major city on the coast. Although Britain and the Ottoman authorities had in 1904 negotiated and demarcated a frontier separating the Ottoman provinces of Yemen from most of the states of the Aden Protectorate, the Imam of Yemen who succeeded to the Ottoman control in 1918 effectively repudiated the border agreement and there was always a state of tension along the boundary. Disgruntled tribesmen in the WAP would always get a hearing in the Yemen, which would also be happy to foster dissent within the WAP states; people out of favour with the Imam would often flee to the WAP and Aden. The WAP states were generally smaller in both size and population and there was nothing comparable to the law and order which prevailed in the EAP, except in the Abyan delta where a major irrigation scheme had been developed and in the part of Lahej state which lay immediately north of Aden.

Thus the problem faced by Britain, Aden Colony and these small states was how to achieve consensus on future constitutional evolution and what form of state and government would be 'viable' – who would be the 'residuary legatee' at independence? Given the differences in the respect for law and order, the level of education, the administrative experience and system of government between Aden on the one hand and the undeveloped protectorate states where tribal loyalties remained strong, this was always going to be a difficult task. The merger of Aden and the WAP states has often been compared with merging the eighteenth-century Scottish Highlands with a twentieth-century Glasgow. Some observers thought the very idea was ludicrous.[1]

Though thought had been given to merging the states of the protectorate as early as the late 1920s, the first officials to think seriously about this in the early 1950s were Kennedy Trevaskis, then British Agent in the Western Protectorate and Sir Tom Hickinbotham, then Governor of Aden. The young Sultan Ali Abdul Karim of Lahej was also making proposals in the context of his interest in the South Arabian League (SAL), which was an early proponent of independence for South Arabia as a single state. Trevaskis was concerned about the viability of the states for which he was responsible in the face of claims to their territory on the part of Yemen, which the Imam continued to make; and he was concerned about the relations of the very traditional small states with the urban and modernising Colony of Aden. Hickinbotham was concerned about the viability of the entire territory; the sharply different degrees of economic development and quality of government; and the implications of improving levels of education. He was also very aware of the rising tide of Arab nationalism, especially following the overthrow of the Egyptian monarchy by Colonel Gamal Abdul Nasser in 1952.

Sultan Ali and his friends among the Jifri Sayyids, who supported the SAL, were well ahead of thinking in the other WAP states, as well as Aden, on questions regarding the future of the WAP and Aden. Indeed, the SAL policy of the 1950s was essentially adopted by HMG in 1964 when the proposal for a unitary state was put forward (see page 31). That the British authorities were unable to keep Sultan Ali and the SAL engaged in the political process and in fact withdrew recognition of the Sultan was a major political failure, with long-term consequences. As Trevaskis put it, 'having lost faith in our intentions, the League turned for help to the Yemen'.[2] They also sought help from Egypt. It is not possible to avoid the conclusion that there was a lack of imagination on the part of the Aden and British governments in their dealings with the political parties generally. It was already quite evident in the 1950s that such parties would play an increasing role in the future government of the country, would be attracted to the emerging Arab nationalism and that the traditional rulers would have increasingly to cede authority in favour of a constitutional construct with greater long-run legitimacy. The survival of traditional rulers in Saudi Arabia and the Gulf since the 1960s does not invalidate that conclusion – the circumstance of unheard-of oil wealth completely changed their situation.

The first official plan for constitutional advance evolved from exchanges between Trevaskis/Hickinbotham and the Colonial Office in the mid-1950s, and entailed a federation of the 21 states in the WAP and a federation of the four states in the EAP as a step towards a federation of the entire Protectorate. The initial response from the rulers was favourable. However, the scheme did not get off the ground. The proposed federation implied considerable loss of autonomy by the rulers in favour of the federal institutions, for which some of them were not ready. In the EAP, there was difficulty in balancing the separate interests of the smaller states with the much larger Quaiti state. In the WAP, some rulers also feared it might be a subterfuge to detach the Protectorate from Aden, which was not to be included at that stage. Some wondered if Britain would stand by them if they took a step they knew would incur the wrath of the Yemen and Cairo Radio. The Imam of Yemen attacked the scheme, perhaps because he feared that it might extinguish forever his claims to territory in the WAP. Egypt opposed the scheme because of its British sponsorship. It is important to note that at that time, no one considered early entry of Aden Colony into the proposed Federation.

The Cabinet's Colonial Policy Committee in London addressed the future of Aden in March 1956. The outcome was a policy with five elements:[3]

- the Colony of Aden could progressively attain a high degree of internal self-government though not, in the foreseeable future, self-determination on account of Aden's strategic military importance;

- any policy which might lead to the absorption of the protected states by Yemen or Saudi Arabia must be absolutely rejected;
- Her Majesty's Government (HMG) had a strong obligation to continue to develop the protected states;
- the future independence of those states would very likely need some form of closer association;
- the Governor should continue discussions with the rulers about such forms of closer association, which should also address the question of management of any future oil revenues.

Lord Lloyd, then Under Secretary of State for the Colonies, visited Aden in May 1956 to see how these policies might be implemented. His report[4] following the visit is a balanced assessment of the situation at that time. He felt that immediate British initiatives towards federation should be dropped and that proposals for federation should be allowed to emerge from the rulers and politicians themselves. He also reported to Parliament and an excellent and well-informed debate took place in the House of Lords on 13 June 1956.[5] The debate focused, among other things, on Lloyd's statement made to the Aden Legislative Assembly on 19 May 1956 in which he said 'I would like you to understand that for the foreseeable future it would not be reasonable or sensible or, indeed, in the interests of the Colony's inhabitants, for them to aspire to any aim beyond that of a considerable degree of self-government', a statement derided by the Economist at the time as 'governessy'. The debate also criticised him for not giving greater scope in the political process to the Aden political parties – the Aden Association, the South Arabian League (SAL) and the United National Front (UNF), thus providing inadequate local outlets for differing opinions in the political debate. However, Lloyd did make it clear in his report that it was not possible to consider the future of Aden and the Protectorate separately, and HMG should actively prepare for the day when some form of amalgamation became necessary.

In 1954, Britain vacated the military base at Suez and in July 1956 Egypt nationalised the Suez Canal. This led to the Franco-British invasion of the Suez Canal Zone, in an attempt to keep the canal under international control, collusion with Israel, US equivocation and a Russian threat to intervene with ballistic missiles. These events and the subsequent withdrawal of the invasion force from Suez completely changed the political situation in the Middle East, and gave a major stimulus to Arab nationalist sentiment.

These events also precipitated the appointment of a new British Prime Minister, Harold Macmillan. One of his early initiatives was to ask for a review of the status and future of the colonial empire. This 'Balance Sheet of Empire' was both to provide a forward perspective on the likely future constitutional and political development of the colonies and assess the economic impact on Britain of the colonial empire. The report on constitutional development is dated May 1957; that on economic and financial considerations July 1957.[6] 'In summary, the review concluded in respect of Aden:

(i) Taking strategic, diplomatic and economic considerations together, Her Majesty's Government has a strong interest in retaining control of the Colony of Aden, which could by progressive stages attain a high degree of internal self-government, but Her Majesty's Government cannot in the foreseeable future consider the grant of self-determination.

(ii) From the point of view of Her Majesty's Government's interests, the Protected States have mainly to be considered in relation to the protection which they afford to the Colony; in this sense, the only policies which must be absolutely rejected are any which would be likely to lead to the absorption of these States by the Yemen and Saudi Arabia.

(iii) Her Majesty's Government has, however, because of its treaties, and for general historical reasons, strong obligations towards these Protected States, which equally lead to the impossibility of allowing them to be absorbed by the Yemen or Saudi Arabia, and make it the duty of Her Majesty's Government to continue to develop them economically and socially so that they may eventually be able to maintain their independence vis-à-vis the Yemen and Saudi Arabia without outside support.

This review was neither published nor made available to Parliament, though it was discussed at the official level, and in general terms at the political level, with both France and the

United States, with whom the Prime Minister was keen to have an understanding about the approach being taken to de-colonisation. It should also be noted that at that time (1957) Saudi Arabia was staking claims to territory in the Aden Protectorate and Muscat/Oman, was weakly governed and had not yet emerged as the stabilising factor in the Arab world which Emir Faisal made it in the 1960s and beyond.

Aden was bound to be strongly affected by the Suez events. Sir Tom Hickinbotham left Aden in mid-1956, just before Suez; his successor, Sir William Luce, arrived just after Suez. Luce had to re-appraise the situation and prospects for Aden in the light of the new political situation in the Middle East at large. He took his time. He sent some initial impressions at variance with Lord Lloyd's conclusions soon after his arrival in Aden. HMG approved an increase in the elected component of the Colony's Legislative Council and the addition of five elected members of LegCo to the membership of the Aden Executive Council. Luce also initiated in 1957 a Public Service Commission and a strong Adenisation programme under a respected ex-Sudan official, Sir Arthur Charles. But it was not until 1958 that his views about the future of the territory crystallised. This timing was certainly influenced by the creation in January 1958 of the United Arab States/Republic between Egypt, Syria and Yemen, which served to extend Nasserist influence into the Arabian Peninsula. The other important event for Aden in 1958 was the decision by the British government to move the HQ of Middle East Command (MECom) from Cyprus to Aden. This meant the rapid growth of British forces based in Aden until they numbered in excess of 15,000, with all the supplies and services required to sustain them. Most of these were a strategic reserve to be deployed around the Indian Ocean as required, not for use in Aden.

In March 1958, Luce wrote to the Colonial Secretary Alan Lennox-Boyd and sent three letters in two days to Gorell Barnes, then Assistant Under Secretary of State for the Colonies.[7] Gorell Barnes passed his three 'rather shattering letters' on to Lennox-Boyd. The first of these letters was an assessment of the British position in Aden and the Arab world generally. Egypt and Russia had common interests in South West Arabia which they pursued through support for the ambitions of the Zaidi Imams of Yemen. Luce concluded that Britain should eliminate its last positions in

Figure 1.3 A Royal Navy aircraft carrier in Aden harbour: strategic flexibility.

the Middle East, attempt to align itself with Arab nationalism and thus provide the basis for a longer-term favourable relationship with Arab countries. The second letter considered the policy options available to achieve these objectives in the context of Aden. The first option was to hang on to Aden Colony indefinitely, a policy which he described as 'utterly bankrupt'. The second was early withdrawal, which he concluded would be unthinkable, implying a breach of faith and ingratitude to those who had assisted Britain over many years. The third option was 'a gradual disengagement from our position in South-West Arabia, with the objective of strengthening our friends in both the Colony and the Protectorates ... and creating a new relationship more in keeping with modern trends and the realities of the situation'. He envisaged about a decade to accomplish this disengagement. The third letter described the rationale newly advanced by some of the rulers of states in the Western Aden Protectorate for a proposed federation: 'the fundamental weakness of their and the Government's position in resisting Yemen was that it stood on nothing more substantial than the preservation of a British protectorate, which in the context of the Middle East today was something of an anachronism'. Under the influence, so Trevaskis asserted, of their sons who had seen more of the world and were better educated, some of the rulers were also attracted to the SAL concept of 'South Arabia' as the future for their mini-states. Luce was careful to point out to HMG that the implication of the policy he advocated was that Britain would have to enter into new treaty relations with the proposed federation; that the latter would have to be given teeth; and that HMG would have to support it financially. He did not emphasise the fragility of relations between the modernising Nasser and the reactionary Zaidi Imamate, which Nasser would later subvert.

In response to queries on his recommendations from London, Luce visualised[8] a three-phase programme of change:

- a simple association of Colony and Protectorate on practical matters of government – communications, customs, health, water supply, etc.;
- a firm constitutional arrangement for merger, the whole (including the Colony of Aden) to have protected status in treaty relationship with Britain, with provision for continuance of the military base;
- independence of the new state, which he now visualised, would occur in less than the ten years he had previously envisaged.

He went on to say that he considered that an attempt to hold the military base by force would negate its value; that to choose this option would very soon create the need for force; and that 'basic to his proposals was his belief that by then HMG are likely to consider that their remaining interests in the Middle East can be better preserved by coming to terms with Arab governments than by the use of military power'.

In December 1958, when Luce's proposals were still under consideration in London, and prior to the creation of the Feder-ation, the Colonial Secretary, Lennox-Boyd, wrote to Luce[9] saying 'I must tell you that this subject is causing me and my colleagues much perplexity', and telling him that the Chiefs of Staff, who considered the Aden military facilities to be vital strategically, were considering if there were any alternatives. In February 1959, Lennox-Boyd visited Aden. He met members of the legislative and executive councils, leaders of the political parties, most of the protectorate rulers and some of their councils. He found strong support for the federation in Aden and much of the WAP, a more equivocal position in the EAP, which stemmed partly from hopes of oil being discovered. He met with the Governor's senior officials who all supported the proposals Luce had put to London. He also heard from the Air Officer Commanding, the senior service officer in Aden, that in view of HMG's experience in Cyprus and elsewhere, he agreed entirely with Luce's proposals, despite opposition in the Chiefs of Staff Committee in London. 'The only way to have a military base was for it to have local political acceptability'.[10]

The Colonial Secretary arranged a full discussion of all the issues with Luce and the relevant ministries in London in May 1959. The Cabinet's Colonial Policy Committee considered his recommendations in August 1959.[11] A principal supporter of the earlier Lloyd policy was Julian Amery MP, who was then at the Ministry of Defence. In September 1959, the Colonial Secretary wrote to Luce[12] giving him a formal response to his proposals. The first object of HMG's policy was to secure Aden Colony as a military base for as long as possible. Thus he could not allow Luce to announce the merger of the Colony and the Protectorate/ Federation at that time. Federation of the states would have to proceed without Aden for the time being. Time would be needed to accomplish a merger given the different stage of development of the parties, and there was no need to hurry the entry of the Colony into the proposed Federation. Lennox-Boyd also pointed out that although both Adeni politicians and Protectorate rulers wanted to merge Aden into the Federation, they did so for very different reasons and they totally underestimated the difficulties which would arise. The Governor was, however, permitted to say that HMG would consider any proposals for a merger between Aden and the Federation if they came up in the future. Thus Luce's recommendations were in essence rejected by HMG.

It seems clear that strategic requirements were the major factor in HMG's decision – the strategic division of labour between the USA and Britain in resisting the communist threat meant that Britain had the principal military and naval role in the Indian Ocean region, extending from the Persian Gulf and East Africa to Indonesia, and for this purpose, the military bases in Aden and

Singapore were essential. Sceptical officials and politicians in London pointed out that treaties providing for defence facilities had not prevented India, Egypt, Jordan and Sri Lanka from repudiating them – the only assurance was retention of sovereignty in Aden.

In June 1959, Iain Macleod became Colonial Secretary. One has to conclude that he never gave the Aden question the detailed attention it required or which he gave to other colonial questions. In May 1960, he gave Prime Minister Macmillan a status report on the various colonies.[13] It is of great interest that he did not find it necessary to say anything at all about Aden, which is omitted from the survey. Perhaps he had concluded that he could not win a battle with the Ministry of Defence over Aden policy and felt he should expend his energies on the many other pressing colonial questions. However in 1961 he did permit talks to begin about an association between Aden and the Federation.

Thus when we look at the record of events in Aden in the 1960s, we should recall that the Governor of the day, Sir William Luce, had in 1958 foreseen almost exactly what would occur unless a different policy was adopted, and that HMG rejected his advice. We have to conclude that the primary responsibility for the failure of British policy in creating a viable South Arabian state at independence lies with the government of Harold Macmillan in 1959. Perhaps the Aden base did in the event fulfill the strategic needs given so much weight at that time – it facilitated the defence of Kuwait against Iraq in 1961 (a precursor of later conflicts) and the disarming of mutinous troops in the newly independent states of Kenya, Tanzania and Uganda in 1964. It also facilitated the major operation of defending Malaysia against communist pressure from Indonesia. However it would require a different analysis to determine if there were viable alternatives to the Aden base. Arguably there was a basic incompatibility between HMG's desire for the military facilities in South Arabia and the policy of creating a viable state to hand over to at independence. From the point of view of policy for the future of South Arabia as an independent nation state, recovery from the decisions of 1959 proved impossible.

If we can permit ourselves a forward-looking speculation at this juncture, had Luce's recommendations been acted on in late

1958, with a commitment to the early ceding of British sovereignty in Aden, there would have been four years before the Egyptians had an army in Yemen, with all this meant for the opponents of federation and for subversion, keeping the initiative in British hands and giving the federation a greater chance of establishing itself. It is possible that the South Arabian League, which had for five years espoused a single state for South Arabia, and Ali Abdul Karim, the former Sultan of Lahej, might have been willing to return and operate within the constitutional constraints. There would also have been a greater chance of keeping the states of the Eastern Protectorate in favour of federation, with all this would have meant for a more balanced representation within the power structure of the Federation and for the future viability of the country. Perhaps as important as anything, a merger of Aden and the federal states in 1958, with Aden as the nucleus, would have permitted the creation from the start of stronger 'government' and institutions in the federation, because an effective government already existed in Aden, and would have had a greater chance of support by the Aden political class. In the event, the Federation of South Arabia never developed effective systems of administration and barely raised any revenue, without which no government can function or survive.

Trevaskis' book *Shades of Amber*[14] is a detailed, knowledgeable and generally perceptive record of events in the WAP and Aden, although he had nothing to say about the EAP, which he never visited, even when he was High Commisioner. However, his descriptions of some of the most important exchanges between Aden and London are not consistent with the actual record, nor with their chronology. He agreed with Luce that had HMG offered to cede sovereignty over Aden and permit its merger with the Federation in 1958, the Adenis would have accepted at once. He regrets that he did not himself adhere to Luce's proposals, ignoring the fact that it was HMG's decision to turn them down, not his. He also suggested that by the time of the appointment of Sir Charles Johnston to succeed Luce as Governor, in August 1960, British officials in Aden were opposed to ceding sovereignty in Aden, which also conflicts with the official record. It is not now possible to reconcile these apparently different records and interpretations of events.

THE FEDERATION OF SOUTH ARABIA

To return to the chronology, the Federation of South Arabia was inaugurated in February 1959 among six WAP states. All federal constitutions have to find a way both to give power to the majority and to protect the interests of the states with a small population against the tyranny of the larger states. The classic case is the constitution of the United States of America, in which each state, regardless of population, has two senators, while the legitimacy of the majority is reflected in the number of members of the House of Representatives. In the case of the Federation of South Arabia, the legislature, known as the Federal Council, consisted of six representatives from each state. Thus population was not a factor in determining representation at that level. Furthermore, these representatives were selected, not elected, which could only be a transitional arrangement (elections were first held in three WAP states and one EAP state in 1963/4). Each state had one member in the Supreme Council, which in view of the status of the rulers and the 'Dawla' (the household of the ruler) in the states, meant that the rulers themselves became the members of the Supreme Council.

Figure 1.4 Inaugural parade of the Federal Regular Army at the Federal capital: al Ittihad in 1962.

This constitution adopted by the initial six states, with advice from Trevaskis and presumably the Attorney General in Aden and advisers in London, was most ill-advised, as it entrenched the position of the individual rulers in a way which they were sure to defend as long as they could and was bound to antagonise elected politicians when they came in. This was realised when discussions began on the merger of Aden with the Federation in 1961, but by then the political environment for the federation was much less propitious, making the necessary changes eventually agreed in July 1964 look like grudging concessions wrung out of reluctant rulers.

When discussions began under Sir Charles Johnston on the possibility of Aden joining the federation, there were two central problems to be solved. First, what form of constitutional advance would occur first in Aden Colony to legitimise a decision by the Colony to join the Federation? New elections to the Aden Legislative Council were required no later than January 1963 and these had to occur if moderate Adeni opinion were to support the merger. For this to occur, the franchise question would have to be re-addressed. Second, what representation would Aden have in the two federal councils; Aden was to be far and away the most significant state after merger and for Adeni politicians to carry the electorate, they would have to insist on adequate representation.

Johnston managed to postpone the 1963 elections with the help of Hassan Bayoomi, a leading Adeni politician, and the exisiting Aden Legislative Council narrowly voted in favour of the merger with the Federation. But this manoevre provided a very weak basis for such an important constitutional change, as was soon to become apparent.

The Aden franchise issue was addressed by the appointment in 1963 of a Franchise Commission. The membership was entirely Adeni Arabs. The Commission held wide-ranging consultations and received representations from both official and non-official sources. It produced an excellent report,[15] which however posed a number of tricky questions for the Aden and British governments. It recommended that those entitled to vote should include any Arab person who was born or whose father was born in Aden; any Arab resident in Aden for 20 years who had a child or children born in Aden; non-Arab Muslims who were born and whose fathers were born in Aden, and who satisfied a language test; and non-Arab non-Muslims who were born or whose fathers were born in Aden and who satisfied a language test. There was to be no property or income qualification; women would be fully enfranchised; those with a foreign nationality would not be entitled to vote; the voting age would be 21 years.

This franchise proposal had the perhaps unintended effect of equating the position of Arabs who were British Protected Persons with Yemeni Arabs (thus equating the Federation with Yemen), which caused the federal ministers much concern. The Aden government estimated that on these proposals, about 10,500 persons would be *dis-enfranchised* (mainly protectorate Arabs, about half the Indian population, most of the Somalis and most citizens of the UK and Colonies), roughly halving the number entitled to vote and keeping electoral influence in the hands of a small number of older Adeni families.[16] The Chief Minister of Aden, by then Zain Baharoon, eventually concluded that reducing the number of eligible voters in this way was unsustainable politically and that the best approach for the purpose of the immediate elections was to accept the principle of those born in Aden or whose father was so born. This would be the most simple and defensible franchise for the immediate elections, putting off implementation of the other recommendations until there was a newly elected government. The British government was anxious about the likely impact of the proposed changes in the franchise on the nature of future Aden governments. The Aden government thought they would be neutral unless women got the vote, when, it was thought, the People's Socialist Party (PSP) (see p. 42) would gain substantially. Mr Besse (see p. 31) thought this was a misreading of the situation. The Aden Council of Ministers felt it was premature to enfranchise women and HMG accepted that view.

The debate about the merger in Aden, which had a free press and fully accepted rights of public assembly, was intense and led to some clashes between demonstrators and the police. The democratic institutions and the judicial system in Aden both permitted the expression of opposition to the merger and made it difficult, even at this stage, to prevent intimidation of officials, jurors and politicians. Despite the opposition, however, the elections in Aden produced a majority of those entitled to vote in favour of the merger, though those who thought the franchise should have been wider predictably denounced this result. The commercial community for the first time began to be concerned; they required a law-abiding community, where business could operate in a predictable manner. The foreign firms in particular, began to think about their future.

The debate in the federation was less public but just as intense. Some rulers were autocratic, but there were well-established rights of access to rulers and the 'Dawla'. In due course, the agreement reached was for Aden to have 24 representatives in the Federal Council out of 85, and four members of the Supreme Council out of 14. The argument made was that since the Yemenis in Aden were to be largely un-enfranchised, greater Adeni representation was not justified. This situation was initially accepted by the Adenis due to the inclusion in the merger agreement of a clause giving the Colony the right of secession from the Federation. Nevertheless, it was not to be long before Aden's representation came to be considered inadequate by most Adeni politicians. This soon became a critical issue.

It should also be noted that while it joined the Federation of South Arabia, Aden remained a Crown Colony, an extraordinary constitutional contrivance, which led to confusion as to where authority lay and served among other things to prevent the Federation taking full control of law and order in Aden. This also became a crucial issue when the opposition resorted to terrorism (see elaboration in Chapter 6).

We do not know what representation the EAP states would have had had they joined the Federation at that time, but when in 1967 HMG tried to put together a consultative body to devise and vote on a new constitution for the future independent state, the Quaiti, Kathiri and Mahra states were to have had 36 votes between them, Aden 24 votes and the WAP states 85 votes, giving the proportions shown in Table 1.1.

Neither Aden nor the EAP could have or should have accepted these proportions, which meant they would always be outvoted, despite their greater population, and it is difficult now to understand how the representation agreed in 1962/3 could have been arrived at. Perhaps the essence of the matter is that having taken the initiative to create the Federation in 1959, the federal rulers were not willing to lose their control over it. HMG should have been more far-sighted and insisted on a better balance from the

Table 1.1 Proposed representation in the Federal Council

	Representation[a]	%	Population[b]	%
WAP states	85	59	550,000	51
EAP	36	25	318,000	29
Aden	24	16	220,000	20
	145	**100**	**1,088,000**	**100**

Note: a Memorandum of Colonial Office to the DOP(O) Committee, 12 January 1966.[17]

   b Memorandum by the Colonial Office to the South Arabian Constitutional Commission, July 1965.

beginning so as to facilitate the later accession of Aden Colony and the EAP.

Just as agreement was reached on the merger between Aden and the Protectorate, though before the British parliament approved it or it could be implemented, the Imam of Yemen died and a republic was declared in the Yemen. A civil war broke out with the republicans supported by Egypt and the family of the Imam, led by the former Imam's son, Prince Badr, supported by Saudi Arabia. Badr had visited Britain in 1957, but was not received with much imagination which encouraged him to think that he might do better with other patrons, especially Egypt and Russia. Events forced a different choice on him. There was considerable sympathy for the new republic in Aden, with its large Shafai Yemeni population, and this had the effect of strengthening the opposition in Aden to a merger with a federation seen to be dominated by traditional rulers. Nevertheless, as it had been agreed, the merger went ahead, the federal institutions were somewhat strengthened and for a while Aden seemed content to support the emergence of the new government. Though there were incidents, 1963 was largely peaceful. It was only at the end of the year that a grenade was thrown at Trevaskis, by then High Commissioner, at the airport, killing two and injuring many. George Henderson, who shielded Trevaskis from the force of the blast, and who died from his injuries, received a bar to his George Medal. In the aftermath, a number of Adeni politicians and other suspects were arrested, including Abdulla al Asnag, leader of the PSP. Security was re-established and there were no more serious incidents in Aden for the best part of a year. However, the political atmosphere had taken a distinct turn for the worse and the events in the Yemen now had increasing ramifications in the WAP and Aden.

A constitutional conference was convened in London in June/July 1964 to address the deficiencies in the Federal constitution and reflect the changing political situation following Aden's accession. Though invited, the Quaiti and Kathiri states decided not to attend. The conference, held under the chairmanship of Duncan Sandys, the Conservative minister, agreed to the following changes to the Federal constitution, which were reported to Parliament in Cmnd 2114, together with HMG's renewed pledge to continue to provide military support after independence:

(i) The legislature would consist of two houses, a National Assembly (Majlis al Watani) and a Council of States. The representatives in the National Assembly would be selected either by direct election or, where such elections were found to be impractical, by indirect election through an Electoral College. The composition of the Electoral Colleges would be defined in the constitution. An independent commission would carry out a census to define who could vote and where. The Council of States would have one representative of each state. The Council would have powers of delaying legislation and ratifying treaties.

(ii) The Federation would have a President elected by the members of the two legislative bodies sitting in joint session, who would appoint a Prime Minister. The Prime Minister would be required to command a majority in the National Assembly.

(iii) The British government agreed to cede sovereignty over Aden Colony to the Federation following new elections in Aden, and to abrogate the advisory treaty with the Federation and the states.

(iv) The British government agreed to convene a conference as soon as practical to work out arrangements for independence of the Federation no later than 1968 and to agree the terms of a Defence Agreement between HMG and the Federation.

Thus much of what Sir William Luce had advised in 1958 and which HMG rejected at that time, was agreed to in August 1964, six years later, providing the basis for the independence of South Arabia. However, the proposed constitution was still not acceptable to the political parties – the PSP, the SAL and the newly formed National Liberation Front (NLF) – which wanted a much reduced role for the traditional rulers (see pp. 39–45 on the political parties). Moreover, by then the political situation had deteriorated seriously and the opposition was beginning to take a violent form. When the Aden elections were held in October 1964 (which happened to coincide with elections in Britain) the principal suspect in the attack on Trevaskis was released from detention without charge and was elected to LegCo on a wave of popular support.

Announcing a target date for independence in 1968 was a mistake; it meant that those opposed to the Federation knew that they had to act quickly if they wanted to determine the nature of the future state. Furthermore, the pre-requisites in the 1964 agreement for addressing the disparity in the number of Aden representatives in the existing Federal institutions were onerous. Elections would have to await the appointment of the proposed Electoral Commission, a census, decisions on the franchise and much further political argument, during the course of which Aden would continue to be outvoted. Meanwhile, the Federal Council was also subject to the actions and decisions of individual rulers, weakening its authority. Despite the fact that all the military base facilities were located within the Colony of Aden, the 'rent' paid by HMG went straight to the Federal government. Despite all these difficulties, Sayyid Zain Baharoon continued to lead the Aden government and it seemed possible to begin to move forward on the agenda of constitutional change agreed in July.

THE IMPACT OF THE LABOUR GOVERNMENT

However, instead of pressing on with the measures agreed in August 1964, the new Labour Colonial Secretary, Anthony Greenwood, prevaricated, and effectively repudiated the agreement arrived at under his predecessor-in-office. He visited Aden in November/December 1964 and, in Trevaskis' words, 'seemed to see the issue as one between al Asnag's Aden and the Federation, seeing Baharoon's Aden as an irrelevance'.[18] However, Greenwood's position evolved, especially when Baharoon proposed on 28 November that the Federation become a unitary state in order to address major weaknesses in the way it functioned. He argued that Aden's interests were inadequately served by the Federation which he felt had entrenched the autocratic powers of the Rulers. The Adeni objective was to end tribalism and introduce democratic institutions throughout the Federation.[19] Greenwood referred to the 1964 conference report as a starting point, but indicated that 'the British government did not wish to be too much limited by decisions taken in the past. They had to take account of subsequent developments such as the move of opinion in favour of a unitary state.'[20]

On 7 December 1964, during the course of Greenwood's visit, the Federal Supreme Council and the Aden Council of Ministers issued a joint declaration of policy affirming their support for the formation of a unitary state comprising the whole of South Arabia. This was a fundamental departure from the agreement reached the previous August. The change should have been welcome to the political parties, as it would have had the effect of reducing the role of the state rulers. It soon became apparent, however, that they remained sceptical. Furthermore, it was also apparent that the implications of this fundamental change of concept had not yet been fully realised by the Federal leaders involved. Nevertheless, Greenwood told the House of Commons that the proposal had HMG's support and that he hoped to convene a further conference in March to work out the new approach.[21]

Greenwood also came to the conclusion that Trevaskis, who had succeeded Johnston as High Commissioner, was not the man to bring Aden to independence. He dismissed him. Sir Richard Turnbull was appointed in his place. It has to be said that, though Greenwood was probably motivated partly by Trevaskis' links with former Conservative ministers, he was right about Trevaskis, who was so closely identified with the rulers of the old WAP who now dominated the Supreme Council of the Federation that it was unlikely he would ever gain the confidence of the Adeni politicians. This point was made at the time in a letter[22] from a well-informed resident of Aden, the businessman M. Antonin (Tony) Besse, to Lord Shawcross, a prominent member of the Labour Party and a director of Shell (for which Besse were agents):

Sir Kennedy, the skilful architect of the federation is known for his pro-ruler sympathies. His appointment unfortunately led to the further alienation of the feelings of the Adenis who were soon to be confirmed in their apprehensions when . . . the High Commissioner turned over his special powers to the Supreme Council of the Federation and allowed a state of emergency to be declared . . . and scores of Aden political and Trade Union leaders were rounded up and detained. Wounded pride turned to anger. The issue was taken to the United Nations where it received both wide publicity and a sympathetic hearing.

It is also the case that Trevaskis had failed to visit the EAP, even when he was High Commissioner, and seemed not to wish to know the rulers and leaders of the EAP states or their views about the future.

Turnbull had had a distinguished career in Kenya and Tanganyika, but those had both been directly administered colonies, unlike the Aden Protectorates. Furthermore, he knew Swahili, whereas he did not know Arabic. In Aden Colony, everyone spoke English, but if you wanted to establish a rapport with Arabs in the protected states, a knowledge of Arabic was almost essential. Seeking to learn about Aden, Turnbull invited some knowledgeable Adenis for discussions. He told them, perhaps following Hegel, that he found Aden rather like an onion; every layer removed revealed new layers and complexities.[23]

Members of the new Labour government in Britain hoped to be able to achieve a greater understanding with the PSP in Aden. In particular, Mr George Thomson, Minister of State for Foreign Affairs, had known Abdulla al Asnag for some years and evidently felt it would be possible to find a solution to Aden's problems by negotiating with him. They also thought they had goodwill with the Egyptian government. Both these hopes proved to be illusory. Al Asnag was happy to exploit his relationship with Labour politicians, as the Federal Rulers had with the Conservative Government, but the PSP wanted power, it had support from Cairo and was not particularly squeamish over the means of obtaining it. Terrorism increased, with the NLF claiming responsibility, putting the PSP under pressure, and becoming more professional with Egyptian training and support.

The idea of a unitary state attracted the interest of Ali Abdul Karim, the former Sultan of Lahej, exiled and now resident in Egypt. In a wide-ranging discussion with a member of the British Embassy staff in January 1965,[24] he argued that the conference proposed by Greenwood for early 1965 was very important, that time was of the essence and the conference must have concrete results – not merely produce a set of general principles. He said the Egyptian government would do all in its power to sabotage the conference and though he would like to attend he was not sure they would let him. He felt UN involvement, or at least attendance of independent Commonwealth countries such as Canada and India, would help in dealing with the franchise and organising elections. He said that he and other Adenis in Cairo had come to realise that they had different objectives from the Egyptians. They merely wanted an independent South Arabia, which could then work out its future relations with Britain and Yemen; Egypt wanted to exert its influence in the Arabian peninsula, wanted to prevail in creating a republican Yemen, make trouble for Britain and get rid of the Aden military base. If Egypt received substantial Soviet assistance, they could cause much trouble. Ali Abdul Karim was particularly emphatic on the need for Britain to keep control of the situation so that it remained worthwhile for residents and federal rulers to support British rule until independence. Thus Britain must retain the initiative in the moves towards independence. He considered the NLF and Qahtan al Shaabi would lose support as soon as South Arabia became independent. Interestingly, he felt Qahtan would be happy to see the base retained once the country was independent.

The planned conference also attracted the interest of the South Arabian League itself, though the League made conditions for its attendance in terms of the ultimate outcome of the conference, which were not helpful in arranging it. It also pressed, reasonably enough, for greater freedom of movement of its members, some of whom were restrained from travel or were living in exile. The Federal government wanted time to hold widely representative talks, including the opposition parties, before the conference.

The March 1965 meeting proposed by Greenwood did not take place, not for any particular reason but mainly because the difficulties of getting attendance on reasonable terms led to the timetable just slipping and slipping. There were questions about who should attend, about freedom of the various parties to consult publicly before the meeting; there was posturing which attempted to pre-determine the outcome of the proposed conference by adherence to UN Resolution No. 1949 of 1963. The fundamental nature of the changes required to create a unitary state raised all sorts of issues and led to second thoughts among several of the parties involved. Sir Richard Turnbull, the High Commissioner, in a note written more than ten years later, considered that the conference did not take place because the leaders of the Federal government 'sabotaged' it.[25]

Meanwhile the problems caused by British retention of sovereignty in Aden escalated steadily. As mentioned above, though Aden was part of the Federation, the Federal government had only limited jurisdiction in Aden, which remained a Crown Colony – how this extraordinary situation was possible is at the least a constitutional curiosity. The political parties' ability to campaign in the protected states was limited both by the autocratic nature of the rulers and by the reluctance of the British advisory staff to permit them to. It has also to be said that the administrative capacity of the Federal government was very limited. Roy Somerset who was working for the Federal government at the time recalls that the Assembly rarely met; the Supreme Council often met informally and support for the Council at the staff level was derisory, depending heavily on a few dedicated Arab and British staff, and certainly not comparable with the quite well-established ministries in Aden. The Federation's revenue situation was parlous and there seemed to be little inclination to adopt revenue-raising measures.

In February 1965, Baharoon resigned as Chief Minister of Aden over a squabble with Federal Ministers, something he had done before, but which had always been rejected by Trevaskis. The new High Commissioner, Sir Richard Turnbull, unwisely accepted his resignation and in early March Turnbull had to invite Abdulqawi Makkawi a member of the PSP and the member having most support in the Legislative Assembly, to replace him. Makkawi had worked for A. Besse & Co. and Tony Besse considers that while Makkawi accepted it as his duty to enter politics, he was ill-equipped and unfitted for playing a major political role. In the event he proved totally un-cooperative with both the Federal government and the British government; knowledgeable Arabs said that he was not a free agent, but under much pressure from Egypt and others. He probably was. He insisted on Britain accepting the Adenis' 'just demands' and the implementation of the UN resolutions on Aden. He appeared not to be interested in the future of the Federation or the non-federated states. Despite his position as Chief Minister, Makkawi frustrated the process of maintaining law and order, even showing tacit support for acts of terrorism. Turnbull found he had to take emergency powers, as combating the terrorism through the courts was proving impossible. Makkawi also refused to cooperate with a Constitutional Commission due to visit Aden and induced the Adeni representatives to withdraw from the Federal Councils.

Despite these difficulties, following further negotiations by Greenwood and the various parties it was eventually agreed that a Working Party should meet in London in August 1965 in order to prepare for a subsequent Constitutional Conference. The working party would seek to agree on an agenda for such a conference and create goodwill between the parties. The Working Party commenced on 2 August 1965 and continued in session for nine days. Representation included Federal and Aden government ministers, officials, members of the PSP and SAL and Quaiti and Kathiri state officials. Despite physical threats made against some of those attending and although it was evidently extremely frustrating for all those involved, the Working Party papers[26] reveal considerable good will among all parties in the search for solutions for the benefit of South Arabia. Concerns about the exiles, the state of emergency and detainees could have been worked out. In the end however, distrust and differences between the parties was such that agreement could not be reached either on the conference agenda or on ancillary preparatory measures for the conference. The PSP stuck too firmly to the tenor of the UN Resolutions; the Federal leaders lacked the imagination to bridge the differences with the party leaders; HMG was not willing to accept the electoral components of the UN resolutions (as it did do eventually). In the end, Greenwood ended the discussions, which proved to be the last attempt to reach an agreement at which all the main political interests were present – except for the NLF (see p. 43).

On their return to Aden, the situation continued to deteriorate. The High Commissioner and Makkawi corresponded on the issues facing Aden. Makkawi articulated with great clarity the reasons why most Adenis were dissatisfied with its membership of the Federation, especially in his letter of 4 September 1965 to the High Commissioner and the follow-up meeting of Turnbull with the Aden Council of Ministers on 11 September.[27] Turnbull could have been in no doubt that re-gaining Adeni support for the federal/unitary concept without addressing these complaints was a very long shot indeed. The differences were fundamental.

Meanwhile terrorist attacks in Aden increased in number and in the absence of support from the Aden government, no progress was made in containing them. The statistics of incidents and casualties in Aden Colony alone make sober reading (see Table 1.2).

Eventually the Labour government had had enough. Late in September 1965, the Aden constitution was suspended; Makkawi was sacked as Chief Minister and the High Commissioner, Turnbull, began to rule by decree. As a step on the way

Table 1.2 Aden Colony: security, incidents and casualties, 1964–7

| | 1964 | | 1965 | | 1966 | | 1967[a] | |
	Total	Month av	Total	Month av	Total	Month av	Total	Month av
Incidents	36	3	286	24	480	40	2980	248
British forces								
Killed	2		6		5		44	
Wounded	25		83		218		325	
Local forces								
Killed	1		9		2		5	
Wounded	—		7		8		43	
British civilians								
Killed	1		2		6		9	
Wounded	5		28		19		31	
Local civilians								
Killed	—		18		32		240	
Wounded	2		86		283		551	

Source: Taken from 'Last Post Aden' by Lt Col Julian Paget, Faber & Faber, London, 1969.
Note: a Nine months only; by October 1967 the situation was so confused that statistics had become unreliable.

to independence, this was a political disaster, though by then the alternatives were not apparent. Turnbull's experiences during the Kenyan Mau Mau emergency may have given him the confidence to feel that with patience the problems could be seen through. This belief was also illusory as the situation in Aden had large international dimensions which were absent in the case of Kenya. Furthermore, Turnbull's direct rule was limited to the small territory of Aden Colony and did not extend to the Federation and the EAP.

On 15 October 1965, Turnbull met with three members of the Federal Supreme Council, Shaikh Mohammad Farid (External Affairs), Sultan Saleh (Internal Security) and Sultan Fadhl bin Ali (Defence). Also present were the British Agent in the WAP, Ian Baillie and Ralph Daly, who interpreted. The record of this meeting[28] encapsulates all the dilemmas facing the British and Federal governments and clarifies the British government's unwillingness or inability to force a way through them. HMG could not hope to conclude a defence agreement with the Federation, or a new Treaty of Friendship and Protection, if the Federation was still split by an undeclared war between Aden and the rest of the states. It was essential that Aden should be persuaded to play a positive and responsible part in the Federation. This required new elections in Aden, which would in turn require a new and wider franchise. That, however, was impossible to achieve so long as Aden was ruled by decree, the Aden political parties would not cooperate, and the Federation had no role in maintaining security in Aden. The Federal delegation pointed out that Adenis were chiselling away at the Federation both internally and externally which was corroding the legitimacy of the Federal government. HMG could either allow the Federation to be harmed in this way or move promptly to cede sovereignty in Aden to the Federal government. The High Commissioner said he could not visualise HMG abandoning democratic processes in Aden in this way, or ceding sovereignty until there was a properly constituted authority in Aden to which they could hand over.

Turnbull actually suggested that if the situation was as grave as the Federal representatives suggested, perhaps the Federation should expel Aden. HMG would then negotiate with an elected government of Aden and agree terms for independence. It would then be for the Federation and Aden to work out their own future.

The shocked federal representatives rejected this possibility, though Baillie did suggest that if there was a total impasse on the matter, perhaps the Federation should ask for early independence.

Commenting on the record of this meeting, Donal McCarthy, a Foreign Office official seconded to the High Commission, said to Turnbull[29] that he thought the series of constitutional hurdles he had put up where Aden was concerned was not only impossible to surmount in the time available, but also unnecessary. Turnbull agreed with the first point and had some sympathy with the second, but he said that he had felt he had to demonstrate to the Federal representatives that it was not easy to get Adeni support.

In the background, two eminent constitutional specialists, Sir Ralph Hone and Sir Gawain Bell, were working away on a draft of a new constitution for the future South Arabian state. Though the Aden government had refused to cooperate with them, they did in fact prepare their draft, which became available for public scrutiny in February 1966, just as HMG announced it would not extend military support to the new state at independence. One of the critical issues was the representation in the legislature. They proposed the following:

Capital Territory (Aden)	28 representatives
Western Protectorate states, including Upper Yafai	83 representatives
Eastern Protectorate states, if they joined	36 representatives

Thus the old WAP states would, as under the existing Federal constitution, always outvote the EAP states and Aden together. This elementary point about the excessive share of power in the Federation of the WAP states seems never to have sunk in. In the event, the recommendations of Hone/Bell were not proceeded with as the conditions in which they could be discussed and implemented never materialised. Turnbull recalled that every specifically Arab constitution in the Middle East was examined for ideas, but that this was fruitless because all the notionally democratic states in the Middle East were in fact military dictatorships.

The British government also faced steady criticism of its Aden policies in the General Assembly and the Committee of 24 of the

United Nations, which debated the situation in Aden and passed resolutions on the subject, notably Resolution 1949 of 1963. The PSP and other political parties gave evidence to the Committee and the Federal government found it necessary to respond. HMG was reluctant to allow any role in the independence negotiations to the UN as it would infringe British authority, lead to a loss of control of the process and complicate the already complex negotiations.

UNDERSTANDING THE VARIOUS PARTIES AND FRONTS

It was very difficult for both Arab and British participants in the events of the 1960s to understand the nature of the different parties, fronts and leagues, the relationships between them and their aims and objectives. Disentangling the threads is even now difficult because personalities were crucial, relationships fluctuated under the impact of events, and the parties and fronts themselves evolved. Furthermore in some respects the policies of the NLF remain unique in the recent history of the Arab world and this was either not understood at the time or did not seem credible even to well informed observers. Nevertheless, no account of the period can be complete without some understanding of the parties and fronts and the way they evolved. It is not necessary to subscribe to Fred Halliday's Marxist interpretation of the Arabia of the 1960s and 1970s to be grateful to him for the rather detailed description of the various parties and fronts in his book *Arabia without Sultans*.[30] The following is only a brief summary of very complex organisations and relationships, but hopefully conveys something of the turbulent struggle among those seeking to take control at the time of independence.

Modern political life in South Arabia began in Aden Colony among the better educated residents, who in 1950 created the Aden Association, which sought through constitutional means to negotiate a degree of local self-government. This association was limited to Adenis and was never a popular party with a campaigning organisation. Separately, there soon emerged ideas for a unitary state of the whole of Aden and the Aden Protectorate, which became the policy of the South Arabian League (SAL), founded in the early 1950s. The League also flirted with the idea of union with

Yemen, but did not pursue the idea. The League had some support among the rulers, including the younger members of the families, especially the Sultan of Lahej, Ali Abdul Karim, but also in Aden, where the United National Front (UNF) emerged to fight the 1955 elections, and to a limited extent in the Hadhramaut, the homeland of Shaikhan al Habshi, one of the leaders of the party. The SAL was heavily based in Lahej, with the sultan and the Jifri family, and it had a tendency to want to confront the British authorities – for example, Muhammad Aidrus, the young Yafai ruler, chose to pick a quarrel with the authorities about the allocation of the proceeds and the management of the Abyan Board, an irrigation scheme; the SAL came to believe that the British authorities would not take them or their political objectives seriously. In 1958, the leaders of the SAL, including Sultan Ali, were expelled.

The reasons given at the time in a letter[31] from Trevaskis to the Sultan's brother, who succeeded him, were as follows:

- Sultan Ali was in correspondence with foreign powers in breach of the Protectorate Treaty;
- the purpose of this correspondence was to help such powers injure HMG's interests and sever Lahej's long-term relationship with HMG;
- Sultan Ali ordered the defection of some of the Lahej forces to the Yemen;
- Sultan Ali favoured Muhammad Ali al Jifri who was openly acting as the agent of foreign powers.

Sir William Luce held three meetings with Sultan Ali on 1 January, 20 February and 5 March 1958, just before the expulsion, during which he sought to persuade the Sultan to modify his position and his attitudes to the future evolution of the country.[32] The exchange was friendly and both parties were frank in their views. If one were to be critical of Luce's position, one could argue that he laid too much emphasis on the reasons why Sultan Ali should cooperate with HMG rather than the political role the Sultan could legitimately expect to play in the negotiations about the future of South Arabia. Luce seemed reluctant to see treaty chiefs engage in politics at the party level. Tony Besse knew Ali Abdul Karim and admired him for his powers of leadership, good education and ideas for the future.

The expulsion was counter-productive as it gave Egypt and Yemen a political channel into Adeni affairs, even in the late 1950s, through their support for the SAL. Trevaskis acknowledges this in his book. Since the essential objectives of the SAL for the future of the country were very similar to Britain's, it is most regrettable that some way could not be found to keep it involved in the discussions. Some Arabs thought the expulsion was linked to the contemporaneous creation of the United Arab States, though no confirmation of this has been found in the British records.

The mid-1950s also saw the emergence, with the support of the colonial authorities, of a vigorous trade union movement in Aden to improve the working conditions of the floating labourers in the port, the refinery, the military installations and in the booming construction industry. Many of them were Yemeni immigrants fleeing repression in the Yemen or looking for work. The formation of the Aden Trades Union Congress (ATUC) in 1956 happened to coincide with the nationalisation of the Suez Canal which had the perhaps unintended consequence of converting the ATUC into an advocate of Arab-nationalistic solutions to the Suez Canal and the future of Aden. The need for reform of employment practices was subordinated by some of its leaders to political objectives. In fact, this tension within the ATUC and the PSP (see p. 42) between the role of the trade unions in representing their members vis-à-vis employers and the wish by Abdulla al Asnag in particular to use the ATUC as a platform for political activity at a national level, persisted until 1966. Militant trade union tactics caused substantial economic disruption in the 1950s and led the Aden government to enact the Industrial Relations Ordinance of 1960, which stipulated arbitration before a strike could be called, a sensible measure, since widely adopted elsewhere in the world.

The Arab Nationalist Movement (ANM), created by George Habbash to fight the Palestinian cause, with members and branches in most Arab countries, and a number of other smaller movements, also emerged in Aden, especially among young people, many of whom joined whilst attending Aden College. Though it shared some of Nasser's revolutionary objectives, its ideological inspiration was essentially Marxist. As the proposals for federation emerged, the Aden Association split into one party opposed to the federation, the People's Constitutional Congress, and one party in favour, the United National Party (UNP), led by Hassan al Bayoumi.

In 1962, the UNF renamed itself the People's Socialist Party (PSP) and sought support among the members of the unions and the ANM. It was opposed to Aden's entry into the Federation and in this endeavour received some support from Egypt. The PSP, whose activities and support were at that time limited to Aden Colony but much influenced by the many Yemeni workers, also mobilised support for the 1962 republican coup d'état in Yemen. However, internal events in Yemen meant that there was little time init- ially among the republicans to concern themselves with Aden. The leader of the coup d'état in Yemen, Colonel Sallal, actually stated in October 1962 that they had no intention of getting involved in the South. By late 1963, however, when the republicans in Yemen were on the defensive and seeking to stop supplies reaching the royalists through Beihan, the notion of supporting the opponents of Britain in South Arabia took greater hold among the republicans and their Egyptian supporters.

The PSP tended to a confrontational approach to politics, which took the form of denying the legitimacy of the government in Aden and the leaders and constitution of the Federation; and condoned occasional violence. It was always confrontational with the British authorities, whether there was a Conservative or a Labour government, trotting out the mantra of implementing the rather impractical UN Resolution 1949. Nevertheless, the PSP was essentially a political movement, not a terrorist organisation and Asnag was keen to keep it that way. It is again unfortunate that the Aden authorities could not find ways to give it more scope for political activity and thus deny the leaders the excuse to run off to Cairo. The nature of the franchise in Aden was one of the PSP's targets, to which the Aden authorities were slow to respond, and the nature of the Federal Constitution, with the powerful role of the traditional rulers really alienated such Adeni politicians as al Asnag, who were more at home arguing their points in street meetings and demonstrations. It was not in Britain's long-term interest to prevent the PSP making their arguments for change in the constitutional provisions of the Federation; indeed it was self-evident that a popular element had to be introduced into the constitution if was to have any chance of surviving.

The response to the airport incident in December 1963 led to al Asnag being detained and, when released, going off to Cairo, where he both became somewhat detached from the realities in

Aden and was exposed to strong Egyptian influences. His absence led al Asnag to misread the situation in Aden and when he led the PSP into a boycott of the Aden elections of October 1964, the boycott failed – turn-out was 76 per cent of those eligible to vote and the 16 seats were contested between 48 candidates. So Zain Baharoon continued as Chief Minister. Once Abdulqawi Makkawi became Chief Minister in March 1965, as a leading member of the PSP, he became an obdurate opponent of both the Federal government and the British authorities. Nevertheless, over the period to August 1965, when the Working Party on the Federal Constitution met in London, the PSP were open to negotiations with the Federal rulers and also with the British Labour government. From 1965, the PSP came under strong Egyptian pressure to merge with the NLF (see below). This forced on the PSP a choice between the political route it had pursued up to that moment and the terrorist route to power adopted by the NLF. The PSP chose the political route, which the Aden authorities should have found more ways to welcome. The PSP also sought to merge with the SAL in order to resist pressure from the NLF's campaign of violence, though this cost them Egyptian support. For by then, the SAL was in receipt of support from Saudi Arabia. The Aden government was well-informed of the PSP's changing relations with the other parties and their decision to eschew violence 'because the country would become another Congo', but it showed little imagination in responding to the PSP's manoeuvres to avoid the NLF's clutches.

The creation of the National Liberation Front for Occupied South Yemen (NLF) in October 1963 put all political parties in a difficulty, though they were able to ignore this for a year or so while the Front created its policies and cadres. The Front had grown up among those who had gone to support the republicans in the Yemen and the members of ANM. Qahtan al Shaabi, formerly of the SAL, became one of the leaders, along with his cousin Faisal and Saif al Dhalai, formerly a civil servant in Aden. The distinguishing features of the NLF from the beginning were: its secrecy; its decision to base itself in the Aden Protectorate, not in Aden Colony; its lack of public figures to represent it in the political arena; its commitment to violence against both Britain and the Federation; and its strong, close-knit organisation. It also gradually articulated the intention to carry through an economic and social revolution when it achieved power and create a 'people's army' not based on tribal affiliation. Thus it evolved from being principally a nationalist organisation into a socialist, revolutionary one with the purpose of replacing the traditional authorities with socialist ones modelled partly on precedents in Algeria, China and other revolutionary countries. Its acceptance of some aspects of revolutionary Marxism was perhaps unique in the Arab world and it is clear that this was not fully appreciated or credited at the time by the Aden authorities, who also took a while to recognise that the various cells of the NLF were actually cooperating effectively. From the beginning, the NLF was also wary of Egyptian offers of support and wanted to base itself solidly on domestic support, though it was willing to receive arms and support from the communist bloc countries and China, as well as ANM.

While the PSP initially opposed the NLF through political means, when the Egyptians realised that the NLF was detaching itself from Cairo, they encouraged al Asnag to combine with the SAL by creating first the Organisation for the Liberation of the Occupied South (OLOS) in May 1965 and subsequently, when that failed, the Front for the Liberation of South Yemen (FLOSY) in January 1966. Both al Asnag and Makkawi belonged to this front and to some observers, FLOSY was 'the Aden independence' party. (John Wilton visited Abdulla al Asnag in Cairo in early 1966 and suggested to him that since Britain would have left Aden within 18 months, it made sense for al Asnag to cooperate with HMG now. His response was to say, 'No – we must be seen to kick you out').[33] Some leaders of the NLF were induced to visit Cairo with a view to joining FLOSY, though the NLF leadership then repudiated them. FLOSY continued to rely heavily on Egyptian support and allowed itself to be, to a degree, controlled by Egypt. This dependence eventually alienated the SAL leaders, who in 1966 created CONFISA (Command National Forces in South Arabia), which was intended to broaden the membership of the SAL and its sympathisers. FLOSY never had the basis of support in the states that the NLF developed, though it did have the political personalities. Some of the Federal rulers, especially Sultan Saleh, attempted to work out a joint position with the SAL/FLOSY/CONFISA in early 1966, but this did not come to anything.

The NLF continued to evolve, gradually becoming more radical, with adherents from the Popular Democratic Union, a Marxist group in Aden, and the Arab Socialist Party in the EAP, and increasing detachment from Egypt. They created a revolutionary army, and in the Radfan and other battles gained experience in protracted warfare based on local support. To avoid Egyptian support they acquired local resources through robberies and also received weapons from communist states. Finally in November 1966, the NLF broke off its contacts with FLOSY and in April 1967, at the time of the UN Mission, the conflict between the two broke out into the open and took a deadly form, with FLOSY creating its own military wing – the Popular Organisation of Revolutionary Forces (PORF).

By mid-1967, it had become apparent to the British authorities that the NLF was the organisation with the broadest support, especially in the army, with the best organisation, and was the most ruthless. Some of the Federal leaders began to talk to them about creating a broader-based government after independence. This was too late and in the event, the NLF eventually seized control without conceding anything of substance to the former Federal leaders and traditional rulers, most of whom then fled the country.

By the time they did so, the Suez Canal had been closed during the course of the Six Day War, and it remained closed for several years. This proved to be fatal to Aden's Port, which almost overnight lost its raison d'être; within eighteen months, Aden's trade had withered away to nothing. Thus the NLF inheritance was a distinctly unpromising one and one which required real business acumen to confront. The NLF government did not possess business acumen. It quickly moved to nationalise significant parts of the economy, a move calculated to persuade foreign-owned businesses in Aden to sell or close down. Though the law required compensation for property seized by the state, none was forthcoming. A. Besse & Co., for example, did not receive anything until after the 'wahadat' (union) with North Yemen, 26 years later.

WHY DID THE EAP STATES NOT JOIN THE FEDERATION

It is important to look into the reasons why the Eastern (EAP) states did not join the Federation, because, as indicated above, they were initially in favour of doing so. The Hadhramis were in significant ways a different people from those in the WAP. Both the Quaitis and Kathiris had become cosmopolitan in outlook from the effects of their centuries of trade with and settlement in countries around the Indian Ocean, from East Africa, to India, Malaya and what was then the Dutch East Indies. The Kathiris had links going back in their history to tribes which lived in what is now Saudi Arabia and Oman. The Mahra also had trading links with East Africa and the Gulf. Furthermore, the EAP had substantial foreign remittances, which were estimated to be worth up to one third of its GNP.

The older Hadhramis remembered the anarchy which had prevailed in the Eastern Protectorate in the early 1930s, when the Bedouin had held the towns to ransom. It was not until the peace negotiated in 1936 by the Quaiti Sultan Saleh bin Ghalib, Sayyid Bubakr bin Shaikh Al Kaff and Harold Ingrams that security was established in the Hadhramaut. This history probably accounted for the fact that the Eastern states initially favoured federation. They felt that a larger state would serve them better in the future, when Britain withdrew. The design of the federation was at that time (in the mid-1950s) a matter for future negotiation. For that design to be acceptable to the Eastern states, and particularly the Quaiti state, the constitutional construct had to reflect (i) the population of those states, which exceeded a third of the total; (ii) the level of remittances and the customs revenue to which they gave rise, which made these states more independent financially than the WAP states; (iii) the higher quality of administration achieved in at least the Quaiti and Kathiri states; and (iv) limits on the power of individual rulers. In addition, the cosmopolitan outlook of the Hadhrami people would have had to be reflected in policy and decisions. Finally, there would have had to be understandings, not unfavourable to the Eastern states, about any possible future earnings from oil.

There were some astute members of the Quaiti Sultan's Council who were highly critical of the design of the federation from the beginning, especially Shaikh Muhammad Abdulqadir Bamatraf, who would soon draft a new constitution for the Quaiti state, and Shaikh Bubakr Barahim. As early as June 1961, before Aden joined the Federation, Arthur Watts, the Resident Adviser in the EAP wrote to Alistair McIntosh, Protectorate Secretary in Aden relaying the essence of their critique and their view that the EAP states could not possibly join the Federation as it was then constituted as the Customs had not been unified and the rulers appeared to have retained their traditional separate powers. They made it clear that their attitude would remain unchanged even if Aden joined the Federation. But they would be deeply interested if Aden and the Western Federation formed a really united government. Bamatraf spoke of the need for a 'United Government of the Arab South'. What they really found unpalatable was the preservation of all the old tribal divisions under a cloak of unification.[34]

Once the Federation of the Western states was created without Adeni participation, the difficulties facing both Adeni and EAP participation were significant, though the Wahidi state left the EAP and joined the Federation by itself in 1960. The tribal nature of the federal authority was felt to be a fundamental flaw; the preoccupation of the Western states with Yemen and Yemeni subversion was deeply unattractive to Hadhramis; and no solid offer to deal with the revenue and oil questions was ever made. It might have been possible to overcome these drawbacks at the time Aden joined the Federation, but by then the High Commissioner and the British government had both become equivocal about the EAP states joining the Federation, for both political and financial reasons. In his 1962 report to the Secretary of State,[35] Sir Charles Johnston commented that

> the sophisticated suqs of Mukalla and the Wadi Hadhramaut are dangerous potential centres from which a union between Aden and the Federation might be infected with the virus of extreme nationalism. The desirability of a wider union includ-ing the Quaiti state will therefore need very careful study. The problem is not urgent as the Quaitis, puffed up with dreams of oil, have no intention whatever at present of federating with their poor relations to the westward.

In view of the political situation in Aden, even at that time, the complacency of this assessment is breathtaking.

In 1962, when the Kathiri Sultan was again showing interest in joining the Federation, the Governor told the Federal Supreme Council that HMG could not contemplate the entry of the Kathiri state, let alone the Quaiti state, into the Federation on account of

HMG's financial situation. The Council sought assurances that it was HMG's policy to encourage the Eastern states to join and expressed the hope that financial resources would soon be found. He responded that it was HMG's policy to allow each state to determine its future, just as the states already in the Federation had done; the Governor would not therefore attempt to force the Kathiri state to join[36]. When Colonial Secretary Iain Macleod visited Aden in July 1962, he was advised by officials

> that the question of this (Kathiri) or any minor state's accession to the Federation is not relevant to the current talks on the merger of the Colony with the Federation; nor has HMG any interest in raising the matter ... the Secretary of State is advised to agree to discuss this only after the talks on Aden have been completed.[37]

For a poker player like Macleod to accept this advice again suggests that he was not strongly focused on the matter, or he would have appreciated the negotiating possibilities of having three parties to the talks on the merger of Aden with the Federation. It is really pretty amazing that HMG and the Aden government were actively discouraging the possibility of the Kathiri state (and by extension the Quaiti state) joining the Federation at that time. It is much to be regretted that Iain Macleod did not use his formidable powers of negotiation to get a constitutional arrangement for the Federation at the time of Aden's accession which had greater attraction to both Aden and the EAP states. As late as May 1964, HMG was still concerned about the financial cost of accession of the EAP states to the Federation, then estimated at about £1.2 million per annum.[38]

In the course of 1964, the Quaiti Sultan and Council decided to accept UN Resolution 1949 of 1963 as the route to independence. In so doing, they associated themselves with the position taken by the PSP and the SAL, though the resolution had major implications for the Quaiti state and the position of the Sultan, which it did not for the political parties. It is not clear how strong that commitment was, but it did mean that the state had not put itself at odds with Cairo-inspired vituperation.

The possibility of the Eastern states joining the Federation was assessed again when the Labour Party came to power in Britain.

The brief prepared for Mr Greenwood's visit in late 1964[39] referred to the earlier attempt made by Bamatraf assisted by the Attorney General in Aden to draft a new constitution for the Quaiti state, which was agreed but never promulgated. It also referred to the discussions about a possible federation of the eastern states, which the Federal government strongly opposed. The Eastern states had been invited to send observers to the London conference of July 1964, but had declined to do so. (This is not strictly correct – they considered sending Sayyid Muhammad Abdulgadir Bafaqih, but he declined to go.) The conference nevertheless decided to invite the eastern states to join the Federation. The brief for Greenwood also referred to the distrust of the Bedouin felt by the urban centres in the EAP, and the view held by some public figures in the EAP that some of the rulers of the Federation were little more than bedouin themselves.

Also of interest is a long letter to the Colonial Office dated November 1964 written by Tom Oates, when he was Acting High Commissioner.[40] The letter displayed no sense of urgency, even at this date, in bringing the South Arabian states to a satisfactory constitutional settlement. In Oates' view, it was the Federation which was now dragging its feet about the Eastern states, although he did report exchanges between Shaikh Muhammad Farid and Sayyid Ahmad al Attas, the Quaiti Minister. He reported al Attas as saying that the internal position of the Quaiti state was weak as the Sultan could not give a lead; the State Council felt it needed to have broader consultations in the six provinces of the state, which they had not yet arranged to have. Interestingly, in reference to the revenue question, Oates raised as a possibility the Federation adopting the Quaiti system of import duties 'bearing in mind that the Federation must, sooner or later, do something about increasing its own revenues'. Oates also reiterated correctly that the conflict between the Federal rulers and Adeni politicians was making the Federation less attractive to the Quaitis.

The record of Greenwood's discussions[41] with the EAP State Councils and unofficial delegates recorded much interest in the EAP in a move towards electoral systems of government and to protection of the rights of free speech. In this sense, Hadhrami opinion was considerably nearer to Adeni opinion than that of the Federal rulers. The discussion with the Kathiri Sultan was most revealing. In particular, he stressed that he felt a unitary state in the conditions of South Arabia would be impossible in view of the strength of tribalism. On the other hand, he felt the existing federation was far too weak, at the mercy of the constituent rulers of the WAP. If a strong federation were to emerge, he felt this would be attractive to the Hadhrami states. He did not feel they would voluntarily enter a unitary state. Both the Quaiti and Kathiri states sent delegates to the July 1965 constitutional working party. They participated essentially as observers, though giving a nod in the direction of UN resolution 1949.

In February 1966, following publication of the British defence review, the High Commissioner, Sir Richard Turnbull, paid a formal visit to the Quaiti Sultan, with the Resident Adviser. Also present were the Sultan's younger son, Umar, the Quaiti Minister, Sayyid Ahmad al Attas, the Naib of Mukalla, Badr al Kasadi, and Qaid bin Somaida of the Mukalla Regular Army. In total contrast to the previously relaxed approach used in discussion with the Quaitis, Turnbull presented the issue of the future of the Eastern states in the starkest fashion.[42] If they did not join the Federation, subsidies would cease, the Hadhrami Bedouin Legion, which was a vital part of the armed forces, would be disbanded and the oil company would almost certainly leave. If they did join, there would continue to be funds from Britain and the first call would be for maintenance of law and order. Al Attas pointed out that both he and the Sultan were bound by undertakings that there would be no change in the government of the state without full consultation with the people and that they would observe the UN resolutions bearing on South Arabia. Turnbull held a similar meeting with the Kathiris.

However, as Turnbull reported to the Colonial Office, by then the Hadhrami townspeople did not think the Federation would survive independence; the tribesmen were more favourable to the Federation, but would accept anything which provided firm government; some of the northern tribesmen would be quite likely to attach themselves to Saudi Arabia; and the poor health of the Quaiti Sultan, combined with the absence of an effective ministerial council, meant there was an absence of adequate leadership which al Attas could not make good. Turnbull concluded that a delegation of Federal Ministers and Eastern leaders should visit Saudi Arabia to ask King Faisal to use his good offices in support of a constitutional solution for the Hadhramaut and

South Arabia generally. Discussing this proposal the following month, the Federal Supreme Council was reluctant to proceed until they were sure the Hadhramis were willing to join in an approach to King Faisal. John Wilton, Deputy High Commissioner on secondment from the Foreign Office, was asked to assist in arranging the meetings in Mukalla and Jedda. (See Chapter 2 on the international context).

In the absence of effective leadership by the Quaiti state regarding the future, and fearful for their future, the EAP tribes began to meet among themselves. The first meeting took place in Jedda in June 1966, organised by Abdulla Said Buqshan, a prosperous Hadhrami trader.[43] The meeting agreed a five-year truce among all the major tribes, a means for enforcing it, insisted that no person or institution could represent them without prior consultation and agreed to a follow-up meeting. This occurred at Qarat Abdul Aziz in the Kathiri state in July 1966,[44] where the truce was reiterated and a 'lujna' or committee was established to represent the tribes and negotiate with other parties. Though these meetings were reported by the Mukalla Residency to the High Commission, there was no follow-up by either the Resident Adviser or the High Commission.

In September 1966, Sir Richard Turnbull visited the Quaitis and Kathiris again. Amir Ghalib had just left school and succeeded his father. He had a private discussion with Turnbull about the options for the Quaiti state.[45] He felt there was little to attract the Quaiti state into the Federation – there was no economic attraction as the Federation was entirely dependent upon HMG and Aden, while the Quaiti state had annual revenues of about a million pounds which would enable them to survive at a low level. If they joined the Federation, he doubted they would receive the same amount back. He doubted the ability of the Federation to offer the EAP security – he felt that when HMG removed its support, the whole edifice was in danger of collapsing. If the Quaiti state had to join another state, he felt that Saudi Arabia was perhaps the best option, certainly not Oman. He wondered if Turnbull could arrange for him to meet King Faisal. Turnbull said he would look into this, but it would have to be handled with great discretion. Turnbull also met the Kathiri Sultan, who also doubted the morale and capability of the Federal armed forces. He commented that the SAL had a good following in the

Hadhramaut, but it was falling into the hands of wild men and that the Arab Socialist Party wanted to seize power and work closely with Egypt. He said that listening to Cairo Radio made people weak at the knees. He asked what hope the EAP states had against Egypt if Britain could not resist them.

In early 1967, the Quaiti Minister, Ahmed al Attas went abroad and did not return when scheduled. The vacuum in policy-making increased; in al Attas' absence Sultan Ghalib had less official or political support. He attempted to consult more widely and called a tribal meeting in April 1967, which was to have been followed by a national meeting, though that was postponed due to al Attas' absence. Eventually, the Sultan dismissed al Attas and attempted to face the future by himself. He realised that there was no support for joining the Federation and in May 1967 travelled to London to meet King Faisal. The discussions did not lead to any decision and the situation then began to run out of control (see Chapter 4).

Figure 1.5 Sultan Ghalib al Quaiti receives visitors: John Wilton (DHC), Jim Ellis (Resident Adviser), Shaikh Barahim and John Ducker.

BRITISH GOVERNMENT HANDLING OF THE
ADEN QUESTION

Chapter 2, which discusses the international context, highlights elements of the British government's handling of the international dimension and a separate chapter discusses the Defence White Paper of 1966. However, there are other factors bearing on the Aden question which are worth commenting on. Responsibility for Aden within the British government lay with the Colonial Office and subsequently the Foreign Office. The constitutional position of the Governor and later the High Commissioner was such that though he could be dismissed, as both Trevaskis and Turnbull were, he could not be over-ruled while in office on security questions. Staff of the departments of state were very respectful of the boundaries of responsibility of each office. It was only at Cabinet and Cabinet committee level that the threads were drawn together. The Cabinet's Colonial Policy Committee and the Colonial Policy (Official) Committee did have representation of the Foreign Office and the Ministry of Defence, as required.

Nevertheless, reading the records of the different departments on the Aden question, sometimes it is almost as though offices were proceeding along parallel lines, not actually touching at any point (see for example the exchange between Sir Paul Gore-Booth and Sir Roger Allen in Chapter 7 on the Defence White Paper). Frank Brenchley recalled that the Colonial Office was 'out on a limb' when it came to formulation of national policy.[46] There were exceptions. We have seen that the Air Officer Commanding in Aden supported Luce in 1958 against the views of the Chiefs of Staff Committee in London; later Donal McCarthy, a Foreign Office official seconded to the High Commission in Aden, worked assiduously to coordinate thinking and action of a policy nature.

Another possible factor was the relative seniority in the British scheme of things of the Commander-in-Chief, Middle East Command and the Governor/later the High Commissioner. Three successive CinCs (Elworthy, Harrington and Lefanu) were made Chief of the British Defence staff on subsequent appointments. By comparison, Governors and High Commissioners, with the exception of Trevelyan at the end, were by no means so senior and almost certainly much less influential at the highest levels in the government. This no doubt reinforced the authority of the policies argued by the Ministry of Defence.

Finally, although HMG made large-scale expenditures in Aden and South Arabia in a military context, it was parsimonious when it came to development expenditure. The funds made available were not commensurate with the ambitious nature of HMG's objectives. A really significant development programme could have been very influential with the people at large.

The three principal objectives of British policy in South Arabia – independence of a single, viable state, maintenance of the military base and harmonious relations with the Arab world – had different requirements and may well have been incompatible. John Wilton commented that the appointment of Trevelyan to succeed Turnbull in May 1967 probably marked the moment when HMG decided that it would have to abandon the first and second objectives and simply withdraw in the best order possible.[47] Perhaps in the end this did assist in realising the third objective. It has to be concluded that it would have helped had there been someone in London with the brief to ensure that the disparate threads of British policy on Aden were drawn together. It was only with the appointment in May 1967 of Lord Shackleton as minister responsible for Aden, with a position in the Cabinet, that concerted direction of policy was achieved, but by then it was far too late to prevent the anarchic end to British rule in South Arabia. His role was limited to supervising the final stages of British withdrawal – a very dispiriting and undignified affair which left everyone feeling betrayed except the NLF who seized control.

THE DENOUEMENT

From April 1966 until mid-1967 various initiatives were taken to get talks going again between the various parties. Federal government rulers visited Jedda and sought assistance from the Saudis and went to Beirut and elsewhere to talk to the various party leaders. At the United Nations, party leaders and federal officials and ministers were able to conduct exchanges. An interesting example is the exchange recorded by David Treffrey, Permanent Secretary to the Federal Supreme Council, with

Abdulqawi Makkawi.[48] Makkawi evidently continued to believe that it was only a matter of time before the British government would have to talk to FLOSY; he continued totally unwilling to have anything to do with the Federal government, despite the latter's eventual acceptance of UN resolution 1949, despite its drawbacks; and he evidently lived in fear of the Egyptian Intelligence Service. He had nothing to say about the NLF. The parties proved unable to bridge the huge gulf between themselves and the Federal government.

The final, farcical and violent end to British rule began with the visit of the United Nations Mission in April 1967, appointed by the United Nations General Assembly in February 1967 'to recommend practical steps for implementing previous United Nations resolutions on South Arabia'. The earlier resolutions had condemned the Federal government as unrepresentative. HMG accepted the mission because they hoped that it might induce the parties to negotiate more flexibly about the future. The NLF and FLOSY condemned the mission as 'UN puppets of British imperialism'; they refused to deal with them unless their claims were recognised. When the mission declined to do this, the fronts launched strikes, 'popular' riots, and demonstrations. The High Commissioner had the unenviable duty of protecting the mission, which was virulantly anti-British, against possible terrorist attacks at a time when most of the population was not at work. On the day the mission arrived, there were 71 security incidents in Aden. The mission told the High Commissioner that they were not prepared to have any dealings with the Federal government. When the mission visited the al Mansoura detention camp, the detainees jeered at them and refused to talk to them. When they wanted to broadcast to the nation, the Federal authorities, who controlled the broadcasting facilities, refused to let them. The frustrated UN mission then decided to leave Aden, which they did amid farcical scenes at the airport.

Their departure was followed by the arrival of Lord Shackleton to review the situation. His visit resulted in the dismissal of Sir Richard Turnbull and his replacement by Sir Humphrey Trevelyan, a seasoned diplomat. Before Trevelyan accepted the appointment, he sought clarification on three points from the British government at a meeting chaired by the Foreign Secretary:[49]

- That there would be no scuttle along the lines of that from Palestine. On this he was told that the objective was to leave behind something stable, consistent with the UN resolutions. On the other hand, HMG could not rule out the possibility that complete disintegration might occur and HMG could not decide in advance what it would do in that situation. Meanwhile the Aden Bill was being drafted so as to provide for the separation of Aden from the Federation in case that was required.
- The final date for independence must be left flexible. It was agreed that no announcement would be made now, but active steps would be taken to prepare for independence and the rundown of the forces would proceed.
- He wanted assurance that the government was flexible on the future defence arrangements for Aden. He was told that though extraction of the British forces was the first objective and no commitment could be made to leaving British forces on the ground in Aden, in practice ship-borne forces would be available, as well as forces based at Masirah.

The evacuation of service families began on 1 May and was completed by 15 July. On 16 May, Lord Shackleton offered to end the Emergency and release the detainees if the fronts would reciprocate by joining the Federal rulers to form a broader-based government and end the terrorism. This was a bold offer which might have worked a year or so earlier, but now was rejected. The fronts demanded British withdrawal from Aden, ending the rule of the Federal government and the surrender of all authority to them. They knew they only had to sit out the time until the end of the year, when power was anyway likely to fall into their laps. Britain then offered to provide air cover for the Federation for six months after independence, from aircraft carriers. This offer was rejected by the Federal government as inadequate. These discussions were going on against the background of rising tension throughout the Middle East, stimulated by bellicose speeches by Nasser about Israel, Britain and the USA. Anti-Jewish riots occured and Jewish shops and synagogues were burned around Aden. This was the situation when the Six Day War broke out between Egypt and Israel on 3 June, which effectively destroyed the Egyptian forces and blocked the Suez Canal.

The Egyptian defeat had a profoundly dispiriting effect on the entire Arab world, where it was also believed that Britain had assisted Israel. Various irrational acts occurred, such as a strike by the Aden dockers just when the best possible service to shippers were needed in the port to retain the traffic after the closure of Suez. The port operation was therefore taken over by the Armed Services, who ran it until the final withdrawal. There were many security incidents all over Aden, especially in Shaikh Othman. Mukalla and Saiyun came under pressure and the Irish Guards were flown to Riyan and Saiyun. The biggest clash, however, occurred on 20 June. Some non-Aulaqi officers objected to the appointment of the Aulaqi Nasser Bureik as first Arab Commanding Officer of the South Arabian Army. The Federation did not handle this complaint very well and a mutiny broke out, initially in Aden and then at al Ittihad, the Federal capital, where for a time control was lost to the mutineers. In Crater, rumours led the Armed Police to open fire on a patrol of the Northumberland Fusiliers, who in a series of ambushes lost eight men. On that day, the British Army lost 53 men: 22 killed and 31 wounded, mostly fired on by their erstwhile comrades-in-arms.

The impact of the events of 20 June was to undermine still further the authority of the Federal government, which had failed to control its forces. On 27 June, Trevlyan advised London that 'radical measures are necessary; the Federal government in its present form will never be able to govern or control its armed forces'.[50] He proposed that the Federal Supreme Council reconstitute the government on as wide a basis as possible. The danger to be avoided was destroying the Federal government without getting another in its place. In the event, the Federal government did not collaborate with Trevelyan's proposal. In a revealing passage in his dispatch of 6 August, Trevelyan wrote

After 20th June, the feelings between the British and South Arabian forces have radically changed. It is now virtually certain that the South Arabian forces will not call on British land forces for help if they get into difficulties, particularly after the recent friction between our forces and the population. They are more likely in such circumstances to do a deal with the terrorists. In the words of the Commander-in-Chief, 'we now have a potentially hostile South Arabian force who pose a real threat to our forces, particularly in the final month when we are reduced to two battalions and an afloat commando. We are now operating on almost the reverse principle to that which guided us before, namely, we wish to reduce to the absolute minimum the interval between handing over to the South Arabian army and our withdrawal.'[51]

Treveleyan advised that the planning date for independence be advanced to a date within the first ten days of December. He wanted a quick decision so that he could put this to the Federal ministers before they left for Geneva. He warned that if the South Arabian Army moved firmly towards the terrorists, we might have to leave even earlier.

In its reply, the Foreign Office said that the change of date would need the decision of ministers as the current target date had been announced to Parliament as recently as 19 June; ministers were currently away from London. It advised Trevelyan to use the threat of the withholding of post-independence military support to keep the South Arabian Army cooperative until the planned date in January 1968.[52] Treveleyan responded that the January date was chosen because we needed that time to strengthen the South Arabian forces, but as it was now clear that they might become hostile, the basis for the earlier decision had changed.[53]

From this moment, authority began to slip away from the Federal forces towards the NLF forces, which began in August to take over state after state of the Federation. The federal rulers seemed to be taken completely by surprise by this, as many of them actually went to Geneva to meet the UN Mission, just as the upcountry states began to fall to the NLF. This even led to charges that the timing of the Geneva meeting was arranged so that the rulers were out of the country at the time the NLF made their major push. After severe fighting with FLOSY in early November, especially in Shaikh Othman, the NLF came out on top and the South Arabian Army then declared their support for the NLF.

The departure from Aden now became a military withdrawal, the politics and diplomacy becoming secondary considerations. The forces retained in Aden had to be strong enough to keep

control in case a government emerged from the Geneva negotiations but also because control had to be retained of the airfield
and the essential services. It was in this context that the departure
described by Peter Hinchcliffe in his Introduction occurred.

CHAPTER TWO

THE INTERNATIONAL CONTEXT OF SOUTH ARABIA AND BRITISH POLICY

John T. Ducker

Whereas the move towards independence in most colonies and protectorates was stimulated mainly by domestic politics, in the case of Aden, international currents played powerfully on the situation. Arab nationalism, projected through Cairo Radio's *Saut al Arab* (Voice of the Arabs) to the now ubiquitous transistor radio strongly influenced domestic Adeni opinion. The British military presence irritated opinion in the streets and was considered increasingly offensive to the younger, better-educated Arabs. More distantly, the Committee of 24 at the United Nations could be relied upon to fan the aspirations of Adenis rather than address the complexities of the process of achieving independence.

Britain's policy in the Middle East in the 1960s was summarised in a despatch dated 17 April 1963 from the Secretary of State for Foreign Affairs to the heads of missions of the British embassies in the Middle East and the Persian Gulf.[1]

First, we believe that each country in the Middle East should be left to choose its own road to salvation, free from outside interference. Our object is to work with whatever governments are in power, or come to power, on the basis of such common interests as exist between us, and to help them within the limits of our means.

Second, we should accordingly abstain from any interference in the internal affairs of Arab states and from inter-

Arab quarrels, except to the extent to which our special responsibilities may make it, exceptionally, necessary.

Third, we must make it clear that where we have special responsibilities and so long as we have them we intend to carry them out. Our action should be prompt and effective and the minimum necessary to achieve our purpose.

Fourth, we must accept Arab nationalism and 'Nasserism', which is one manifestation of it, as a fact of life. We must take account of it and adopt as sympathetic an attitude as is compatible with British interests.

Fifth, we must avoid any general anti-nationalist, anti-Nasser or anti-revolutionary posture, both because it would be ineffective and because it would provide Arab nationalists, even though they may be working against us, with a convenient target against which to rally other Arabs against the West and to inflict greater harm on our interest.

Sixth, we must continue to keep in close touch with the United States Government and ensure that our policies are coordinated and each properly understood by the other.

The principal British interests in the region at that time, beyond the maintenance of good relations with all countries to facilitate trade and other normal civilian exchanges, can be summarised as follows:

- stability in the Persian Gulf to facilitate the production, refining and flow of oil into international markets;
- support for the large British commercial interests in the oil industry;
- continued access through the Suez Canal and through over-flying rights to facilitate trade and the deployment of the armed forces in the Indian Ocean region, including South East Asia;
- in concert with the USA, minimisation of Soviet influence exercised mainly through the USSR's relations with Egypt, Syria and Iraq.

In implementing these policies, HMG had to take account of several important factors. Arab public opinion widely viewed Britain through the prism of their dispute with Israel. Britain had been the mandated authority in Palestine until it renounced the mandate in 1948, which enabled the Jews to create the state of Israel at the expense of the Palestinian Arabs. This conflict distorted British relations with most Arab states, but especially with those adjacent to Israel – Egypt, Jordan, Syria and Lebanon. Britain had had complex and by no means entirely harmonious relations with Egypt for about 100 years and this too influenced Egypt's policies. At the time of the Suez crisis in 1956, most Arab nations had broken off diplomatic relations with Britain, and it was only in 1963, for example, following a meeting between Lord Home and King Faisal at the UN at which the Buraimi issue was also discussed, that Britain was able to re-open diplomatic relations with Saudi Arabia. Gemal Abdul Nasser's mesmeric hold over Arab public opinion, projected through the medium of, Cairo Radio's *Saut al Arab*, forced Britain on to the defensive on numerous issues and in various contexts.

Nevertheless, among the Middle Eastern states, a number were equally on the defensive vis-à-vis Nasser's republican populism, and against the National Socialism emerging in Baathist Syria and Iraq. In particular, the monarchies in Jordan and Saudi Arabia, the Persian Gulf states run by more or less autocratic rulers, Sudan (whose relations with Egypt were of a love/hate nature), Iran, and in North Africa, Libya, then still a monarchy, and Morocco were all wary of Nasser and the populism he thrived on. In 1961, Britain deployed forces based in Aden to defend Kuwait when it was threatened by Iraq. Thus, there was plenty of room for diplomatic manoeuvre.

The rise to power of Emir, later King, Faisal in Saudi Arabia in the early 1960s was a major new factor making for stability in the Middle East. He was not cowed by Nasser, and, on account of Saudi Arabia's oil riches and geographical scale, and the ultimate assurance of US protection, Faisal could exert his influence for stability in the face of Arab republican nationalism at many points. Furthermore, Arab nationalism was by no means a monolithic phenomenon – for example, the United Arab States, created in 1958 between Egypt, Syria and Yemen, quite soon fell apart and the dreams of its further expansion to encompass Iraq were not realised.

This complex international context complicated the task of bringing South Arabia to independence. Unlike most African and other colonies, where the context was largely domestic, international currents and events constantly buffeted policy-making in South Arabia, and they will be alluded to below. The official papers of the period reflect all of these conflicts, either directly or indirectly, though it was events in Yemen which impinged most directly.

The situation inside Yemen frequently created difficulties on the borders with the Aden Protectorate, both before the creation of the Yemeni republic in 1962 and afterwards. Several attempts had been made by Britain to establish better relations initially with the Ottoman authorities and then with the autocratic Imams of Yemen, making use of earlier treaties wherever possible, but they always lapsed into new conflicts. Trevaskis' book[2] describes many of the exchanges which occurred between 1952 and 1965. In 1957, the young Prince Badr, the eldest son of the Imam, paid a visit to Britain, where he was received without much imagination or forethought about his potential importance to Britain when he would succeed his father. By contrast, he received much greater attention in Moscow and Cairo. When the Imam died in September 1962, republicans supported by Egypt seized control of Sana'a, though Badr escaped and made his way to northern Yemen, where he could obtain support from Saudi Arabia. A civil war ensued between republicans, strongly supported by Egypt, which at one point had over 50,000 troops in the country, and royalists, supported logistically and diplomatically by Saudi Arabia.

HMG's approach to the recognition of governments in the event of civil war or revolution was essentially pragmatic, as indicated above in the policy statement. The principal question was who controlled the country. If a government was in effective control, Britain would normally recognise it. In the case of Yemen, relations between Britain and Egypt had not recovered from Suez and Egypt was virulently opposed to British influence in South Arabia. Britain's official position in the civil war was neutral, though HMG did not welcome an Egyptian-supported republic, so it prevaricated in the hope that the tide would turn against the republicans. (There were in fact strong differences of opinion within the British government on the issue of recognition, both at the official and the political level. There were those who argued that a friendly gesture towards the republicans could have served to detach them from the Egyptian occupiers. There were others who wanted HMG to strongly support the royalists, a position encourged by the expulsion by President Abdulla Sallal of the British Charge d'Affairs in Yemen, Christopher Gandy. Thus, HMG policy vacillated.) By 1964, the royalists had extended their control from the northern regions to encompass much of the country outside the triangle formed by Sana'a, Taiz and Hodeida, inclining Britain even less to recognise the republican regime. It allowed the royalist legation to remain in London.

By contrast, the US government was quick to recognise the republican government. In February 1963, officials of the US State Department seeking ways to arrange mediation in the Yemeni civil war, met with British officials led by Sir Roger Stevens, Deputy Under Secretary of State at the Foreign Office to discuss their different approaches to the Yemen.[3] The US emphasised the internal political situation in Egypt, the impact of Egyptian policy on the world at large and was keen to wean Egypt away from diplomatic, economic and military reliance on the Soviet Union. They felt Nasserism tended to weaken the appeal of communism. By contrast, HMG paid more attention to Nasser's impact on the Arab world, in particular in the Arabian peninsula and the Persian Gulf, whose rulers were not at all attracted to his republican populism, and which is where British interests were greatest. Sir Roger Stevens pointed out that with the possible exception of Algeria, no Arab state approved of Nasser's intervention in the Yemen. If we were to recognise the Yemeni republic, this would be widely interpreted as a gesture in favour of Nasser.

The US recognition of the republican government in Yemen later became controversial in Washington. This was apparent when in August/September 1964, the US ambassador to Saudi Arabia, Parker T. Hart, who had served three times in the country and whose views were respected, visited London.[4] The ambassador had recommended that the US government closely coordinate its policy on the Arabian Peninsula with Britain and Saudi Arabia. He was particularly concerned at the possibility of South Arabia becoming independent as a satellite of Egypt. There was initial discussion about the possibility of Saudi financial aid to the Federation of South Arabia. He was keen for the South Arabian League (SAL), and ex-sultan Ali Abdul Karim, to be accepted as having a role in the political future of South Arabia. He felt the SAL could help to strengthen local nationalism to counter Egypt's influence, and to help bring the Eastern Protectorate states into the Federation. He reported King Faisal as thinking that Britain was moving too rapidly towards the independence of South Arabia and felt that King Faisal would be willing to visit the Federation, though lower-level contacts would have to precede such a visit. It is the greatest pity such a visit could not be arranged for it could have helped to stabilise the situation sufficiently to facilitate the emergence of a South Arabian state with a longer-term, more conservative regime than the radical, violent republic which in the event seized power.

The ambassador was warned by officials in London about the difficulty of the federal rulers accepting Ali Abdul Karim as a participant in the political process, but this warning is not convincing. Had HMG been resolute in encouraging a rapprochement with the SAL and Ali Abdul Karim, the Federal rulers would have had to accept the situation – they would have had no alternative.

Immediately after the 1962 Yemeni revolution, Egypt was too busy in Yemen to bother about South Arabia, but as the royalist cause prospered and Egypt concluded that Sherif Hussein of Beihan was acting as a conduit of supplies to the royalists, their attentions turned increasingly towards South Arabia. From the time of Nasser's visit to Yemen in December 1963, they increasingly opposed both Britain and the Federal government in South Arabia. They found it easy to facilitate attacks on the British installations and the Federal rulers through training, supply of weapons and actual direction of operations. Egypt was not interested in the future of the country, per se, but on removing British influence from the area. A number of South Arabians who had fled from South Arabia to exile in Egypt eventually realised that Egypt's objectives were different from their own, regretted their move and sought to extricate themselves from Egyptian influence.[5]

As the Yemen civil war ground on, and approached stalemate, President Nasser and King Faisal met in Alexandria in late 1964 and later at Taif and Jedda and arranged for a conference of both parties to the war to be held the following year at Haradh, whose purpose was to seek an end to the war and determination of a new constitutional construct for the Yemen. Nasser hoped to get a government friendly to Egypt's international objectives. Faisal hoped the conference would lead to the creation of a sovereignty council as an interim government for the Yemen until a new constitution had been adopted by domestic consent. He also hoped that by the time of the conference the position of the Egyptian army in Yemen would be untenable, and Nasser keen to withdraw it.

On 17 December 1964, the American Charge d'Affaires in the Yemen, Harlan Clark, visited Tom Oates, Acting High Commissioner in Aden, to brief him on the internal situation in the Yemen.[6] He described a situation in which the republican areas of the country were dominated by the Egyptians, who were 'cordially detested' by the majority and the responsible republicans were desperate to find a way out of the impasse. Iriani (Zaidi) and Numan (Shafai) wanted to establish a common basis of action with Zubairi (Zaidi) and Ali Muhammad Mutahhar (Shafai). He thought it very important for HMG to make it known to the more reasonable republicans that it sympathised with the situation in which they found themselves and would respond helpfully if the opportunity presented itself. He also argued that there was also strong opposition to the Hamid ad-Din family (the family of the former Imam) and support by the Saudis for them discouraged many of those most keen to get the Egyptians out. As a result of this spreading demoralization, Clark thought the Eastern Bloc, which had played their cards very well, were potential beneficiaries of the civil war.

Various attempts were made by Yemenis outside Egyptian control to find a way to end the war by themselves. On 31 December 1964, the royalist Foreign Minister, Sayyid Ahmad al Shami, visited London and described[7] the so-called 'third force' of republicans which it was hoped would gain support among Arab governments for a nation-wide conference to call a cease-fire, seek complete withdrawal of the Egyptian army and an end to Saudi support to the royalists. He talked of victory being in sight. He said the 'Young Yemenis' were acting entirely independently, and that they were important in Yemen. Their initiative had King Faisal's blessing. He said that the Hashid confederation of tribes would shortly be deserting the republicans. He said that the impetus for a national conference was increasing. The Imam Badr had recently approved a charter, drafted by him (Shami) which provided for an Imamate Council and an Executive Cabinet. Its purpose was to convince all Yemenis that neither the royalists generally nor the Imam himself wished to return to the autocracy of the old Imam;

those days were gone. He intended that the new Yemeni government would recognise the Federation of South Arabia and work for
good relations with it. Al Shami warned that even if the 'third
force' was successful, Egypt would try to keep some of its army in
the Yemen.

Some 'young Yemeni republicans' were visiting Beirut at this
time, having previously visited Jedda, and held a press conference
at which they outlined their ideas.[8] They said that the present
regime in the Yemen was not the republic they had been seeking;
Yemenis now had no say in their own affairs; Yemen had become
a battleground between outside powers; the people eagerly awaited
the conference agreed upon by King Faisal and President Nasser,
but it had fallen through because the Yemeni leaders were not
representative; those fighting Sallal were not all royalists, but they
were all opposed to the Egyptian-supported regime. The Yemen
needed help, not fire and slaughter. They wanted all outside forces
withdrawn to be followed by a national conference to choose an
interim government capable of preparing elections or a referendum on a new constitution. The pro-Egyptian press in Beirut
and elsewhere attacked these young republicans as traitors, hired
mercenaries; the Baathist press was more balanced and supported
the withdrawal of all outside interference in the Yemen; the independent press concluded that the Yemeni republic had collapsed.
The group was planning to visit a number of other Arab countries
to gain support for their approach to Yemen's future.

Separately, the US Embassy in Yemen reported to the State
Department[9] that other Yemeni republican leaders struggling with
Egyptian control had had a showdown with President Sallal on
27 December 1964, insisting that full power be returned to a
Republican Council. Sallal and his principal supporters visited
Cairo to discuss the situation. A Foreign Office assessment of the
internal Yemeni situation dated 12 January 1965[10] indicated that
General Hassan al Amri had been given an enhanced role in
improving law and order in the country and that this seemed
to indicate that Egypt had reverted to the search for a military
solution to the civil war.

With the rise to power of Emir, later King, Faisal in Saudi
Arabia, a strong mutuality of interest emerged between Britain and
Saudi Arabia over the future of Yemen and South Arabia, which is
well reflected in the report of an exchange of views between the

British Ambassador and King Faisal in early January 1965.[11] Faisal had led Saudi forces into Yemen in the 1930s and thus was very well informed about the country. The ambassador reported Faisal as saying

> it did not matter who governed in the Yemen so long as no Egyptians were left in the country. He was prepared to recognize any regime in Yemen, so long as it was the choice of the people after the withdrawal of all Egyptian troops. There was no question of recognizing any Yemeni regime before that happened.

Nasser had gone back on the agreements Faisal had reached with him at Alexandria and Taif providing for the phased withdrawal of Egyptian forces and installation of a provisional government. He was not worried however as he felt that before long Nasser would be finished there. He also felt that US aid to Egypt was facilitating the Egyptian intervention in Yemen. In meetings with the US Ambassador to Saudi Arabia, also reported to London in January 1965,[12] King Faisal elaborated on this point. He reiterated that Egypt was not entirely a free agent and Egyptian dependence on eastern bloc countries for weapons meant that Russia and possibly China were behind it. He argued that Nasser could not easily get out of the Yemen even if he wanted to. Faisal encouraged the US to use its naval resources to interrupt and interdict Egyptian military supplies to the Yemen along the Red Sea. The US ambassador felt this would be counter-productive and said that after an explanation of the nature of US aid to Egypt, the King had shown greater understanding of it.

In regard to South Arabia, the British ambassador reported Faisal as saying

> he recognized the full value for the stability of the region of what we were doing and intended to do in connection with the future of South Arabia; we could rest assured that he fully realized how closely Anglo-Saudi interests were linked in preserving the security and stability of South Arabia. Saudi Arabia had not the slightest desire to intervene in the internal affairs of that area, but she would of course be glad to assist economically and otherwise after independence.

In fact, Kemal Adham, a brother-in-law of King Faisal, visited Aden about that time and reiterated Saudi willingness to assist the Federation economically. In July 1965, there were exchanges[13] between the Foreign and Colonial Offices in London about encouraging Saudi influence in South Arabia 'as an insurance for 1968', in which the possible role of Muhammad bin Ladhin, Osama's father, was mentioned. In 1966, John Wilton, visited Jedda and met bin Ladhin. He recalls that the discussions were highly nebulous. He made no proposals as to how the Sultans might be brought to embrace the Federation and the discussions led nowhere. They were not pursued further by either side.[14]

In retrospect, it is the greatest pity that these diplomatic exchanges between Britain and Saudi Arabia concerning South Arabia were not more productive. For associating Saudi Arabia with a constitutional construct for South Arabia would have shown that there was a long-term conservative alternative to set against the populist pan-Arabism propagated by Egypt. Certainly, Saudi support would have been influential in the Eastern Aden Protectorate as a number of Hadhramis had made fortunes in Saudi Arabia and there were growing ties between the two countries. Part of the explanation for the disappointing outcome can perhaps be accounted for by differences of view within the Saudi royal family – in the view of Sir John Wilton and Frank Brenchley, both of whom served in Jedda, King Faisal and Saud favoured a settled and united Yemen, with or without Aden and the Protectorates; Amir Sultan and probably Fahd tended to think that a divided and feuding set of southern neighbours would prove less of a threat to Saudi interests.[15] Thus Saudi policy vacillated and Faisal tended to wait and see. It would have required a more determined diplomacy on Britain's part to get more consistent Saudi support for a new South Arabian state, and a willingness on Britain's part to bring the SAL in out of the cold. That, in mid-1966, when Britain had already announced the intention to leave Aden without a defence agreement, the Federal government and the High Commission should still have been debating how to open discussions with the Saudi authorities suggests that they and the British government were reacting to events, rather than actively seeking to engage the Saudis.

In February 1965, the US Charge in Taiz told the High Commissioner in Aden[16] that the Egyptian-supported Sallal regime had gone onto the offensive again, both politically and militarily. They were destroying whole villages and using poison gas. He expected increased support from Egypt for the opponents of the Federation of South Arabia.

Al Shami visited London again in October 1965 with other ministers when he met with the head of the Arabian Department of the Foreign Office, and again briefed officials[17] about the efforts being made to end the conflict and the plans for the Haradh conference. If the conference were successful, Egypt and Saudi Arabia would recognise a new provisional government and it was hoped that other countries would do so also. On 20 October, he and two other royalist ministers met Mr George Thomson the new Minister of State at the Foreign Office, and three officials. The ministers said[18] that they had come to Britain to give HMG news of the current situation in the Yemen, to thank HMG for not recognising the republican government and to seek assistance, especially medical aid and food. They needed this assistance to counter the effect of the issuance by the republicans of the new Yemeni currency. They also stressed that they sought self-determination for the Yemeni people; the Jedda agreement provided for an interim government and they were confident of success in the proposed referendum. People had to experience Nasser before they learned to distrust him. They felt that if Nasser withdrew his army, he would seek ways to continue exercising influence in Yemen. The main danger now was not Egypt's army, but rather their activities in the fields of propaganda, diplomacy and Yemeni politics.

The new Labour Government, which came to power in Britain in late 1964, had some hopes of being able to forge a new relationship with Egypt. Mr George Thomson had known Abdulla Al Asnag for some years and hoped to be able to influence him in regard to Aden. Al Asnag visited him in London in August 1965[19] and argued that Egypt was looking for a way out of Yemen if this could be done without humiliation. There may well have been an element of wishful thinking on Asnag's part and again there was no sign that Egypt was modifying its policy in regard to either Yemen or Aden. Thomson planned a visit to Cairo in late 1965 for a wide-ranging discussion of Anglo-Egyptian concerns. In preparation he had lunch with the Egyptian Ambassador in London. His report of these discussions on South Arabian matters is of interest.[20] The ambassador implied that Egyptian interference in South Arabia must be seen as a reaction to British interference in the Yemen. He instanced the mercenaries and said that while he did not expect Britain to recognise a new Yemeni regime until it had been accepted by the Yemenis, he felt the continued presence of the royalist Yemeni mission in London was a source of misunderstanding. The Labour government's hopes of better relations with Egypt proved to be illusory. Whatever the prospects for Thomson's dialogue in Egypt in September 1965, they were undermined before he even met Nasser. Turnbull's dismissal of Makkawi, Chief Minister of Aden, occurred the day before he was due to meet Nasser and Nasser cancelled the meeting – very poor diplomatic coordination.

The British Defence Review, the results of which were announced in February 1966, was ineptly handled so far as South Arabia was concerned. (See Chapter 7 for a more detailed discussion of this matter.) Though both Lord Beswick, a junior minister at the Colonial Office in November 1965, and Denis Healey, the Defence Secretary in January 1966, had specifically reassured the Federal government of Britain's intention to continue to provide military support to the Federation, in February 1966 Healey announced that the Aden base was to be closed and that no military support would be provided to the new state. Closing the base was not a matter of great concern to the Federal government, but the denial of defence support was. It gave the Egyptians an immediate pretext for going back on their declared intention of withdrawing their troops, an entirely predictable result, and effectively repudiated the encouraging noises made by King Faisal. Senior British officials, including Turnbull, had advised HMG against announcing the decision on the military base at that time, but they were over-ruled. In the whole sad history of Aden and South Arabia, it is difficult to point to any other decision on the part of HMG which had such predictable and malign consequences. It was not until the Khartoum summit of Arab states after the Six Day War, that Egypt finally signed an agreement with Saudi Arabia for the withdrawal of its troops, but by then British troops were already being withdrawn from Aden and it was too late to influence the outcome in South Arabia.

In April 1966, members of the Federal government visited Jedda for talks with King Faisal. By then they were also talking to the

SAL, perhaps a result of Saudi advice. King Faisal[21] advised the delegation to 'steal the clothes of the enemy', descend from their thrones into the arena and fight the enemy with their own weapons. He wanted them to get together with the SAL and any other group not in Egyptian pay, to use the UN resolutions and set up a provisional government which would gradually enact the terms of the UN resolutions. Elections could be held when peace was restored. He said he would use his influence to ensure the Hadhramis came into the new state as soon as the Federation had set its own house in order. He promised financial support and diplomatic recognition and promised to ensure South Arabia would get recognition at the UN. These exchanges occurred out of deep frustration and a sense of betrayal among the Federal ministers at the decision of the British government to deny them military support after independence, and were encouraged by some British officials in Aden. However, the talks were fruitless – the Federal ministers did not follow, or were not capable of following, King Faisal's advice, they were not able to persuade the parties to actively engage with the Federal Governement in discussions about the future, and Faisal was not able to commit himself to a government which was so plainly likely to fail.

Although there were tactical differences between HMG and the United States over policy in this region of the world, they shared a broadly similar strategy. The US government had a long-standing policy of encouraging de-colonisation, though they were supportive of the measures being taken by the British government in bringing its colonies to independence. The United States fully realised the strategic importance of the Aden base and made no secret of this in their discussions with Saudi Arabia. Though they tried to keep Nasser free of communist influence, in the event, Egypt's decision to buy arms from the eastern block in 1955 was the first of many such contracts, which in the end escalated the scale of conflict between the Arabs and Israel to the point where the US had in the early 1970s to use its full diplomatic and military strength to resist Soviet influence in the Arab world and defend Israel.

The Soviet interest in South Arabia was strategic more than ideological. They would support any party which was opposed to British and American influence in the area. Initially, they felt Nasser to be the best agent for them to exercise their influence, but over time they became stronger supporters of Syria and Iraq. In the 1960s, however, they provided support to Egypt and Yemeni republicans and to other groups which would fight against the more conservative regimes and British influence. When the NLF detached itself from Egypt's support, they continued to receive military supplies from the Eastern bloc. In the months before the independence of South Arabia, Russian fishing and other vessels were already appearing off the coast of South Arabia. After independence, the Soviet Union and East Germany soon became patrons of the South Yemeni regime and looked into the possibility of creating a naval base on Socotra. (Like all previous naval powers in the Indian Ocean, they found this not to be practicable.)

The major impact of the United Nations on South Arabian affairs was through the debates in the De-Colonization Committee and General Assembly resolution No. 1949 of December 1963. Opponents of the merger of Aden Colony with the Federation went to the committee to seek support for their opposition. In general, Britain resisted UN involvement in the process of de-colonization because they feared it would just complicate an already complex political process, that it would lead to pressure for UN involvement in other domestic policy matters and lead to loss of control of the process. It was only in cases of impending deadlock – such as Palestine, Cyprus and Aden – that it encouraged the UN to play a role. In the case of Aden, it was the failure to find a way to organise elections in Aden Colony and deadlock in the relations between the Federal ministers and the Aden government that brought UN involvement in April 1967. This proved to be fruitless – the UN mission declined to meet the Federal Ministers and the mission was greeted by violent demonstrations organised in the streets (perhaps by Federal officials) – the UN were unable to broker a negotiated future for the country.

In May 1967, only a month before the Six Day War and six months before the date set for the independence of South Arabia, King Faisal paid a State Visit to Britain. Frank Brenchley, who attended the meetings, considers that Prime Minister Wilson was taken by surprise at the vehemence of the King's support for the Palestinians who were under relentless Israeli pressure.[22] The King, who was accompanied to London among others by Ali Abdul Karim, the former Sultan of Lahej, received some of the

Federal ministers and Sultan Ghalib al Quaiti during his visit. These exchanges did not accomplish much. Ghalib was evidently surprised to find Ali Abdul Karim in the King's delegation and unsure what to advocate for his state. He indicated that he had to consult the people through the medium of the proposed National Council. The King evidently did not want to push for any particular solution for South Arabia. It was too late for the Federal leaders to merge or combine with the SAL or FLOSY and the NLF were not willing to concede anything to them in their grab for power. Astonishingly, however, the King did persuade the British government to announce a reversal of its defence policy and persuaded them to agree to provide military support for six months to the Federal government when it became independent, perhaps a gesture or sop by Wilson towards the King. In the event, the Federation soon crumbled under the assault of the NLF and Britain extricated itself from this commitment as soon as it could. Whatever hopes the Labour Government may have had for al Asnag and his colleagues in Aden crumbled just as thoroughly as those of the Federal rulers and their erstwhile supporters in the Conservative Party.

Overall, it has to be said that the form of our departure from Aden amid the accession to power of a virulent and violent revolutionary party, the over-throw of all the traditional rulers with whom Britain had had treaties of protection and advice, the loss of the military facilities provided by the Aden base and the rapid penetration of the country by the Soviet Bloc was a major foreign policy reversal. In most colonies, independence was arrived at with much goodwill on both sides, albeit with some scepticism among the British officials about the likely outcome. In Aden, there was no goodwill. There was a strong and justified sense of betrayal on the part of large numbers of both British and Arab, and much bloodshed. It was a poisonous experience for nearly all those directly involved. No one came out of South Arabia with credit.

CHAPTER THREE

THE POLITICAL OFFICERS IN THE WESTERN ADEN PROTECTORATE

Peter Hinchcliffe

INTRODUCTION

I had very much hoped that, even after 40 years, I would have been able to tap the experiences of more of my former colleagues who had worked as Assistant Advisers (AAs) (or Political Officers as they tended to be called) upcountry in the Western Aden Protectorate (WAP) as it metamorphosed into the Federation of South Arabia than has proved to be the case. One has died very recently, three felt so bitter about the shabby way that our former Arab friends were left in the lurch that they are just not prepared to dredge up painful memories. Others feel constrained, even now, by the provisions of the Official Secrets Act. For any short-fall in the quantity of witnesses, however, I have made up with quality and what you now read is only a very small proportion of the voluminous material from which I have so generously been allowed to select the bare bones for this chapter. John Ducker's Chapter 4 on the Eastern Aden Protectorate describes the lives of Political Officers in that (for most of the time) better administered and more peaceful region.

Robin Young's guidance to Assistant Advisers below gives some idea of what the Political Officers were meant to do in what sometimes seemed a vague and undefined employment. We did not have executive powers and success or failure was largely determined by the personal relationships we built up with the local rulers within our area of responsibility. It could be a lonely and

Figure 3.1 Peter Hinchcliffe on tour in Eastern Fadhli Sultanate in 1962. The antelope strapped to the landrover was his contribution to the evening meal!

socially isolated life – good Arabic and an understanding wife were great advantages. We sometimes seemed over-influenced by what George Brown, the Labour Foreign Secretary in the mid-1960s told one of our number was our 'worm's eye view'. It was difficult to focus on the bigger picture, nationally and internationally when we were immersed in very local affairs. Even events in Aden sometimes seemed to be happening on another planet and of little relevance to me as near as 50 miles away. I for one had very little appreciation of how potent the forces of Arab nationalism were to prove – despite having little boys shout 'Aysh Gamal!' – ('Long Live Gamal (Abdul Nasser)!') at me wherever I went – and despite so many passionate conversations with Arab colleagues, military and civilian, who from the outset had very little respect for the Federal government and its viability nor for many of the Federal rulers whom they wrote off as British clients, doomed once Britain lost interest in the area. Many may not have liked Nasser and his own imperial expansionist (Egyptian) ambitions but they believed that he would destroy the Federation one day and ensure our withdrawal from the area. The Defence White Paper of 1966 (see

Chapter 7) may not have come as much of a surprise to educated Arabs inside Aden and in the Protectorates, nor I believe to many senior British officials who had expected something of this sort once the Labour party took office in 1964; see, for example, Robin Young's sense of impending doom as recorded in his diaries. The White Paper did, however, come as a surprise to me – I was enjoying my exotic life and had a faith that we British would see Nasser off and leave the Federal government as a viable post-colonial regime. I wonder how many of my younger Political Officer British friends had their heads as buried in the sand as mine was, but I do know that to many of them our planned withdrawal and abandonment of the base came as a rude and unwelcome shock. Even after 1966, however, I worked on with enjoyment and some lingering optimism that things might yet work out well.

THE POLITICAL OFFICERS IN WAP

A Joint Intelligence Committee (JIC) Cabinet paper of December 1965 covers an analysis by Don McCarthy, a Foreign Office official, at that time Political Adviser with Middle East Command about the difficulties of gathering intelligence upcountry. Referring to the part played by political officers in frontline intelligence work he describes how 'many of them live in mud huts, working on trestle tables without secretaries or ciphers, in rooms from which the windows are shot up from time to time. They are harassed by callers and the great effort required to achieve the simplest thing.'

I lived once in a (very comfortable) mud brick house[1] and in a series of attractive stone ones but accept the description of an often harassed existence coping with the most basic of facilities. My letter of appointment (text at Appendix 3) had prepared me not to expect too much of an easy number. Miss A. Chambers of the Department of Technical Co-operation[2] warned me that 'the conditions of desert life are comfortless and most rigorous'. And if I were fortunate enough to be posted to 'the settled states of the Protectorate where I would be responsible for guiding the states towards stability and the first foundation of ordered government', I would be unwise to relax too much. 'There is a constant risk of the breakdown of law and order, and conditions will also be disagreeable and dangerous.' I was relishing the prospect of 'supervising the activities of Government security forces and in *guarding the frontier from foreign intrusion and intrigue.*' I imagine that these letters were deliberately over-egged to deter the faint or half-hearted and the thoughtless, after any old job. To me, however, it was an irresistible summons to a romantic Beau Geste existence so unlike the careers offered by the ICIs, the Metal Boxes, the Home Civil Service so prized by my fellow students. And the money was good thanks to a generous inducement element, better than most other starting salaries being offered at home!

In 1966 Robin Young produced a guidance note for Political Officers, which covered all aspects of the job, if only in the Federation. Somewhat late in the day one might think. By that time the cadre of youngish Assistant Advisers, as Political Officers were called, who were doing their first substantive post-University job (although Bill Heber-Percy had been 'co-opted' from the Welsh Guards) had been reinforced by army officers on attachment (such as Tim Goschen in Wahidi) and a number of older men who had served in other colonial territories or retired from military service. These included Bill Reid, Jack Wright (both ex West Africa), Patrick Holmwood, John Shebbeare (Indian Army), John Reader (British army) and (a younger example) Hugh Walker, who had come from Kenya. These experienced officials found service in the Federation totally different from their previous careers in more orderly and more stable places and were initially at sea in the unfamiliar waters of WAP.[3] So this very comprehensive handbook was mostly for their guidance and I am indebted to Hugh Walker for a sight of his copy.

Robin's explanation of the Assistant Adviser's position is worth quoting. After explaining the context provided by the advisory treaties between HMG, as represented by the High Commissioner, and the individual states and delegated to the WAP office headed before the creation of the Federation by the Adviser and British Agent, now Assistant High Commissioner (Federation) Robin continued:

> The difficulties besetting the Assistant Adviser in his day-to-day work are many and various, and caused in the main by the fact [that] he has no executive authority. He is not a District Commissioner but, as his title implies, he is stationed in the

States to advise the local authorities on the good government of their territories. This advice is not only confined to the broader aspects of local government such as constitutional development, financial policy and the reform of the court systems, but covers a far wider field and extends to more mundane matters such as the planning of villages, the provision of domestic and agricultural water supplies, drainage schemes and other public health matters. In brief, there is hardly any aspect of local life in which the Assistant Adviser may not find himself involved.

He warned:

The Assistant Adviser is not only a dogsbody, but everyone's dogsbody. Blamed when things go wrong and generally forgotten when all is quiet and apparently well. He is the recipient of many grievances when even if well founded, by no means always the case, he has little authority to rectify . . . In brief his lot far from being a romantic idyll, is hard, often frustrating and sometimes dangerous.

Quite a job description, and an increasingly daunting one as the security situation upcountry in many states deteriorated and the work of development and encouraging good governance often seemed secondary to counterterrorism and sheer self preservation.

I was fortunate to have my first posting as Assistant Adviser (AA) in Ja'ar[4] the administrative centre of the Lower Yafa' Sultanate and within the Abyan area – the Protectorate's major cotton growing region. At that time it was peaceful, with a competent administration; nor was it isolated. It was only about 40 miles from Aden, which was not too demanding a journey depending on the state of the tide, as the beach was the only road – both east and west.[5] There was a small, mostly British, expatriate community comprising the senior staff of the Abyan Cotton Board and of the Cotton Ginnery/Research Station. There was a club with a bar and a regular cinema and during my time there I introduced golf, building a fairly basic course at Zingibar, the Fadhli capital.[6]

I enjoyed the support of a very experienced Adeni Arab in his mid-50s: 'junior' Assistant Adviser (JAA), Mr Ali Qassim. Stephen Day who was the AA at Zingibar, had a year's start on me so was my informal mentor until Robin Young returned from leave some two months after my arrival. Stephen had been in Ja'ar as my immediate predecessor, as had Godfrey Meynell before him, in 1959, and it was obviously regarded as the ideal training post for a young cadet[7] Political Officer.

Godfrey Meynell[8] describes the Abyan Cotton scheme as something of a showpiece for Empire – at least compared with anything else in the Protectorates.

The Fadhlis held the south and east of the delta, and the bulk of their people lived in less hospitable country further to the east. The northwest portion of Abyan was occupied by Kaladi maktab[9] of the Lower Yafa'i tribe, most of whose population lived in tangled hills to the north. The Wadi Bana debouched into the northwest corner of the plain, so the Yafa'is had first sight of the seasonal floods. The smaller Wadi Hassan emerged into Fadhli territory to the east. During the previous decade (the 1950s), two remarkable men, Hartley[10] and Congden had established a highly successful cotton scheme, with a reliable market in Liverpool for the product. This had so revolutionised life for both Fadhlis and Yafa'is with land in the area that a *modus vivendi* had been found between them despite centuries of hostility. A system of dams was established in the wadis – built at first of earth. These diverted the rich chocolate floodwater to an increasingly intricate system of canals, whence it was fed into the high-banked fields. It stood in each field a few hours before the bank was broken and the water admitted to the field below. As the years passed, the great earth dams which could only be built and broken once a year were replaced by permanent fixtures with gates.

The Abyan Board was established on a spectacular rock, above the principal Yafa'i town, Ja'ar. It had a manager, engineers, electricians, agricultural officers and accountants, mostly British. Frank Downing, the Chief Engineer or Bash-Muhandis had the complete trust of the local population. He was an elderly, quiet Evangelical Christian, rather delicate, with a passion for his job. He had made hair-raising little bridges across the canals for the Board's landrovers – approachable, as a rule, only at right angles. His word was law and his decision final. Ted Eyre, the Manager and Guy Hudson his successor were Sudan sahibs of the old school. They both hit it off well with Robin Young and accepted the complications of local politics.

In a chapter mostly about Political Officers I agree with Godfrey's stricture: Political Officers might think they were calling the shots but probably the best work in the Empire was done by the Downings, Takis (-Stephanides, a Greek ginnery engineer), Ogborns (an agricultural officer) and Anthonys (the Head of the Cotton Research Station) who ignored the politics as long as possible and did what they could for the people. You can add to this list many others in the Protectorates such as Terry Hague (an Agricultural Officer), Graham Hunter (a Doctor) and the legendary 'Buck' (a peripatetic government engineer).[11]

Kennedy Trevaskis the British Agent had instructed me to learn the ropes from Mr Ali and to pick up some Arabic. There had been neither briefing, nor any guidance either in London before I left or in Aden when I arrived. Johnny Johnson detailed one of his very junior domestic staff, Abdullah Sha'abaan, to be my 'cook bearer'. He was as green as I was and being from Seiyun in the Hadramaut (EAP) was not familiar with WAP. At Mr Ali's suggestion I spent several uncomfortable days on a camel learning 'my' district and practising my very primitive Arabic on anyone I happened to encounter. It left me with a lifelong dislike of the supercilious, evil tempered and unpredictable 'ship of the desert' but at least I learned my way around, becoming something of a high profile figure (and one of fun, too, I suspect!).

Rex Smith[12] had a similar lack of orientation. He at least had the experience of spending 18 months in the Aden Students' Office in London, helping to look after young men from South Arabia studying in the UK. Several senior South Arabian figures called on the office when in Britain and Rex got to know them. He also had the advantage of having studied Arabic although he felt his knowledge of mediaeval Arabic texts was of little practical use in mastering the colloquial language of the Arabian Peninsular.

I think we were all thrown into the lion's den without any notion of the broad Middle Eastern picture (so important) and indeed without an adequate briefing on the overall South Arabian scene.

Rex's lion's den was a posting to the Wahidi Sultanate:

> with a wife and 5-month-old son with the nearest medical help
> in Ataq five hours away by road! There I already knew the
> State Secretary – Muhammad bin Said as he had visited
> London several times, with whom I like to think I established
> some sort of rapport. Here the regime was tough, nothing was
> done without his say-so and appalling punishments were dealt
> out. My predecessor had withdrawn into himself and I gather
> made no attempt to communicate with state officials. I felt that
> I should try and make some sort of impact but I was clearly not
> in a position to do so.

This was a common problem with brand new political officers
who, by definition, lacked any previous experience in dealing
with local powerbrokers in unfamiliar surroundings. But Rex
struggled on:

> A pleasant surprise was that Bin Said regularly told me what
> was going on (but only of course what he wanted me to know!)
> and was generally and genuinely (I felt) ready to communicate.
> His hold was such, however, that nothing happened without
> his knowledge and my early naive thoughts that the head of
> the Wahidi FNG [Federal National Guard] 2, who came to
> see me regularly and slightly furtively and who projected an
> ever-so-slightly anti-state establishment line, was genuinely
> desirous of my knowing exactly what was going on, soon
> brought the realisation that this was all part of Bin Said's plan
> to control everything, even the AA! And that was the nearest I
> got to organising 'political intelligence'; it just was not possible
> there. My favourite occupation in Wahidi was the relatively
> large amount to spend on development and Ralph Daly [Senior
> Adviser in charge of Eastern WAP] had paid an early visit to
> Wahidi in order to set this in motion. It was he who largely
> prevented the money all going into Bin Said's and his cronies'
> pockets and this left me with an easier job to chase up the
> actual work (roads, wells, irrigation schemes, etc.). I found
> the annual estimates very taxing with totally unreasonable
> demands for increases in this and that, but I had a good help
> in the State treasurer. I could travel widely without fear of

bad security and I did so, mainly chasing up the development schemes, but also I learned much linguistically and of life in the area. The one bit of clout that Rex had: 'if one could prod "Aden" into action over something, it gave one sometimes the only real standing one had with the local ruler'.

Michael Crouch's[13] first experience of WAP came after a spell in the Eastern Aden Protectorate (see Chapter 4). Like Rex his wife accompanied him.

Our arrival in Aden early as a married couple in mid-February 1963 seemed an auspicious reminder that when I had been first introduced to South Arabia, I had known nothing. Now I had acquired a self-assurance of someone who had 'been there, done that', partly explained of course by the experience acquired in the EAP. Perhaps it would have been more appropriate for me to have acknowledged that life may have been pretty easy to date.

I was now embarking on something entirely new, in an environment about which I knew very little and, because I had come out to Aden just ahead of my generation in the WAP service, I was the most senior of them and called upon to act in the next position above mine in the hierarchy. My callow ignorance was perhaps balanced by fluency in Arabic, but a conversational version learnt hundreds of miles away. My only other attribute that could be regarded as an asset was a determination not to become a casualty statistic. I remembered Johnny Johnson briefing me for Northern Deserts and talking casually about a dead political officer being a nuisance. I had certainly learnt to be a professional coward!

It said something about the cavalier attitude, not to say desperation, of the WAP Office that they were prepared to take such a risk in using me, someone as unprepared as I was. It was pure expediency that I was so used; it had nothing to do with any sort of career path planning for me. To employ me in so many jobs was to mean that I acquired a wide but shallow experience of both Protectorates. As the demands grew for someone with a degree of first-hand experience and, concurrently, the numbers of such officers shrank, so I was to be catapulted up the tree. It resulted in my being the officer who had served in most places in both Protectorates, by the time the whole framework had come crashing down.

His first posting was Lahej:

an oasis-type centre, out across the barren 40 miles or so that separated Lahej from the Aden township of Sheikh Othman. Our residence was a former 40-roomed Sultanic palace, which included a cinema gallery we converted into a badminton court. Actually the WAP Office only intended to allow us to spend a couple of weeks out there, before temporarily installing us in a modern flat with all conveniences (in Al Ittihad) to take over as acting Senior Adviser (West). This was the first of many acting senior positions I was to occupy over the next five years. But I managed to persuade the WAP Office that I could do the job equally well from Lahej and, with some reluctance, we were allowed to stay put, and still relieve the Senior Adviser (West), to go on leave.

Michael was to act for Robin Young:

he was large, avuncular and hospitable. He was most welcoming and kind to us on arrival. He lent us his personal motorcar, to which he had given the unlikely name of 'Esmeralda'. Driving down from Government House on the day after we arrived, with Lynette at the wheel, we gently ran into the back of a car stopped in front of us. The embarrassment I experienced in telling Robin of the mishap was much worse than confronting the owners of the car we had run into (we bought the vehicle we had damaged). I expected Robin to be understandably annoyed, but he barely showed it. His strangely husky voice, no doubt damaged by his incessant pipe smoking, might have thickened a bit at the news, but he remained polite, making some joke about, 'Poor old Esmeralda'. I should have preferred more of an overreaction.[14] It was not a good start to a relationship with Robin, but somehow I doubt if our association would ever have been more than cordial, Esmeralda or no. I would have had to have started in the Political Service at Robin's knee, as it were (as did some of my colleagues who were deeply fond of him), for it to have been closer. I was always rather in awe of him.

Roy Somerset[15] came to Aden in 1957 after a stint in Nigeria as District Officer (DO) in Brass in the Niger Delta.

For a bachelor a DO's job was the best in the world. Magistrate, Sheriff, Superintendent of Police, Court of Appeal from all Native Courts, Tax Collector, Architect, Surveyor and amateur Civil Engineer. But with constitutional advance in Nigeria – the advent of self-government this delightful job was about to disappear. So I became divorced from Nigeria and entered a second marriage with Aden, but I was never happy with it. To appreciate the WAP I think you needed to come to it fresh and without experience elsewhere.

Roy at least had some familiarisation and an attempt at basic briefing.

Trevaskis (British Agent) put me up on my arrival, and in a series of anecdotes tried to introduce me to the difference between the WAP and normal colonial administration. I never came to see the WAP clearly through Trevaskis' spectacles, but then and later he was always courteous, patient and never openly exasperated by my unwillingness to be involved in bribery with rifles, ammunition or money.

(A point of difficulty with many Assistant Advisers) His first upcountry experience was a posting to Ahwar (Lower Aulaqi Sultanate) in January 1958. He flew up: 'I saw the WAP moonscape below me. Why should anyone wish to live there and why should anyone wish to administer it?' He experienced the sorts of problems which were so familiar to all of us operating in what often seemed an anarchical society 'they emphasised the truth of Doreen Ingrams'[16] opening sentence on government inthe Aden Protectorates: "Government is a misnomer for the type of misrule which prevails throughout the Western Aden Protectorate."'

Roy may have been particularly disillusioned coming from the orderly environment of Nigeria, but his first few weeks in Ahwar did little to give him hope that the British would bring law and order, never mind justice, to his part of WAP.

> Two incidents made me wonder whether our presence in the WAP was beneficial. The first was the sight of a boy, aged no more than 10, shuffling with irons around his ankles and an iron bar between them, which he had to lift to move. I gathered he was a hostage, released from prison to take his daily constitutional.[17] The second was the GGs' (Government Guards: the predecessor force to the Federal Guard) reaction to an incursion one Friday evening when Kazimis[18] stole five goats. The GGs managed to wing one of the robbers, who fled leaving two cooked goats, which the GGs ate, the wounded man's jambia (dagger) and mushedda (headdress) and the three remaining goats. The JAA (Arab assistant political officer) reckoned that the GGs had blackened the raiders' faces.[19] 'Would it not have been better if they had killed some of them?' I enquired. 'Certainly not, this would have led to endless trouble until the Kazimis had killed one of the GGs'[20]

Roy Somerset's other upcountry posting was to Dhala. Like his predecessors and those of us who came after him, he had an exiting time. I think all of us (Godfrey Meynell, Bryan Somerfield, James Nash, Hugh Walker, Michael Crouch, Julian Paxton and myself) who spanned the 1960s, were shot up in the house, or ambushed away from it, at one time or another. I was there for a couple of months in 1964, and for seven months (this time with my wife) in 1966. In that latter period the house was attacked by 'dissidents'[21] five times – once seriously from very close range and I was lucky to survive.[22] None of us, however, could match Roy's claim to international fame. In April 1958 he and a detachment of GGs reinforced by Aden Protectorate Levies (APL), the immediate predecessors of the Federal Regular Army (FRA), were besieged for several days by a large force of dissidents on Jebel Jihaf, the 7000-foot mountain that dominated the Dhala plateau. It took several air strikes by RAF Venoms and the participation of troops from two British Battalions[23] to raise the siege and drive the attackers back across the Yemeni frontier. Sensational accounts of this action (in which one National Serviceman lost his life) appeared in the

British press – one headline screamed 'Last of the Plantaganets besieged in Arabian Fort'.[24]

Some Assistant Advisers had the good fortune to spend lengthy periods in one area – the longest I ever had in one post was a full tour of ten months.[25] Those who had longer time developed an unrivalled expertise in the affairs of their region. In my time Stephen Day[26] became quite an expert on Abyan, especially the Fadhli Sultanate. He describes a former Fadhli Sultan, Nasser bin Abdullah as his 'greatest friend to this day'. Like many of us there is more than a hint of nostalgia in his recollection:

> The Aden Protectorate was my first job and it was there that I met my wife Angela and where our eldest daughter was born. The experience left its mark; the Arabs whom I worked with became friends for life. I lived most of my time in the Fadhli capital, Zingibar, in a mud fort. Tribal Guards occupied the ground floor, we lived on the main floor and the roof was used for sitting out in the summer and for guards at night.

Stephen and I shared a boss in Robin Young whom we both liked and admired. Robin, who attached great importance to punctuality, especially in junior officers, sometimes, in exasperation referred to Stephen as 'the late Mr Day'. On two occasions, however, tardiness came to Stephen's rescue. The first time was when he missed being involved in the Aden Airport bomb attack on Kennedy Trevaskis, which cost George Henderson his life.[27]

> It dawned on me that the reason that I had not been to the airport was quite simply that I had overslept, so I learned the first lesson of countering terrorism – never be predictable. It is amazing how many have died because of an inability to follow such a simple precept. 'The late Mr Day' was evidence that it worked and, although it pained me to keep Robin in the dark when I was chasing Angela around Aden, it saved my life when the Bin Lahmar brothers[28] waited for me at El Qeru (Political Officer's house at Zingibar), killed a young engineer instead and claimed on Sana'a and Cairo Radio that they had got me.

When I had been working in Abyan in 1962 under Stephen Day's supervision I had found it a peaceful and undemanding assignment. By early 1964 with an upsurge of rebel activity elsewhere in the Federation it was heating up politically. It was near enough to Aden to be particularly affected by developments there, especially after the Aden airport bomb referred to by Stephen. The fall-out from the bomb attack had bizarre consequences for Stephen as he describes:

Recall the context – Sultan Ahmed, head of police and some 25 other Fadhlis wounded; George Henderson (my greatest friend) dead; Ken (Trevaskis) dumps on me all the politicos of Aden to keep in jail. The situation in Fadhli was grim, and as the politicos got to feel their oats and mount an international campaign to improve their conditions, even getting beds, mosquito nets, etc., so the jail became untenable. We had a stream of journalists, UN reps, etc. ending with the three MPs[29]and a man from the International Federation of Trades Unions or whatever.

The Fadhlis argued, reasonably enough, that no MP had ever shown the slightest interest in their lot. The guards on the prison were mutinous and I was seriously concerned that they would either walk out and leave the jail open, or kill a few prisoners. Asnag was leading the crew and I warned him twice that I could not ensure his safety.

I did at that point organise a demo of tribesmen, requiring Asnag[30] to walk through them on his way to my office; I thought, since he wished to run South Arabia, that he might meet one or two. (When we met years later in London he remembered it well; I also became a great chum of another in the jail who ended up in Tunis as my Yemeni colleague: we walked around receptions hand-in-hand, he was so proud of the anti-colonial accolade of having served time in one of our prisons.) When news of the MPs' visit spread, a delegation of young Fadhlis came and asked for permission to demonstrate; they made good arguments for a bit of democracy, free speech, etc. Was not a demo part of the great British tradition? I was very uneasy but couldn't think of a reason to go against them, especially since I would have to ask the FG2 to stop them, and they were on the point of mutiny. So I agreed the basic guidelines and warned them that I would be driving the MPs; they were on my face and I would defend them, if necessary by shooting.

I forgot that most of the Zingibaris were not nice tribesmen, prepared to keep their word, but a motley crew from the north and elsewhere. I drove the delegation through the crowd (I still have the photos of the event and there were some lovely banners, including my favourite – 'Labour MPs, go back to Soho') then the stones started, smashing all our windows and leaving the MPs on the floor of the Land-Rover, cut and alarmed. The Trades Union man – I think he was from behind the curtain – never turned a hair. [Stephen is presumably referring here to what he believed were the Trade Unionist's communist leanings.] Hadi [Stephen's Federal Guard [FG] bodyguard] opened up with his Klashnikov over the crowd and winged Fadhl Mohsin who happened to be walking by and wanted to join in.

There was a sequel, if not several. I had to answer to the Chief Justice, accused of torturing the prisoners; Sultan Ahmed pushed off to Cairo (to my great relief) and we installed Nasser, to whom I owe a vast amount; it was clear that Britain had no stomach to run the place, and I was keen to stay alive. I had just met Angela.

If Stephen Day had an extensive knowledge of the Fadhli area, Godfrey Meynell will always be to me synonymous with Radfan. He too, however, spent a significant period in Abyan, having found himself in Aden having failed to get a job in ICI (India) and rejected Nyasaland: 'I happened to read how people passed their time there by shutting all the windows and then exterminating the flies inside.' Aden struck a chord: '"tent floor diplomacy" was the phrase that stuck in my mind. It sounded the closest I could get to the life my father had led before being killed in action on the Northwest Frontier.'[31]

Godfrey arrived in Aden in January 1959. Kennedy Trevaskis was the British Agent in charge of WAP office – at that time in Champion Lines, the Government Guards' headquarters.[32] I was always in great awe of 'Uncle Ken', and so, I think were the rest of us, including Godfrey:

A massive, subtle man, of great charm, with a great affection for the Rulers, he was a convinced imperialist. His politics were pretty far right and he was highly sceptical about the wisdom of the too hasty development of democratic institutions or a political middle class. He liked the tribesmen of the Protectorate and felt they would prosper best under their traditional rulers.

Godfrey had a lot of time for Robin Young who was to be his boss in Abyan:

A bachelor of 34 in 1959, Robin with Trevaskis, was the model of Sir Charles Johnston's evocation of the Colonial Service 'a rugged Victorian pipe-smoking virility'. He looked back with pleasure to the special camaraderie of the Sudan Service. But unlike the West Africa hands and others who had served in the fully administered colonies, he took to the WAP like a duck to water. His affinity for the Arabs, his enthusiasm for development and his belief in the British mission all made him a very suitable mentor for a beginner.

Godfrey had free board and lodging with Robin in Zingibar for seven or eight months until the latter went on leave.

During that time I had plenty of opportunity to learn the language, and get the feel of the job. Thus I organised a PT display by Zingibar secondary school children for the Alan Lennox Boyd visit.[33] I encouraged the poor creatures to do the kind of bone shattering exercises that were fashionable at my prep school, in contrast with the ideas of the Egyptian PT master, which I am sure, were more advanced. But the children were warm and friendly, and I found my Arabic improving with their help. Thereafter I always made a practice of visiting the schools and talking about the future. My line was 'we shall not always be here and the future is up to you. Learn hard and be ready for it. Don't believe all you hear on the radio. At the moment we need the base and the refinery, but we are keen that you should benefit as well.' Such remarks, of course, were addressed to the teachers as well as the boys. I didn't attack Abd el Nasr head-on, because people lived in several mental compartments. In some houses you would see the Queen's portrait and Abd el Nasr's in the same room. This approach would not have worked in Lahej where the atmosphere was already more sophisticated and more hostile. But in the areas where I worked, there was much confused goodwill for Britain, as well as anxious assessment of which horse to back if the choice finally had to be made.

Godfrey soon got a feel for Fadhli affairs – and the role of the Political officer in all its permutations according to the structure of the state and the effectiveness of its administration. In Abyan most of the shots were called by the 'Naib'[34]: Ahmed bin Abdullah, the effective ruler, as the Sultan Abdullah bin Othman confined his activities to the fishing village of Shuqra and playing with his smart red sports car.[35]

Because Ahmed was forceful and articulate, the running of the state was very much in his hands. There was a mud-built, white secretariat, with smart office peons. We had an office there. There was a state treasury, an agricultural office and two courts – for Common (Urfi) and Shariya (Islamic) law. These operated largely without our interference, though we helped with the annual estimates, took up what appeared to be injustices, tried to get health and prison conditions improved and were consulted over major investments. Our real job was to be an informed presence in the area, conveying the good will and also the power and confidence of the British Protectorate.

Up on the Eastern Plateau, Sultan Nasr bin Abdullah, Ahmed's older brother was responsible for the tribal areas. He collected their taxes, settled their disputes and kept himself informed. Two key issues were contact with the north (the Yemen) and local blood feuds. Of these, that between the Ja'adinis and the Fathanis of neighbouring Dathina was the most serious. Of the tribal sections, the most isolated and interesting were the Merqashis who lived in the dry coastal hills east of Shuqra. Their land was the poorest and their culture the most individual. Owing to their isolation they had retained a number of pre-Islamic customs, including mixed dancing. Virtually my only experience of them arose when some of them went to the north to collect arms from the Imam's representative in Beidha. For this we dropped warning leaflets on them and then machine-gunned their goats. Had there been money for peaceful development, such measures might not have been necessary.

Indeed this is a theme referred to by many of Godfrey's colleagues – we tried to run the Protectorates and later the Federation on the cheap and it didn't work.

Hugh Walker[36] arrived in Aden in July1964. He had spent 11 years in the Colonial Service in Kenya, serving mostly in the Northern Frontier Territories. Like Roy Somerset before him he found the transition from the ordered discipline of a Colony on the verge of independence to the apparent institutionalised anarchy of the Western Aden Protectorate something of a challenge. After a spell working with Lionel Folkard[37] in the WAP office management section he was posted to Dhala in early 1965. For a man used to an orderly existence he had an unfortunate initiation. His predecessor Assistant Adviser was not a good administrator and had departed with no handover. The Arab JAA immediately followed suit on compassionate leave. Walker's notes recorded: 'No clerk, no handing over notes of any kind, no inventories; no lists of stores; no cash – not even an imprest; no state estimates; no state treasurer (absconded); no development plans (letters unanswered). No filing for seven months. Office in indescribable mess.'

Perhaps not surprisingly Hugh Walker had a jaundiced view of Dhala from the beginning. At the best of times it was not an easy post. Godfrey Meynell spent some time there:

Dhala had a bad reputation. Its inhabitants grew and chewed a great deal of Qat. Its ruling family lacked the wealth of the Lahejis or the Fadhlis, and its hold on its tribes was correspondingly weak. The Yemen border was only a few miles away. The Amir's local soldiery were considered fickle and potentially treacherous. Peter Davy, the Political Officer [a convert to Islam], had been killed as he tried to arrest the Ahmedi Sheikh, head of an affiliated tribe to the Southwest.[38] An unfortunate Agricultural Officer, Mr Mound had been shot in my office, from outside, around 1955. Sayyid[39] Mohammed Darwish, a much-loved holy man who rode a white donkey with red trappings and charmed everyone he met, was killed in cold blood at about the same time. During negotiations, somebody took him by the hand, as though in confidence, led him behind a rock and shot him. Basil Seager the former British Agent had been attacked with a dagger and badly cut about – saved only by the courage of his wife.

We have noted Roy Somerset's misadventures, Robin Young had a torrid time there and while Godfrey had a much happier posting, he had his JAA murdered and was present when an FRA Colonel, Sandy Thomas was stabbed on Jibel Jihaf. Godfrey himself was ambushed coming down on foot from Shaib and in his own words: 'I missed been killed by a whisker.' (Some years later he met one of his attackers at a British Yemeni Society function in London and had some fun comparing notes!)

On the whole Godfrey has positive memories of Dhala and warm feelings for the Amir, Sha'aful bin Ali Shaif.

Figure 3.2 Dhala town taken from the Political Officer's house in 1964. The white building on the hill is the Amir's Palace; that at the other end, the prison dating from Turkish times.

I spent 23 of the most rewarding months of my life there. I found the Amir improved greatly on acquaintance. Being 'Pol [Political Officer] Dhala' was more fun than anything else I have been paid to do, except, perhaps, 'Pol Habilayn'. There were the glorious country, the optimism of the time, the spectacular characters I had to deal with, the hard exercise and the occasional breakthrough. There was also the fun of our first baby. Before we left the sky had darkened, but exhilaration is my abiding memory.

Indeed Godfrey and his wife Honor arrived in Dhala in autumn 1961 when it was still possible to live a fairly peaceful, normal life, to be able to tour the Amirate and the other two little Sheikhdoms for which Pol Dhala was responsible (Muflahi and Shu'aib) and not be pinned down in one's house by threat of attack or unable to drive around for fear of mines as was the lot of most of his successors. Godfrey became involved in road building. In one project he had the assistance of

Colonel Sandy Thomas, Crete veteran, author of *Dare to be Free* and *Malice in Blunderland*, happy, burly New Zealander [and the target of the would-be assassin, referred to above]. There was a Turkish gun road up Jihaf, too narrow for vehicles. He set his fourth battalion of the Federal Army to widening it. Before long, you could get up Jihaf by a spectacular road, and the scope for tourism was a gleam in my eye. The top of Jihaf was stunning – lush crops, fat animals, accessible groundwater, banks of terraced fields and only the vileness of the qat weed to spoil it. The Amir was delighted.

But the situation had deteriorated by the time Hugh Walker arrived more than two years later.

Hugh not only took over a chaotic office but the sharp end of a counterterrorist policy with which he profoundly disagreed, in principle and in practice. Long before his posting to Dhala he had strong misgivings over the whole thrust of HMG's policy over the Federation and especially worried that the powers that be in London did not know what was being done in their name on the ground in South Arabia. He poured out his worries to a friend

'Eric' in a series of letters to his 'safety valve'. In one, dated 13 August 1964 he wrote:

> I had started a letter to you but got so carried away with what I can only describe as my own revulsion for my own people that I abandoned it. I don't quite know why but I have hated this place from the moment I set foot in it. Although I now have an absorbing job . . . it is such an inefficient and corrupt place and has no *esprit de corps* whatsoever that one feels the effort to do anything well just isn't worthwhile. [He goes on:] Every serving officer I have met who has been in other colonial territories is appalled at what we see here and most are determined to get out just as soon as they are able to without financial loss.[40]

Thus within a month of his arrival in Aden Hugh was already appalled and repelled by British policy. It seems that working in the WAP administration exposed him to what he regarded as undesirable practices and particularly the use of arms and ammunition[41] as a means of bolstering the position of what he regarded as 'feudal Federal Rulers' and the channelling of all aid for development through the same rulers with no accountability. So strongly did he feel about what was happening on the ground that he asked Dennis Healey, the Secretary of State for Defence, whom Hugh had met in Kenya when Healey was in opposition, if he could write to him about Aden. The Minister's response (1 November) in a handwritten note was welcoming and he suggested: 'Perhaps in view of our present responsibilities it would be better if you wrote to my home.' He added: 'In view of the speed with which events are moving, the sooner you can write the better.'

Hugh duly wrote to Dennis Healey on 15 November. He explained:

> I deliberately refrained from writing before the election[42] as I felt it would have been improper. I still in no way wish to appear disloyal to the service which employs me but I have been unable to satisfy myself that HMG is fully aware of everything that is done in her name. If, in fact, all is known then I have no worries. If not, then at least I have passed it on to a quarter where it can be objectively evaluated.

He then spelled out in considerable length (27 paragraphs!) his objections to HMG's policy as implemented in South Arabia (paragraphs on the arms and ammunition handouts and particularly unstinting support for the 'feudal, tribal rulers'. He felt that any Colonial-sponsored Federation was bound to fail unless it has the support of the people. 'Here, and in Aden State and the Protectorate, it has not. It does have the support of the majority of the rulers and others with vested interests in it and in whose hand power lies.'

The key paragraph probably is:

> The support of these rulers (and some Aden politicians) is due to several factors amongst which are
>
> (a) Gifts from HMG although it is in the name of the States (through the High Commission.
> (b) Facilities afforded by HMG to purchase arms in the UK from which vast profits are made locally (afforded to rulers only).
> (c) The increase in their power and influence by a) and b).
> (d) The channelling of all aid for development in the States through the Rulers but about the actual use of which few questions are asked.
> (e) The presence of British Advisers in States often supported by British Forces but for whom local antipathy for the Ruler's corrupt and unjust rule would have long since led to their ejection/overthrow.

(There was no reply from Healey)

Perhaps Hugh was not the ideal officer to be sent to Dhala, of all places, in that frame of mind but he volunteered to go if only to cover a gap! Hugh is now a bit abashed about this whistle-blowing exercise, but (pace Michael Crouch's *An Element of Luck*) his views were widely shared by many British officials. He did moderate his position in later correspondence, however. He wrote to Eric in April 1965, from Dhala

> I have seen nothing since coming here that makes me apologise for what I have said from Aden previously. I can, however, begin to see that the 'blame' (for want of a better

word) lies more squarely on HMG's previous parsimony than on any other one cause.

He went on to serve elsewhere in the Protectorate including a spell in Wahidi which he rather enjoyed and where he bent his principles sufficiently to sell some rifles to finance a development project! His boss Robin Young had a high opinion of Hugh. He wrote in his diary on 27 June 1966:

> I had a talk with Hugh Walker. Doubtful if he will come back from leave. Taken 'scunner' to arms and ammo policy. Likes the job of AA (and is good at it) would like a straightforward Admin job. Can't find a place for him in this office. It would be a pity if Hugh leaves us. In many ways he is an excellent fellow.

Hugh did leave, having served out his notice in Mukalla.

Some British people living in Aden tended to regard upcountry Political Officers as 'cowboys' swaggering around in the company of armed retainers up to goodness knows what skulduggery. Clint Eastwood or Victor Stallone plays Lawrence of Arabia. James Nash[43] was one that may have fuelled the image. Tall, rugged, usually wearing an Arab head dress, a pistol holstered at his belt, accompanied by some roughish-looking Federal Guard soldiers, said to be up to dark deeds, all fitted the bill.[44] James had indeed specialised in tough assignments and tended to have an irreverent and sometimes cynical, approach to them.

> I had been the Political Officer on the ground in Radfan, guiding and advising a brigade group of British troops in a punitive operation against the tribes in this mountainous area who owed allegiance, more theoretically than actually to the Amir of Dhala. The Amirate was a frontier state that lay across a principal trade route between Aden and the Yemen and the Radfan tribes had a long history of descending from their mountains and raiding the trade route. This time their crime had been ambushing an army Landrover and shooting a War Office Brigadier in the bottom, which some people in the army, the Colonial Service and the population of South Arabia in general might have considered a virtue rather than a crime.

James, later based in Dhala (Hugh Walker took over from him) became involved in 'Rancour', which was an 'unattributable' covert counterterrorist operation carrying the war across the frontier to the rebels and their Egyptian paymasters and controllers.[45]

> In South Arabia one lives on the upper floors of houses, for ground floor rooms with large windows are perfect targets for disgruntled tribesmen. An English visitor to one of my predecessors had already been murdered [as referred to by Godfrey Meynell above] while sitting in what became thereafter the office rather than the sitting room. My ground floor store room soon became filled with rifles, mortars, bazookas and machine guns; my office with cases of Maria Theresa silver dollars and my days were spent occasionally inspecting schools or the Amirate accounts, but much more often in training and arming my locally recruited gang of 60 merry bandits, making and despatching bombs and the bandits[46] across the frontier and generally playing a happy game of cowboys and Indians with Her Majesty's (unattributable) sanction. Not many people have had the privilege of being paid to play cowboys and Indians when they were grown up.

His activities put him at risk. Egyptian sponsored gangs retaliated. 'During moonless nights, my house, the British and Federal Army camps some half a mile away and sometimes the Amir's castle came under fire from bazookas, mortars, rifles and machine guns.' This could happen three times a week. 'A rocket blew my front door half way up the stairs just missing my bodyguards who were sleeping behind it.' But the greater risk came from his own side.

> The worst period was when the British army camp was garrisoned by a badly-led company of Royal Marines. After they had opened fire at my house and the FNG fort in a couple of little nighttime battles, they were given very strict fields of fire. The next night they ignored them completely and an armoured car troop under their command fired its 76 mm guns into the fort and the side of my house, wounding eight of the Guard. The Guard, who felt they were having a fairly hard time bearing the brunt of my activities without any financial benefit, had had enough – they mutinied. Thus I had a particularly bad

night being shot at from two sides by the rebels, one side by the rather heavier armament of the British army and all around the house by the mutineers. My beloved bodyguards bundled me up to my bedroom at the top of the house and slept outside the door.

James recounts how the Marines were changed immediately but the FNG company was left there six weeks. (James was sent to Aden for a few days but it was decided to let him back.) The situation improved with a Coldstream Guards Company and a new FNG detachment: 'A well-disciplined combination of British and local forces started to inflict casualties on the night riding dissidents' and there were successes inside the Yemen with a number of important defections to the Federation. James himself was exhausted and developed an ulcer

I began to jump at the slamming of a door or a vehicle backfiring. But we had broken the back of the tribal rebellion. The local opposition was dispirited. My first private army retired rich and happy and were replaced by another gang who had already been trained by the Egyptians, but thought I was a more congenial employer and a lot more generous!

Not long after James left[47] the Egyptians changed tactics and targeted the centre of government: 'Aden with its amorphous, ever-changing and detribalised population was a much easier target for the bomber.' And this was a battle that the bombers and the assassins were going to win.

We will leave Dhala at the end of the story – a finale told by Julian Paxton[48] who had taken over as Political Officer from me in late 1966 having been a Federal Intelligence Officer seconded from the Army. As 1967 progressed and with the steady deterioration of the political and security situation in the Federation, Julian, plus the Secret Intelligence Service (SIS) representative, maintained an official British presence in Dhala. An army company garrisoned the British Camp. In Dhala, as elsewhere, with the knowledge of an imminent British withdrawal

it became difficult for many Yemenis who owed their position to us to remain loyal. It became clear that it was not just the dissidents attacking us at night, but the local people and the police. I was friendly with the local police chief, who had trained at Mons Officer Cadet School in Aldershot, but there was little that he could do and eventually I had a row with him saying that we would retaliate with even greater force and not be so careful about avoiding civilian casualties.

On 20th June the situation boiled over. The suq began to buzz with rumours about the violent events in Aden. [The mutiny and the killing of 22 British soldiers, mostly in Crater.] One company of the Arab Army (formerly FRA) battalion in Dhala mutinied, parading with pictures of President Nasser and shouting slogans, while the British seconded staff took refuge in the British army camp. The British couple who shared my compound[49] had gone to Aden for a short visit, leaving a wireless operator in their house. From the roof of my house where we usually enjoyed our 'sundowners' we could clearly see the events unfolding – the Arab soldiers advancing and joining with the mob to make their way to the Amir's palace. There they made various demands – the Amir must expel his British advisers and the flag come down – all prisoners to be released. The mob had been joined by Ali Ahmed al-Bishi (aka Ali Antar)[50] the leading Shairi dissident with about a dozen of his men in combat fatigues, who had regularly attacked us over the last few months. After a lot of shouting and firing into the air they advanced towards us but stopped short of the compound when our guards fired over their heads. There was then a standoff with much unaimed shooting from both sides. Ali Said, my escort had ordered me off the roof, telling me to keep out of sight! The Amir sent a leading Dhala contractor as his emissary stating that he had no option but to comply with the demands made upon him. When we lowered the flag and it was announced that we would leave, the mob dispersed, one prisoner leaving behind a 'shackle of imperialism' which I later picked up noting that his leg iron had been manufactured from some piece of British army equipment since it bore the War Department arrow and a part number. As we prepared to leave the contractor reappeared with another message from the Amir saying that we should come back once he had restored order and the situation had calmed down.

But Julian (evacuated by helicopter) and the British couple only came back briefly to pack up (with no problem). The Amir and his family soon followed them to Aden, and on to exile in Saudi Arabia. Amiri and Federal 'rule' in Dhala and a British presence thus ended five months before the final departure from Aden.

'Godfrey's services in Radfan deserve recognition more than any one else's have done these many years in South Arabia' confided Robin Young to his diary on 21 December 1966, a week after Godfrey had left Aden for the last time. And there are many references in the diary (see Chapter 5) to Godfrey's development efforts in Radfan (and Dathina 'A Vale of Evesham' according to Robin). Many people have commented that had more money being spent on development upcountry in the early 1960s then much tribal discontent could have been headed off with local people being given a stake in their community worth defending against outside subversive influences. In Godfrey's view:

> The influence of Sawt al Arab[51] was immense. Its appeals to Arab and Islamic pride touched chords everywhere. Then, in the hinterland, the distribution of Federal largesse could never satisfy everyone, whether it took the form of salaries for jobs or just stipends to tribal leaders to keep them on-side. There were plenty of disappointed 'notables', and plenty of poor, idle-handed tribesmen to follow them.

And Radfan with its fiercely independent tribes was a hard case. 'Feuds could flare up at a moment's notice and fields exposed to the enemy remain uncultivated for years. Sheer ennui must have led many such tribesmen to head north when occasion offered.'

Following the militarily successful Radfan campaign Godfrey went back to Habilayn, the administrative centre. He was notionally the Amir of Dhala's Naib (representative)[52] as he continued to claim jurisdiction over the Radfan tribes. His main task was resettlement and development.

> About £30,000 was available for my first year's loan scheme for Radfan. We had a bit of security for the loans through the small stipends that had been agreed for the sheikhs and senior Aqils (headmen) in the aftermath of the campaign. Repayments, interest free, were to be made over four or five years and

recycled into further lending, together with any new money I could get my hands on.

Godfrey was heavily involved in water schemes.

The high Radfan hills were very short of water. [Much of it was carried by women with] great Jerry cans of water on their backs. (Often they carried loads of brushwood from the wadis instead.) I made some comment (to local Quteibis) about how in England men would be expected to participate in such a chore. 'We couldn't carry those loads' someone replied 'and neither could you'. [Well-digging on the hilltops was not successful.] We turned therefore to small catchment dams. These were generally short stonewalls across gullies, coated with cement. We progressed by trial and error, learning first that an admixture of lime made the cement more durable; secondly that protection was needed from the direct heat of the sun. Naval and Air Force helicopters flew in cement, whitewash and crowbars, together sometimes with slender metal pipes for roofing materials. Each dam was normally started with a loan of a thousand shillings – enough, in theory, for 200 man-days of paid work. To begin with nothing happened but once it became clear that there would be regular inspections the scheme began to roll along pretty well. We must have started 70 or more and before long small quantities of evil-looking water were being retained. Heaven knows whether any of the dams were of long-term value. They may just have brought malaria [and possibly Bilharzia] and Women's Liberation! For the moment they kept some people busy and spread the money around.

Godfrey was also involved in the rather more expensive exercise of well-digging. With backup from pneumatic drills powered by Ferguson tractors and the occasional use of explosives

80–100 wells were dug. We also gave loans for pump purchase. We hired a tough, competent Hadhrami mechanic to help farmers maintain their machines. Small new patches of green began to appear – never quite as impressive as my dreams, but pleasing all the same.

All this needed monitoring and Godfrey insisted on inspections which could be combined with a 'flag wave'. Sometimes by foot with the Federal Guard

> at other times we would be dropped by helicopter, perhaps with a single section (eight men or so) and a Bren gun, arranging to be picked up at another landmark either the same day or the next. We would visit all the schemes we could and sometimes stay the night with a local notable. It was important to involve local people with us as soon as we arrived. We were a worry to our hosts I am sure, as there were sometimes dissidents in the area, but they chose not to attack us. Indeed the only times I came under fire during my time as the Amir's Naib in the Radfan were in my house or when I was out with the army. I remember this infuriated a friend of mine, a Royal Marine Officer, who felt that I had compromised myself. I felt differently, since I really did believe that if we honestly tried to help people and were ready to spend money on it, we could win them over. The alternative, I said, was to adopt a siege mentality and help create the world of one's fears. The truth was probably less glamorous. To hurt us in somebody's back yard would have been to bring retribution on his head.

I have a vivid memory of Godfrey in Habilayn on Federal Day 1966 (I came down from Dhala). Godfrey again:

> Shortly before we left we had a celebration of progress in Radfan, to which a number of Federal rulers came – putting a good face on things as the world darkened around them. Tractors, bulldozers and well-digging gear were paraded [I remember all the Health Assistants driving by on their brand new motor bikes]. FNG and children from all our new Radfan schools marched. The children played various games, and then did PT displays. The Da'ar al Hareth made a pyramid, three children high. On top of it a minute six- or seven-year-old acknowledged our applause: 'Long live Gamal Abd el Nasr' he cried![53]

John Harding[54] was I believe only one of two people (the other being Michael Crouch) who in the 1960s served in EAP, Aden

103

Colony and WAP. These excerpts from an entertaining paper give some idea of the contrast of working in a relatively sophisticated and peaceful state where it was possible to get things done.

The nine months I spent between June 1964 and February 1965 as adviser to the Abdali Sultanate of Lahej and the Aqrabi Sheikhdom,[55] an area two-thirds the size of Wales, were the most rewarding of my five and a half years service in South Arabia. During that time I witnessed at first hand the strengths and weaknesses of absolute rule but also had the satisfaction of devising development schemes to bring belated aid to Subeihi, Radfan and Dhala, three of the Federation's most sensitive security areas.

By WAP standards, a posting to Lahej was a cushy number. Apart from the odd suq riot, bomb incident or the bazooka which did for my long drop lavatory, my 40-roomed house-cum-office with its permanent staff of Junior Assistant Adviser, clerk, cook, gardener, dhobi[56] man and armed guards provided a haven for me, my friends and visitors. Fortress-like in construction, it looked across Lahej's spacious Maidan[57] to the grander palaces of the Sultan and the Amir. The current Sultan Fadhl bin Ali, was the senior Federal ruler and Minister of Defence. His father Sultan Ali, although reckoned to be a good and loyal friend, had been accidentally killed by British troops during the First World War when mistaken for an enemy Turk. Sultan Fadhl was an urbane imperious man with a weak lower lip whose marriage to a vindictive Jordanian wife, Hala, was deeply unpopular in Lahej. Ostensibly, the Sultan took little part in managing Lahej's internal affairs which were left to his altogether more robust brother the Amir Abdullah bin Ali, Lahej's Chief Minister or '*Rais al Mudirin*'

Life in Lahej was never dull. A typical day might involve me in a pre-dawn 45-minute drive to the Royal Engineer camp at Al Anad to review the road's sporadic progress; sort out labour disputes and negotiate new terms and conditions of employment with local Naibs and contractors and then press the Amir to authorise ever bigger Lahej National Guard detachments to counter dissident mortar attacks. Sometimes before and sometimes after my sessions with the Amir, I would

drive another 25 miles from Lahej across the desert road to
Al Ittihad to report back to my imperturbable boss Robin
Young, preferably over early breakfast. After this I might
attend the High Commissioner's Office 'Morning Prayers'
as it reviewed external and internal security but more profit-
ably I would do my rounds of Federal Ministries such as
Agriculture, Health or Education to chivvy and chase or seek
advice and support for the development aid schemes for
which I had become responsible.

Back in Lahej, I was everyone's dogsbody[58] fielding
complaints from the Lahej police about the misbehaviour
of passing British military convoys; from Lahej contractors
grumbling about Army rates of pay; from Lahej farmers
claiming they were owed money by the Sultan, the Amir or
sundry Abdalis or Aqrabis and even from the Aqrabi State's
harassed Treasurer who had come all the way to Lahej for
me to sign his cheques. At almost any time of day, there would
be a stream of visitors from Aden private and public who
wanted to something of 'Real Arabia' who would then stay on
for a drink, a meal or a game of Badminton on the top floor
of my palace.

Space does not allow an account of Harding's development
activities in the wilder and neglected areas of the Abdali Sultanate
but his introduction to that passage is worth including as it
resonates with what was happening elsewhere in the Federation.

From the earliest days, it had been generally been British
policy not to interfere or attempt to develop the Western Aden
Protectorate on the grounds of political expediency and cost.
Now, half a century too late and in the locust years of Britain's
mandate, niggardly funds were belatedly being made available
for limited development. Although I had no direct executive
powers, I had a much greater degree of influence than ever
I had in Mukalla and now, with Robin Young's support,
used this to persuade the Amir that those parts of his state in
greatest need were Amoor and Subeihi. Thus was born the
Subeihi and Amoor Aid Scheme and with a paltry £35,000
of British taxpayers money we re-built two primary schools,
improved a string of run-down health units and most

importantly, boosted agriculture with loans for well-digging and pumps and the purchase of bulldozers and tractors.

John Harding was the last Assistant Adviser to serve in Lahej, According to his diary Robin Young wanted me to take over (a good posting for a newly married person) but the Sultan apparently felt that Lahej had moved on beyond the point that it needed a British representative on the ground.

Of the contributors John Harding, Rex Smith and Hugh Walker all left Aden before the curtain came down, for a variety of reasons. Rex went on to a distinguished Academic career having caught the bug of *academe* during his time in the WAP, influenced by his contacts with Professor Bob Serjeant, of Cambridge University, a frequent visitor to the region. James Nash departed not long after his last spell in Dhala. Michael Crouch's last days are vividly chronicled in *An Element of Luck*. Godfrey Meynell exited suddenly and rather stormily. He shared the widespread feeling of disgust at what many regarded as British perfidy – articulated by his outburst during Lord Beswick's visit – described by Robin Young in Chapter 5. Had he been offered a worthwhile job for the final months up to independence he might have been prevailed upon to stay. One or two others, also left at an earlier stage, sharing these sentiments, including a very senior former member of WAP office whose bitter comments on why he resigned I have been asked not to reveal. A contemporary of mine, who declined to be involved in this project, suggested that this book should be called *The Great Betrayal*. Despite feeling badly let down, Godfrey, for one, was far from negative about his experiences: 'My whole orientation is different as my memories are focused on a time of optimism and even Radfan seemed to be going forward most of the time I was there.' But the British 'cop out' did for all that, almost at a stroke.

Stephen Day passed the Foreign Office entrance exam and went on to enjoy a distinguished career in the Diplomatic Service. Of all of the 'young' Political Officers of my generation he and Bill Heber Percy probably still have the best links with our Yemeni contemporaries.[59] Roy Somerset stayed on almost to the bitter end, as did Robin Young and I. Julian Paxton also left after his abrupt expulsion by the NLF. I at that time felt no sense of being part of a colonial disaster – just grateful to have survived and to be able to rejoin a young wife and a small baby. Not so fortunate was Tim Goschen,[60] murdered in a sabotaged plane when serving as Assistant Adviser, Wahidi. So to all upcountry political officers and those others – agricultural advisers, medical personnel, Educational Advisers, Health inspectors[61] whose memories I have not been able to include, this chapter is gratefully dedicated.

CHAPTER FOUR

THE EASTERN ADEN PROTECTORATE (EAP)

John T. Ducker

The WAP was normally reached from Aden by road. The Eastern Aden Protectorate (EAP) was normally reached by air to Mukalla (350 miles) or Saiyun (450 miles). Aden Airways was the lifeline. The EAP was both physically and psychologically detached from Aden and the WAP. It seemed and in some measure was a different world.

By 1960, the Eastern Aden Protectorate (EAP) had enjoyed about 25 years of improving security which had made possible a steady improvement in the effectiveness of government, though the means at the government's disposal remained very limited – HMG had very little to spare during the Second World War and for several years afterwards. The Hadhrami Bedouin Legion (HBL), formed by Harold Ingrams the first Resident Adviser in the 1940s as a neutral force recruited from all tribes, financed by HMG and responsible to the Resident Adviser, had gradually been handing over responsibility for internal security to the Quaiti and Kathiri Armed Constabularies, with the Mukalla Regular Army held in reserve in the event of particular threats in the Quaiti state. The HBL had two companies permanently based in the Northern Deserts, on the borders with Yemen and Saudi Arabia, and smaller sections at Ghail bin Yumain and Musaina'a on the border between the Quaiti and Mahra states and at Hadibu on the island of Socotra. They could be deployed elsewhere as required.

The District Naibs and Qaims were the principal government officials responsible for law and order. In 1949, Colonel Boustead, recently appointed from Sudan as Resident Adviser and British Agent in Mukalla, issued a note entitled 'Advisory Relations and the Executive in the Eastern Aden Protectorate'. The Naib was the equivalent of a District Commissioner in a typical British Colony; the Qaim the equivalent of his Assistant DC. The note described the responsibilities of these posts. These officials could only do their job if they travelled around their districts and had a strong sense of priorities. The task of the British Resident and his staff was to assist the state administrations to strengthen their capabilities – the task was advisory only, not executive. The effectiveness of the advisory staff would depend on personal relationships built up with the state officials and an ability to demonstrate the efficacy of any particular course of action.

The institutions established after the famines of 1943 and 1948 had matured, especially the Hadhramaut Pump Scheme (HPS) based in Saiyun. As a result, the Famine Prevention Scheme (FPS) which had provided loans to farmers for irrigation and other works and the Famine Services Fund (FSF) which had held stocks of grain for issue in times of shortage had become largely redundant. There was also a system for reporting on and combating the movements and breeding of the desert locust. These various schemes were supervised by the Residency staff in Saiyun to overcome the problem of state rivalries. The East Road from Mukalla/Shihr to the Hadhramaut, which was little more than a rough though graded track for much of its length, was supported by a system of tolls which permitted regular maintenance at a basic level. Remittances had recovered from the sharp decline in the Second World War and following the independence of Indonesia, with the increase coming mainly from Saudi Arabia and the increasingly rich Gulf states. Wealthy Hadhramis living overseas, including the Buqshans, bin Mahfoudhs, al Amoodis and bin Ladhins regularly provided funds and materials for installing piped water supplies, public electricity supplies and other public works. The general atmosphere was of a steady, predictable if slow improvement.

The principal city in the EAP was the Quaiti capital, Mukalla, with a population of about 35,000, rapidly expanding in Sharaj on the west bank of the wadi and also upstream in Dis. Mukalla was the principal port of the EAP, with a steady flow of small freighters arriving, together with a larger number of sea-going dhows, trading along the coast of Arabia, to India, the Gulf and East Africa. There was also a Shell oil distribution depot. There were other smaller ports at Shihr and Dis Ashariquiyah, which lay to the east of Mukalla.

British staff in the Mukalla Residency were about 15 in number. Apart from the Resident Adviser, his deputy and his secretary, there were normally two or three other Assistant Advisers (this was their title, though the term Political Officer was also used and sometimes was more appropriate to the task they performed) working on the development projects and various other functions in the Coastal Area. There was a Military Adviser, Colonel Eric Johnson from 1960, and a training officer, Major Philip Hillman from 1961, who trained the Quaiti and Kathiri forces. The HBL was commanded by Qaid Pat Gray, a South African who had also served in the Arab Legion in Jordan and in Oman. He had a deputy, Major David Eales and an MT officer, Gordon Dawson. In addition, there were a doctor and a surgeon who attempted to improve the local health services, supported by Vera Dawson, who was an SRN, and a second nurse. There was a talented Fisheries Officer, Alec White, who lived in a ramshackle house on a promontory east

Figure 4.1 Mukalla – a beautiful Arab port and town.

of the town, and for a while a public health specialist. Colonel Johnson devoted all his spare time, and probably much of his own money, to the Bedouin Boys and Girls Schools; he had lost his own family in a plane crash. There was a fluctuating number of British wives and children. The only other British personnel in Mukalla were the two managers of the branch of the Eastern Bank, and their families. Twenty miles away there was a small RAF station at Riyan, which acted as an over-flying airport, facilitated any military activities in the region and supported the activities of Aden Airways. Technical specialists in agriculture, cooperatives and other sectors visited regularly to assist those administering individual projects.

One of the Assistant Advisers at the Residency had the job of managing the modest development budget allocated to the EAP by HMG under the Colonial Development and Welfare (CD&W) Scheme. John Lanfear had this task for two years and was responsible for drawing up in consultation with the states the plan for the use of available CD&W funds for 1964–7. Later one Adviser was allocated to the education projects alone – for much of the time this was Abdulla Muhairez. The EAP had very few natural resources and rainfall was slight and variable. Much of its income came from remittances from Hadhramis working abroad. The Residency took the view that expanding educational opportunities was the best way to maximise such foreign earnings in the long term. Creation of modern schools had begun in the 1940s and it was decided to concentrate most of the available resources on this sector. Thus the building of schools, the engagement of teachers from abroad and the provision of scholarships for higher level education and training were the major feature of the plan. For the last four years of British time in the EAP 12–15 new schools were being added each year and teacher training was expanding rapidly. Fisheries were a major resource but the funds made available by HMG to develop the resource were nowhere near consonant with the opportunities. The remainder was spent on a variety of projects, principally roads, water supply and health facilities. There was a political dimension to the education programme. The teachers brought in, mainly from Sudan and Jordan, became local advocates for republican nationalism. In 1964 the Quaiti state came under public pressure to employ Egyptian teachers, to be financed by Kuwait. The Resident decided that this would be impossible in view of the difficult relations between Britain and Egypt at that time and was able to get the Quaitis to accept the situation by increasing the budget for teachers from elsewhere. There were demonstrations and stone throwing around the town, but the problem was surmounted.

One function of the EAP Advisory staff which was of great value to the inhabitants at a time when visas were required for travel to most countries was the issuance of passports. People resident in or qualifying descendents of residents of the Eastern Aden Protectorate were entitled to British Protected Persons' passports. This was a great convenience to people such as the Hadhramis, who travelled a great deal. The task of issuing these passports was given to the Residency offices in Mukalla and Saiyun, where the Advisory staff had the final responsibility for signing the passports. State officials and junior Residency staff had the task of screening the documentary evidence of entitlement submitted by applicants. John Harding who was concerned with the subject in Mukalla came to know more about it than anyone else and has written a monograph on this little-known subject which is to be found at Appendix 2. As an example of pragmatic British administration it is a gem.

Life in Mukalla was pleasant, though it was not easy to make friends with the residents. The women adhered strictly to the rules of purdah, so except for those engaged in medical practice, our contact was largely with men. The Residency compound was open to the townspeople – it contained a workshop, a health unit, the state guesthouse, a tennis court, a cinema once a week, and a number of staff houses. Many visitors from other parts of the EAP visited the Residency as a matter of course. The Residency's relationship with Sultan Awadh, his family and household, who lived in a palace across the road, next to the sea, was cordial, though it became more detached as the Sultan's health deteriorated. He died in late 1966 and was succeeded by his eldest son, Ghalib, who had just left school in England. His accession was marked by a day of colour and ceremony in December 1966. The State Council had not functioned well during Sultan Awadh's declining years. The Minister, Sayyid Ahmed al Attas, was not the man to give leadership; some of the older members such as Shaikh Barahim and the propertied interests represented in the National Foundation were very conservative;

and the younger members of the council, such as Sayyid Muhammad Abdulqadir Bafiqih, and some of the foreign-trained officials in the government were out of sympathy with the older ones. A policy-making vacuum was the result. There are suggestions that al Attas's sympathies lay with the Arab Socialist Party, which is not impossible. Despite excellent drafting work on proposals for constitutional reform carried out in the early 1960s by Shaikh Muhammad Abdulqadir Bamatraf, the State Council had not kept pace with events; it had failed to broaden its political base and thus did not adequately represent the views of the provinces, the poor and especially the tribes. This was to prove a fatal weakness.

While Arthur Watts was a knowledgeable and ebullient Resident Adviser, with a fine command of Arabic, no significant steps were taken among the EAP states during his term of office (1959–63) to prepare for independence. The reasons emerge clearly from the correspondence and minutes of the period. As early as 28 June 1961, Watts wrote to the Protectorate Secretary, Alistair McIntosh, saying

> Both Bamatraf and Bu Bakr Barahim say categorically that the EAP states could not possibly join the Federation as it is constituted at present; the Customs were not unified, and the Rulers all appeared to retain their traditional separate powers. They have made it clear that their attitude would remain unchanged were Aden to join the Federation. But they would be deeply interested if Aden and the Western Federation formed a really united Government.[1]

In regard to the possibility of an Eastern Federation, Sultan Hussein bin Ali al Kathiri told the Governor, Sir Charles Johnston on 19 December 1961 that the Quaiti state had initiated what they (the Quaitis) referred to as a 'wahdat' (unification), whereas the Kathiri state was only interested in 'ittihad' (federation). They would have been prepared to agree to ittihad if the Quaitis had allowed them to have two-fifths of the voting power.[2]

Watts' successor was Ted Eyre, ex-Sudan Political Service and the Abyan Irrigation Scheme, but very much a Secretariat man. He was Resident Adviser from 1963 until 1966 and though assiduous, had neither Watts' knowledge of the EAP, nor his command of

Arabic, nor the leadership quality which might have persuaded the states to be more decisive in facing the future. Thus, to the British staff, there was a sense of drift, watching the emergence of the Federation in the WAP, supported by HMG with substantial sums, with little expectation that the Quaiti state would join it, or that anyone was seriously considering any alternative. It was as though we were waiting to see what would turn up. In the circumstances, life went on at a relatively slow and pleasant pace. Meanwhile the Federation was receiving proportionately far greater financial support from HMG than the EAP, though its population was not very different. In 1959/60, expenditure for non-development purposes in the EAP was about one third of that for the whole of South Arabia. By 1966/7, that proportion had declined to one twelfth. The allocation of CD&W funds for development in the EAP during the period 1965–8 was £1.01 million; in the federated states outside Aden, it was £4.2 million and even in Aden with its much greater revenues was £1.22 million.

However, security remained much better in the EAP than in Aden or the WAP up until June 1966, when the first attack on British personnel occurred. By and large, none of the British personnel carried arms. I only remember doing so when following the hearse of Sultan Awadh along the narrow Mukalla street in late 1966, and on a few other occasions when we felt it might be sensible to do so. It was a sort of confidence trick – we depended on our relationship with the rulers and trusted the HBL to look after our security. Until mid-1966 the trust in the HBL was justified.

The Residency housing was good and spacious and domestic servants were readily available so domestic life was comfortable. Most of the British staff lived either within the Residency compound or next to it. The British Commandant of the HBL and his British Deputy lived near the HBL lines and there were also some staff in housing built a mile or so inland near the Bedouin Boys School. From time to time there was a parade and display in the Palace courtyard to mark some occasion, and the Residency staff would be invited to attend. The military units would go through their parade ground routines led by the silver band, under the baton of Pakistani Lt Deswendi Khan. The Bedouin Boys School would put on a splendid and amusing display. The residents of Mukalla would sit on the walls and the overlooking hills to watch the proceedings. Friday was the Muslim day of prayer and relaxation, which the Residency also observed. An Anglican chaplain based in Khartoum would visit Mukalla from time to time, when he would hold a service in one of the houses. The coastal situation permitted excellent swimming on the beach, snorkelling along the rocky coasts, and fishing for those who wished. There was a quite marked seasonal rhythm in the ocean, with clear water and pleasant temperatures from October until April. Then as the monsoon system moved northward, the temperature rose, the on-shore winds increased, the sea became cool from an up-welling of water from the deep and was dis-coloured by an explosive increase of marine organisms which attracted large shoals of fish. David Eales used to motor down to the beach late each afternoon to watch the sun go down and read his copies of the airmail edition of *The Times* in chronological order, one edition each day.

Outside Mukalla, there were normally two assistant advisers in Saiyun, one in the Wahidi state until it joined the Federation, one assistant adviser in the Northern Deserts and, from 1963, one in al Ghaidha in the Mahra state. Saiyun was the perfect district office. The town had a mixture of old and new buildings constructed with mud bricks on a stone foundation, but finished in a form of lime plaster which was very durable in the dry climate and gradually aged into soft colours. The Wadi with its palm trees, extensive agriculture, beautiful architecture and the ever-present cliffs rising up on both sides was extremely picturesque. The climate for much of the year was wonderful and the duties not very onerous. The people were on the whole friendly and our relations with them excellent. The rulers and people knew that we represented order and advancement; we respected the civilization and traditions embodied by their lives and customs. An experienced and know-ledgeable officer could influence many aspects of State affairs. The Kathiri Sultan, Hussein bin Ali, the last of the line descended from Badr abu Tuwariq, was a shrewd and well-intentioned individual whose ability to determine the future of his state was circumscribed by the fact that the Quaiti state surrounded it. Had Hussein been the Quaiti Sultan, the outcome for the EAP could well have been very different for he was generally more favourably disposed to the notion of federation from the beginning. He lived in an amazing palace which looked like a large iced cake. He was a connoisseur of food; meals were beautifully prepared and presented and most diverse. His family included the first fully trained doctor from the EAP and a number of others who served in public positions.

The Residency had two houses in Saiyun, one a traditional building with small rooms and steep staircases; the windows contained no glass, only carved wooden screens and shutters to keep out the heat in the summer days and the cold during the winter nights. The other house was more modern and had a colonnaded balcony. These houses stood within a single garden compound, and had their unusual features. One was the long-drop lavatory in the old house – these were typical of nearly all housing in the EAP; the other was the 'jabia', a small pool which could be used for bathing and was emptied every other day to irrigate the garden, including the precious lime tree, which grew within its own goat-proof wall. In the garden, both vegetables and flowers were grown, and on one occasion, Jim Ellis arranged there a demonstration of a new agricultural tool bar to be used for cultivation and other agricultural operations. The garden also contained 'naghl' – date palms – whose fruit would ripen in the hot summer heat. Electricity was usually available from the town supply during the evening hours. The only other British personnel in Saiyun were the manager of the HPS until the early 1960s, a nurse at the new hospital and Alan Wren the manager of the branch of the Eastern Bank and, in time, Heather his wife.

Extending east and west of Saiyun in the Wadi Hadhramaut were numerous towns and villages, the most notable being Tarim to the east and Shibam to the west. Tarim had been a centre of teaching of the Shafai rite of Sunni Islam since the tenth century, which was in time carried by Hadhrami settlers to the Far East, especially modern day Indonesia, to India and to East Africa. Shibam was noted for its extraordinarily tall housing, made of mud bricks but towering seven or eight stories above the narrow streets. Beyond Tarim to the east was the tomb of the prophet Hud, thought to be the patriarch Eber of Genesis 10, and refered to in the Koran (Surah XI) as being sent to the tribe of A'ad, descendents of Noah through Shem. Genesis 10 also shows Shem to have had a descendent, a son of Jokhtan, named Hazarmaveth, which some argue is the origin of the name Hadhramaut. Thousands made the pilgrimage to Gabr Hud each year to remember the prophet and the way in which the tribe of A'ad 'denied the revelations of the Lord and flouted his messengers'. About 40 miles to the west of Saiyun, the wadi opened out to the south where there were two densely populated wadis, Wadi Duan with its two branches, Leissar and Leman, and Wadi Amd. Muhammad bin Ladhin (now generally transliterated as Ladin) Osama's father, came from Duan. In these three valleys an estimated 75,000 people lived, supported by the remittances of the men who worked abroad. Arriving at the top of the pass into Wadi Duan early in the morning, one could pause and look down hundreds of feet to where the villages stood above the wadi bed, with their date palms and tiny green fields, where they would not be washed away by the seasonal floods, or 'suyul'. The early morning sounds of children playing, cockerels calling and dogs barking floated up to the rim of the wadi.

The Residency staff in Saiyun kept an eye on the Hadhramaut Pump Scheme (HPS). The HPS was established in the 1940s and 1950s, following severe draught and famine to support mechanical pumps installed in the wadi to pump water for human and animal consumption and for agricultural purposes. By 1960, there were over 1700 pumps installed. In addition, the HPS had some larger equipment which it would rent out for particular purposes, including bulldozers, graders, standby generators, etc. The HPS was for some years managed by a bachelor Scot. However, he neglected his health and had to be sent home for treatment. Richard Etridge was put in charge of the HPS in the interim, and found himself dealing with the minutiae of stock control and job cards in the workshops. To his surprise, he became fascinated by the potential of the HPS and began to think of other tasks it could take on, including repair of lorries imported for the development projects. It soon became part of his preoccupation to ensure that the HPS was active wherever it could be useful.

Earlier British officers had expended much energy seeking ways to rehabilitate and strengthen water control structures (*sudud*) in the various wadis, designed to prevent erosion of the rich alluvial soil and conserve water. In the post-war world, Colonel Boustead had managed to secure some now redundant anti-submarine nets previously used by the Royal Navy to protect anchored ships at Trincomalee in what was then Ceylon. They proved to be a useful ancillary technique for stabilising the banks of streams and dams constructed to pond up the silt flowing down the wadi bed. By the early 1960s, the Residency staff had also become administrators of a number of development projects financed by HMG's CD&W Scheme. These included the building of numerous schools, the creation of a hospital and a major road project.

Over a period of decades, Hadhrami road builders encouraged by the British staff had evolved a method of surfacing simple roads using stones set like cobbles in a mortar of mud. Since it rained only rarely, the mud hardened into a brick-like consistency in the hot sun, holding the stones tightly together. The road surface was protected after the occasional rains by being banned from use for a day or two until it had dried and the binding mud had hardened again. The expert in building roads in this fashion was Said al Ingleez, so nicknamed after his and his family's close association with earlier British officers. In the early 1960s, a CD&W grant was received to build a road using this cobbling method through the central section of the Wadi Hadhramaut from Furt to Tarim, a distance of about 45 miles. The Assistant Adviser had the task of leading the state officials through a time-consuming negotiation with owners of land, palm trees and irrigation channels along the route of the proposed road. This was accomplished and construction began. A particular problem was how to carry the numerous irrigation channels across the roads, since they typically ran on banks above the level of the roads. Phillip Allfree's design of a syphon to take the water under the road seemed like magic to the road builders and farmers, who then adopted it wherever they could. Allfree also created something of a precedent with his design of an 'Irish' bridge, a concrete structure laid into, rather than above, the bed of the river, which was a good hard crossing when the river was low or dry and not prone to damage when the river was in flood. 'Allfree's folly' was certainly still in use in the mid-1990s when some of us went to call on a now blind Said al Ingleez at his house in Tarim.

The Wadi Hadhramaut was connected to the coast by two roads, the east and west roads. The east road, originally financed by Sayyid Bubakr bin Shaikh al Kaff, was maintained by tolls collected from lorries driving over it; the west road by Quaiti state funds. It was always felt it should be possible to build a single, shorter road which would serve the wadi better, using a route between the two existing roads. Richard Etridge had the task of surveying the route following the line of a pass known as the aqabat Abdulla al Qharib. He collected a team of Said al Ingleez, an escort and some camels to carry supplies, and set off on foot from Mukalla. Nothing was heard from him for more than a week, but eventually he arrived in the wadi having marked out a route which seemed feasible and short. In the 1980s this route was largely used when a tarmac road was built with funds mobilised by the World Bank.

The beauty of the Hadhramaut, which is one of the glories of Arabia, had become quite well known and one of the features of life for British officials posted there was a steady flow of visitors. Until 1966, there were no suitable hotels so, per force, many had to stay with the British staff. Some visitors were of great interest, character or fun, some a penance. Among them there were several politicians, senior service officers, successive Governors and High Commissioners, the odd scholar and of course friends from Aden or Mukalla. Among scholars, Professor Bob Serjeant from Cambridge was a regular and welcome visitor and Sir Mortimer Wheeler also did some archeological work. Denis Healey visited with his wife when he was Minister of Defence, as did Earl Mountbatten when Chief of the Imperial General Staff (CIGS). I recall receiving Admiral Lefanu, then CinC Aden, and his wife who was crippled and needed a wheelchair. Struggling up the narrow stairs of the housing with Lady Lefanu in her chair was quite a task. Joanna Ellis recalls the need to brief visiting ladies on the idiosyncrasies of Hadhrami lavatories! John Weakley recalls a visit by Princess Hohenzollern, a relative of the Duke of Edinburgh, accompanied by a lady-in-waiting. A small marquee was erected at the Ghuraf airstrip. John Lanfear who received them was confused by the introductions and thought the lady-in-waiting was the princess. It was sometime before he realised his confusion!

Sir Sayyid Bubakr bin Sheikh al Kaf died at Saiyun in 1965. Harold Ingrams has described in his book the crucial part he played in negotiating the tribal truce in the 1930s and in establishing law and order in the Hadhramaut, which had the consequence of leaving him impoverished. He was in the finest traditions of the Sayyids, very devout, a peacemaker, a man who tried to right wrongs and who was notably independent of spirit. He always regretted that Britain had not had more influence in South Arabia as he had seen the benefits which accrued from good government in Malaya and Singapore. John Shipman was given access to some of his correspondence after his death – letters from various sultans and tribal leaders asking him to intercede in disputes; requests for Britain to send officers to place the administration of the country on a better basis; a letter from the Turkish commander in Yemen in the First World War trying to persuade the Sayyid to get the rulers of the Hadhramaut to desert Britain and help to drive them out of Aden. When Sayyid Bubakr received the KBE from Queen Elizabeth in 1954 he was exempted from kneeling as he said that as a Muslim he would only kneel before God. John Shipman and I attended Sayyid Bubakr's funeral. We called on his relatives and sat while prayers were said and incense passed around. After lunch we joined the throng following his coffin to the mosque and then to the tomb where he was to be laid. Drummers beat a dirge, the dust rose in the air and was lit by the hot sun as the crowd moved between the houses and gardens across the flood plain of the wadi and into the old town.

Though the carrying of arms in the towns and the settled areas was forbidden, there remained potential for insecurity to break out in the tribal areas, where the men remained armed. One perennial problem was the attempt by the camel-owning tribes in the Southern Jol (the hilly plateau lying between the coast and the Wadi Hadhramaut) to protect their traditional trade of carrying goods by camel from the coast to the wadi. Normally, these tribesmen got a regular share of the traffic by agreement with the merchants in Mukalla and Shihr, but in March 1961, attempts to ban the carrying of arms on the west road led to some clashes. In July 1961, the insecurity spread to the east road. Khamai and Awabitha of the Saiban confederation feeling aggrieved about the quantity of business being diverted to lorries fired on troops sent to keep the roads open. Two platoons of the Mukalla Regular Army (MRA) and supporting HBL troops were ambushed in a wadi, losing 16 men with 35 others being wounded, by far the largest casualty count of any such incident in the EAP. This required a major operation commanded by Colonel Johnson, to re-assert the government's control on the ground. He mobilised the HBL, the remaining MRA soldiers and armed Quaiti and Kathiri police, arranged for an RAF spotter plane and had access to carrier-born jet aircraft from HMS Centaur and Hunter aircraft from RAF Aden. In this kind of situation, the objective was to get the tribal chiefs to submit to the government, to punish the perpetrators by destroying their buildings after warning the inhabitants, and imprisoning those responsible. Casualties were normally light. Stewart Hawkins (on a sabbatical year from Oxford to enhance his Arabic) played a role in this exercise, ensuring 'rear echelon support' to the HBL and MRA units engaged in the operation.

On the borders with neighbouring states, there was also potential for insecurity. Until the late 1950s, Saudi Arabia was assertive regarding its southern borders, not least at Buraimi in Oman. In 1955 two Arabian American Oil Company (ARAMCO) oil-drilling parties crossed the sands of the Rub al Khali from Saudi Arabia and were test drilling in land within the EAP boundary with Saudi Arabia recognised by Britain. The Military Adviser at the time, Captain Jim Ellis, assembled a force of HBL and surrounded both drilling camps. He explained to the Saudis accompanying the party that they had strayed over the boundary and to the ARAMCO team that their equipment would be impounded. A guard was placed on the equipment and the drilling parties taken to an airstrip from which an RAF plane could take them to Aden, for their return to Saudi Arabia.

In 1960, Stewart Hawkins was asked to enquire into a disputed border at al Khabr between the Wahidi Sultanate (then still in the EAP) and the Upper Aulaqi Sultanate. Hawkins, supported by a platoon of the HBL, spent a month walking the area, with its valleys and hillocks and its patches of millet and date cultivation, looking into the problem, listening to the extremely argumentative tribesmen to whom a dispute of this kind was part of their way of life, talking to anyone who wanted to have a say. He gained the impression that both the states and the tribesmen were perhaps happy to perpetuate the dispute, but eventually proposed that the border be demarcated as running down the middle of a watercourse. He was gratified later to hear that this decision was endorsed in Aden and in due course conveyed to the two sultans by the Governor.[3]

Michael Crouch and Stewart Hawkins were faced by one of the last cross-border raids by bedouin in late 1960. The raiders were Dahm, a Yemeni tribe from the essentially un-administered northeast of the Yemen. The HBL at Al Abr were informed of the raid and Crouch, Hawkins and the HBL set out to catch them. The raiders were spotted from Jebel Thaniya moving along the

Figure 4.2 Camel caravan near Shabwa, on the edge of the desert.

edge of the Ramlat Sabatain, an area of shifting sand dunes. The HBL patrol deployed to bring them in 'to help with our enquiries'. Several camels were injured and had to be put down and the leader of the raiders was badly wounded – he died the following day. The HBL soldiers had little restraint in using their weapons. Hawkins recalled that later they had to account to HQ for all the ammunition used in the 45-minute action – 3453 rounds fired, of which he could explain the use of 11 – seven used to put down wounded camels, three wounded the raider and one was found on the ground![4, 5]

In the summer of 1963 a party of Kurab who lived around the Ramlat Sabatain raided into Wadi Markha in the WAP and made off with 14 camels belonging to the Nissiyin. The raiders were followed in pickups and were caught in the open, when a fight ensued. Fortunately for the Kurab a dust and rainstorm came up and they managed to get away. When I heard about this, I immediately drove there from Al Abr with an HBL escort, crossing the sands of the Ramlat Sabatain, and with the local Quaiti commander at Khirwa examined the place where the fight had occurred. There were four dead camels and shallow hollows in the sand where men had sought shelter. Expended cartridge cases and other debris littered the ground. It was the practice on these occasions to demand hostages from the tribes involved to ensure their good behaviour. The local Kurab muqaddam provided two hostages against the surrender of those involved in the raid. He also brought in two wounded men of the raiding party. They were sent off to hospital under armed guard and there then ensued a frenetic debate between the Kurab and the Nissiyin over the facts of the case, the object being for the parties involved to swear statements which would then be taken to Hakm bin Ajaj, a traditional judge, for examination, before being handed over to the Governor of the Quaiti state province for the trial. After much frantic and wearing argument lasting several days, both parties were willing to make their sworn testimony. A space was demarcated in the sand to represent a mosque and each group in turn then stood in the space, faced Mecca, and swore the statements which had been hammered out earlier. They then went off to the Hakm under guard and I returned to Al Abr mentally exhausted by the fractious exchanges. Fortunately, on this occasion, trial by fire, which was still sanctioned under tribal law, was not resorted to, though there was known to have been one such case in recent years. If the testimony on a crime was disputed, those involved could be required to place their tongue on a knife heated in the fire. Those whose tongues healed would be believed.

One evening late in 1964, I was called by Michael Crouch, who was acting Resident Adviser in Mukalla, and told a dispute had broken out between Quaiti and Wahidi tribesmen in a remote hill area. He asked me to go there to try to separate the parties to the dispute; a Political Officer would also be sent to the Wahidi side. This event can stand as an example of the genre. I set out at about 9.00 p.m. with an HBL escort and wireless vehicle and drove all night through the Southern Jol to the small settlement of Tilh where the local Quaiti official (Qaim) had his office. I was informed the Qaim was at the place of dispute, Amroos on the Raidat Basaid. Arriving there in the afternoon, I found the Quaiti force installed in a fortified house in the village. All was quiet so I sent off messages to my opposite number on the Wahidi side and set up camp at a distance from the village. Just after sundown, as a meal was being prepared and I was having a drink, a fusillade of shots rang out and bullets began to kick up the dust around our camp. There was a bang as a bullet passed through a pressurized primus stove and several busy minutes dodging bullets and flying gravel, as my party sheltered behind the vehicles. The party eventually found their way to the village. No casualties except the primus stove and a few holes in the vehicles. There followed a terrific uproar with shots exchanged by both sides, though I did manage to prevent a couple of Quaiti soldiers firing a two-inch mortar at the Wahidis. The night was reasonably quiet, but it all began again in the morning.

The Arab Political Officer with the Wahidis, whose name now eludes me, and I managed to arrange a ceasefire to permit talks. We sat in the open where everyone could see us and agreed that further clashes could only be avoided if both state governments and the Federal government gave simultaneous instructions to withdraw their forces and the male inhabitants. We arranged to continue the ceasefire for 24 hours to give the state governments time to take action and then departed. Both states procrastinated, so the shooting began again. This was mostly ineffective and there were only a few casualties. It was then agreed to establish another ceasefire through a leaflet drop from an RAF Shackleton. That was nearly a disaster as an error in the message had the Quaiti Sultan giving instructions to the Wahidis! Eventually Harry Conway, another Political Officer sent up to the Wahidi state, and I, were asked to go back and supervise the evacuation of the village pending a settlement. We gave instructions for all the men to leave immediately, the Quaitis to the north, the Wahidis to the south, to be followed by all troops and then by ourselves.

As the men were leaving, two women came to see me and explained that they had no home and were in fact living in a condition of slavery. I asked if they knew they could get manumission by applying to the Resident Adviser. They said they did but they had always lived with their master's family and their children were by him; they had always been well treated by him and they would prefer to stay with him but wondered what would happen if he didn't return. I told them what to do if they wanted to clear up their status, and invited them to visit me in Mukalla. By late afternoon, everyone was on their way and I began my own withdrawal. As I came over the hills behind Amroos with the HBL escort, to my alarm firing suddenly broke out ahead. Fortunately, it was merely that the soldiers in front had come across a pack of baboons in the crop fields and were trying to drive them off.

When I was first posted to the EAP, I received my briefing from Willie Wise, then acting as Resident. He told me to go to Saiyun, pick the brains of Jim Ellis, an experienced officer, and then go to Al Abr in the Northern Deserts. He told me he did not expect to hear from me for three months. There were no terms of reference for the job, and in practice this was probably wise as I doubt if it could have been described. I immersed myself in the minutiae of tribal relationships, worked on my Arabic, got some sort of feel for the way the HBL operated and sought to deal with events as they arose. The kind of thing Jim Ellis said (this was just after the 1962 revolution in Yemen) was, 'I should visit Khirwa from time to time if I was you; they feel a little lonely at times like this'. Khirwa was about five hours away, on the other side of the Ramlat Sabatain sands. In fact this was a useful activity as I got to know the Quaiti soldiers at the post they maintained there and word got about that we were keeping an eye on the area, which was in a frontier zone never properly demarcated. This paid off later when I needed assistance from them in trying to bring some offending bedouin to book.

Figure 4.3 The Hadhrami Bedouin Legion (HBL) fort and Residency rest house at Al Abr.

There was no house as such for the officer posted to the Northern Deserts. I used a rest house at Al Abr when I was there and rooms in various other forts when I was travelling. Often I would camp out. I had a sort of awning attached to the side of my Landrover which could be rolled out and give a little shade from the sun. The weather could be terrible, especially in summer, when the temperature would rise above 50°C, and the relative humidity would fall to almost unmeasurable levels. A wind often got up in the afternoon, blowing dust and sand, and all one could do was find a little shelter until evening. In winter it could be beautiful, though cold at night.

From the time the forts were established at the watering points in the Northern Deserts – in 1939 at Al Abr, a group of wells on the desert route to Najran and the Hedjaz, and then successively at Bir Asakir, Zamakh, Minwakh, Thamud, Sanau and Habarut in the 1950s – in order to impose law and order political officers had recorded information about the tribes in the Northern Desert Book, kept at Al Abr (now in the British Library), to which anyone could add new information. Jock Snell and Jim Ellis, who were largely responsible for the establishment of these forts and the early imposition of security, made most entries in the book. From the beginning, tribesmen from each tribe were employed as irregular Desert Guards (DG). The latter came into the forts from time to time, to receive their stipend and kept the British officers informed about events in the desert region, acted as guides, interlocutors in disputes and, in general, interpreters of situations as they occurred. Some of these were great characters, including the Mulazim, Nasser bin Zaid, a Kurbi who though a bit of buffoon always tried to be helpful; Naji bin Amr al Kurbi, a very steadying influence among both Kurab and Sa'ar, who was actually a somewhat superior DG who acted as Tribal Assistant; Mubarak al Kahar al Sa'ari, who had been an inveterate raider and who had a mischievous sense of humour. He was the best guide through the sands of the Empty Quarter. Others included Abdullah bin Ndail al Sa'ari, who often wore a brilliant orange turban; Tomatum bin Harbi al Minhali (literally, 'tomato son of warlike'; he called one of his sons 'Jerrican'), who became a great friend and colleague to successive political officers in the desert region; two of Wilfred Thesiger's companions from his great desert journeys, Salem bin Kabina and Amair, both of the Ruashid who generally lived in the sand sea to the north and east of Thamud and Sanau. Amair was a dour individual, though very competent. There was also a Mahri called Abdulla, who told me that as a young man he was wounded in a raid on the Abida in Yemen, 500 miles from home, and survived the return journey on the back of a camel with two bullet holes in him.

Apart from the DGs, the political officers came to know well some of the tribal chiefs. They were very different from each other. Asker bin Salem al Kurbi was charming, though a hothead whom I never visited without taking Naji bin Amr with me – Naji could calm him down. On one such occasion, we found his tent and learned that Asker had been away for over a week and his family didn't know when he would return. As we were sitting drinking tea with them, he actually turned up. He had been riding a camel for over three days he told us and, though it was extremely hot, he took no water until he had cooled down and drunk qahwa zinjibil (coffee with ginger). The etiquette in these tented camps was both formal and informal. The women were unveiled, shy but friendly; the children were beautifully mannered and were expected to serve the adults before accepting food and drink themselves. The Sa'ari chief we saw most of was Sarur bin Mursil, a somewhat grave man, who had nevertheless a wonderful, winning smile. On one occasion I brought his two boys back from the Bedouin Boys School in Mukalla at the end of the year. When we arrived at his camp, he was absent, but his wife was there with other family members. She was overcome to see her boys again; they were shy, like boys coming home from prep school in England at the end of term. Arabic specialists said that the Sa'ar spoke a particularly fine form of Arabic, with very few additions from other tongues. They also had the distinction of not having to observe Ramadan because they had saved the Prophet's life at the battle of Uhud in 625 AD. Aidha bin Hariz, a principal chief of the Manahil, was a particularly impressive and sage individual who kept his distance from government officials and only visited Mukalla for the first time in 1966. He performed his role as tribal chief with distinction. Though he was illiterate, it was possible to talk with him about any aspect of life, manners or ideas.

There were two principal chiefs of the Sa'ar tribe. One was a frail old man, Yeslam bin Jerboa who lived in the desert and used to come in from time to time in his smelly clothes to harangue the Political Officer, his single tooth wobbling in his mouth as he spoke. The other, bin Rumaidan, lived in a remote part of the northern jol. It was agreed to build an access track to his house. The Quaiti state provided money for a foreman, a gang of road builders and explosive. I set off with the road gang, an HBL guard and two Sa'ari DGs. The flat-topped country was very broken up by eroded gorges and the surface of the ground was littered with stones shattered over the centuries by sun and frost. A track was made by clearing the stones as the party progressed, the soldiers singing lilting and sometimes bawdy songs to keep time to as they worked. At intervals the party had to prospect the route ahead or use explosive to clear some obstacle. At night we camped in the open. After a long day, one of the DGs, Saleh bin Rahgan, set off with his rifle to find meat. Saleh was without one toe, which he had shot off some years earlier after a snake had bitten him on the toe! No sooner had he disappeared over the top of the hill than there were two shots. Several soldiers ran up after him and, incredibly, returned carrying two ibex, a good reward for hard labour. Eventually, the party finished the track to the chief's house and were well received by him. That night as we ate out under the stars someone spotted a light moving over the sky. This was one of the first earth satellites passing over, the year being 1963.

Life in the Northern Deserts was in general full of interest and variety. The only thing resembling a home base was the rest house at Al Abr, which consisted of two rooms which could be used as bedrooms, a small communal room, a scruffy kitchen and an even scruffier washroom/toilet. At any given time there would generally be up to two hundred camels watering there, roaring away among themselves, together with many goats and sheep. There was a steady stream of trucks and pickups coming from or proceeding to Najran and the Hedjaz. If there was no current incident or event to deal with, it was quite relaxing. However, the communications room of the HBL fort was within earshot and at any time this could burst into life as Morse code messages were transmitted or received. We used a primitive coding system for those messages we sought to keep confidential, referred to as Jock code, devised I believe by Jock Snell. This was a simple letter-substitution code combined with five letter word groups, the letter code being changed once a month. Later, as the civil war in the Yemen broke out and began to have foreign policy implications we were supplied with One Time Pads. These were a real pain as there was no safe to keep them in even at Al Abr, and observing the higher level of security required was a real chore, especially when on tour. There was a health unit at Al Abr and quite often the health assistant would ask for help in getting very sick patients to hospital in Shibam, about five hours' driving away – pregnant women with complications, people with snake bite (who mostly died on the way) or gunshot wounds, and very sick children.

One of the attractions of the proximity of the fort was that the guards would often sing and play beautiful flute music to keep themselves awake while on watch at night, especially on moonlit nights, when they would sit up on the tower of the fort silhouetted against the starlit sky. Some used a simple flute; one or two others used the 'mizma'ar' (from 'zamar', to blow or play a wind instrument with a reed), which was a two-reed instrument with a highly reed-like sound. Sometimes one would be invited to attend some bedouin celebration, when typically there would be dancing. A circle of onlookers would form to clap to the rhythm of the flute, cymbals or a drum. People would take it in turn to dance in the circle, singly or in small groups. The bedouin women, who typically were not veiled, would join in. Some of the dances involved intricate gestures with the jambia, the dagger most tribesmen wore. Weddings would take much longer and involve sitting around sipping tea or coffee until the meal was ready. This was normally quite simple, rice cooked with ghee, with baked or grilled meat. Often this would be served quite late at night when it could be cold. Eventually, the guests would be invited to make financial contributions to the bride and groom, the amount of which would be called out as made.

Every couple of months or so, one would go down to the Wadi Hadhramaut, to stock up, relax and get clean. The first irrigation channels one came across had a magical, sparkling quality after two months of rock and sand. The date palms and crop fields of the wadi, set among beautiful houses, mosques and tombs were highly therapeutic. To collapse into a cool jabia was bliss. Several times I visited Ataq, a military post in the WAP, where there was usually a British army unit stationed, to collect supplies sent up from Aden by Cowasjee Dinshaw, a Parsee trading house. The soldiers posted there thought they were pretty remote and were very surprised when I told them I was based as far north of Ataq as Ataq was from Aden. The officers were always hospitable and gave me meals and other refreshment in their mess.

Travelling with the HBL soldiers was generally a pleasure, though Michael Crouch did have a difficult time once when he found his escort vehicle was carrying smuggled weapons. The soldiers were always cheerful provided they had their food and drink. Water would often be carried in goatskins tied onto the side of the vehicles – as the skin sweated, the water was cooled. The soldiers carried a Lee Enfield .303 rifle, with their ammunition on a cartridge belt. The cartridges were not only used for shooting – they were also used to open tinned milk (always Dutch Baby!) – point the cartridge at the top of the tin and give it a sharp blow to create a hole to pour by! The soldiers slept on the ground rolled in a blanket, which was all right most of the year, but not enough in winter. They hated camping at a place called Arain, where, they said, the snakes would get into their blankets to keep warm. The forts would always have an HBL guard at the entrance and if one turned out at night to relieve oneself, they would line up, spring to attention and present arms, until someone persuaded them that this really wasn't necessary. The soldiers often cooked their meat on stones made hot by burning a fire over them, giving the meat a barbecued flavour. After the goat or sheep was slaughtered, the bedouin often ate first the still warm stomach lining of the beast, which they considered nutritious and therapeutic. The liver and kidney were prized for their high level of protein and iron.

It has to be said that the HBL tended to regard the Quaiti and Kathiri authorities and forces with a degree of condescension which sometimes verged on arrogance. Their pay and equipment was better; they felt their relationship with the Resident Adviser placed them above some normal constraints; and their commanding officer was not always inclined to rein in his men when they transgressed. Though soldiers from the same tribe were prone to cling together, nevertheless, the force had a major impact in establishing security and breaking down tribal barriers and enmities. However, as we shall see later, they also played a major part in the seizure of control by the NLF when we left the EAP.

In September 1962, Imam Ahmed of Yemen died and a number of military officers with Egyptian support proclaimed a republic. I heard of this while attending a gathering in the officials' club in Saiyun. It was not clear what this portended at that time, but

I was on my way to a posting at Al Abr. It was not long before the Yemeni civil war began to stray across the frontier zone. The HBL company commander, Abdulla Bagarwan, informed me one evening that a large convoy of vehicles carrying weapons and men had arrived from Najran, under the control of a man named Qadhi Ahmed al-Sayaghi. He wanted a guide and safe passage through the EAP to Marib, in Southeast Yemen. Al-Sayaghi was unknown to me, to Allfree (who was at Al Abr recovering from a fever) and to Bagarwan. I sent a message to the Residency asking for advice. Arthur Watts replied promptly that al-Sayaghi had been the Governor of Taiz and Ibb under the former Imam of Yemen and should be treated courteously until further instructions were received. By early the following morning, Watts had sent instructions that the convoy should not be permitted to enter the EAP, but should be given a guide and be escorted to the desert route to Marib. This was potentially tricky as the force at the disposal of the HBL was far less than the size of the convoy. I arranged with Bagarwan for an escort and local guide and then explained my instructions to al-Sayaghi, who fortunately accepted the situation with good grace and a smile. I accompanied him until his convoy was on a clear route to Marib. Al-Sayaghi may well have been given reason to think that the British administration would support the royalist cause, but at that time that was news to me.

On another occasion in the same war, the royalist garrison of Harib withdrew to Beihan in the WAP in the face of republican forces supported by Egyptians. I was informed that they were to be flown from Beihan to the airstrip at Al Abr and be met by vehicles to be sent from the nearest Saudi post at Sharora. These lorries arrived at Al Abr driven mainly by drivers of the Yam/Duwasir tribe, under a man called Abdulla bin Shuwail al Dawsari, who had led a major raid against the Sa'ar in the late 1940s. I had met him once before at Al Abr and warned him to leave at once to avoid trouble. As there were many old blood feuds between the local Sa'ar and Kurab bedouin and the Yam, Bagarwan put his entire force on alert, including a couple of Ferret scout cars. Despite this, when the Saudi tribesmen lined up to pray that evening, some Sa'ar opened fire, wounding four of the Yam, including bin Shuwail. Bagarwan acted immediately to control the situation by placing the Yam in his fort and their vehicles under his own men. It was arranged to move the trans-shipment point to the airstrip at Zamakh some 40 miles away which was on much more open ground. The following day, in the early dawn, Bagarwan and I led the entire cavalcade of some 20 lorries out to Zamakh, under HBL escort, taking a little-used route to avoid a reported Sa'ar ambush; the airstrip was then cleared of bushes and shrubs so the RAF Beverleys could land. This time, when the Yam prayed facing the setting sun, they kept their weapons strapped on and the HBL were put on guard. The night was quiet except when a sentry trod on a snake. The following morning, the planes arrived disgorging about 500 men and relatives. They climbed down and into the Saudi vehicles and away they went to Sharora. The wounded Yam went with them, refusing the offer of a flight to hospital in Aden – if they died they preferred to die in their own country.

A tour of the northern deserts from Al Abr required over a thousand miles of driving. Sometimes the desert was a smooth hard gravel and sand surface, which was a pleasure to drive on. After rain, these plains would become pale green with knee-length grass and flowers. When dry in the intense heat and wind of summer, they could be hell. Sometimes there were large sand dunes to negotiate. Often the ground was either hard or crumbling stone encased in a fine dust which billowed up as the vehicle passed and meant one was constantly dusty and dry. Heading north from Al Abr, the first fort was at Zamakh, where there is a well used mainly by Sa'ar for watering their livestock. The depth of the well to the water exceeded 200 feet, and pulling up the water was a great labour. Often camels would be hitched to the ropes running over pulleys to pull up the water, with young girls riding the camel and guiding the animal to and fro. The sides of the well were grooved by the constant friction of the ropes. On one occasion a camel slipped into the well; men had to be lowered down to cut up the animal, then everyone hauled water from the well until it had been cleansed. The next fort at Minwakh was a beau-geste affair on the hill above the well; the wadi below was one of the hottest places I remember. On one occasion, heading for Thamud, I camped in the Uruq ul Zaza, huge seif dunes in the Rub al Khali which stretch for miles in a SW–NE direction. During the night we saw lightning on the southern horizon. Coming out of the sands at Wadi Hazar the following morning we found the wadi

Figure 4.4 Lifting water from the well at Zimakh.

in full spate, a remarkable sight. As far as we could see to the north into the sands the water stretched like an inland sea, with sand dunes standing up like islands. We had to wait for several hours until the *sayl* (or flood) subsided, the water sank into the sands and the vehicles could safely cross.

The following day at Thamud, an ancient well where there was also a fort, a dust storm blew up, to be followed by another rainstorm, an unusual event at that place. Thamud is an ancient name, also mentioned in the Koran, Surah XI, to whose people Salih was sent with a camel of Allah – the people 'ham-strung the camel and disbelieved the Lord'; after three days they were found 'prostrate in their dwellings'. The well at Thamud had been used for so long that its mouth now stood twelve or more feet above the surrounding land – the accumulated droppings of thousands of animals over the centuries. Further east still was another fort on the well at Sanau. By mutual agreement, this was the least attractive of these forts. Huge numbers of animals would sometimes come there to water. This water had the effect of loosening the bowels of the animals and humans who used it. The flies were dreadful. There used to be a mad girl resident who would creep up on you and whose bizarre behaviour disturbed the young soldiers posted to the fort. It was to the east of Sanau that I saw an Arabian cheetah (*fahd*), then most unusual and now surely extinct – their principal prey, the oryx and gazelle, also now largely gone. Even the bedouin with me had never seen one. There were two types of gazelle, 'rim' and 'dhabi' on which they could prey, both the most elegant of animals who managed to get enough moisture from the dew on the sparse vegetation. The cheetah evidently got sufficient moisture from the blood of its prey as the only running water in that area was a hundred miles or so away.

Moving on eastward, eventually you arrive at Habarut on the borders of Oman. There is a perennial stream and many date palms at that point, very unusual in the desert. At the time of the kharif, when the dates are picked, the HBL guard was beefed up to prevent fights over the ownership of the palms and dates. Visitors stayed at the fort on a bluff above the stream, an attractive place to spend a day or two. I was there once at the time of the Īd ul-Fitr, the celebration marking the end of the fasting month of Ramadan. I received a message from the local Bait Za'banat Mahra muqaddam, Ali bin Hizhaiz, asking me to join him for a meal to celebrate the Īd. I found the muqaddam living in a cave nearby and sat down to a disgusting meal of cold rice and cold, fatty, gristly meat. The only good part of the meal was the tea at the end. After an hour or so of chatter, I took my leave and was able to retire to the 'privacy' of the fort. (Stewart Hawkins recalls that bin Hizhaiz, though illiterate, with very little help from Stewart's Genesis and St Matthew, could recite the generations of Shem through Qahtan (Jocktan) to the present day.) John Shipman came to know bin Hizhaiz well and respected him as a mediator and patriarch of the Bait Za'banat. At the fort, I found young boys offering flint arrows and spearheads found nearby. I visited the site with the boys and was amazed at the number of Neolithic implements just lying around on the hillside. I made a report to the Director of Antiquities and took a small sample of implements to show the kind of things found there – they were donated to the Mukalla museum. Others had done the same; Stewart Hawkins took a collection back to Oxford and contributed with a curator of the Ashmolean Museum to an article about them in the journal *MAN*.[6]

In the 1950s, a subsidiary of the Iraq Petroleum Company carried out geological mapping and other studies of the Eastern Aden Protectorate to see what the prospects were of finding oil. They were not encouraged by what they found and abandoned the concession in 1959. However, in 1962, the Pan-American Oil Company, part of AMOCO, obtained concessions from all three states, acquired IPC's data and began renewed geological and seismic studies. Their initial geological party consisted of two Americans, a French Canadian and an Argentinian. They were an eclectic bunch and good company who enjoyed their work and took an interest in the place in which they were working. They ran into some difficulty from some tribesmen in the Northern Mahra area. The Sultan had signed a concession, but the tribes on the ground did not always accept the Sultan's authority. I went there taking two DGs, Sulayim bin Duwaish, (considered by some to be a 'snake in the grass', but nevertheless a shrewd and influential member of the powerful Bait Samuda Mahra) and Tomatum, whose father was Manahil and mother Mahri, as well as a section of the HBL and a wireless vehicle. The geologists followed. All went well until halfway through the day when shots were fired at the leading vehicles. My vehicle was hit on the front axle and an HBL vehicle had a bullet through the front mudguard. The HBL soldiers immediately deployed and seized two Mahra as hostages against future good behaviour. Fortunately, one of them turned out to be a relatively important section chief, Ahmed al Nissi, who later became a member of the Mahra Tribal Council. The hostages were sent off to Mukalla under escort and the geological work continued. The evening of this event, while meat was being taken around a campfire, Sulayim was stung on the thigh by a scorpion. This caused much amusement among the HBL soldiers who felt he had allowed the party to fall into a trap!

The drilling parties who followed the geologists were of a very different nature. They worked 12 hours on, 12 hours off for three weeks at a time, and then went to Aden or East Africa for R&R and a blinder. They did not seem to care whether they were in the desert or the ocean, in America or Asia. As with US naval ships, alcohol was banned while they were in camp. Their caravans were plastered on the interior by centerfold pages from *Playboy*. They just drilled and showed no consideration for the HBL escorts who accompanied them. It was typical of these people that when they eventually gave up the concessions in 1966, they left explosives lying around the desert and abandoned the dogs they had taken as pets.

Exploration for oil was not then possible in most of the Mahra state, which lay south of a steep escarpment. Sultan 'Isa bin Ali bin Afrar, the Sultan of Qishn and Socotra who was in treaty relationship with Britain, lived on the island of Socotra, off Cape Gardafui in Africa and 300 miles south of Mahra. He was recognised by the Mahra as their suzerain, but in return he was obliged to undertake not to bring the British into their territory. Our relations with Sultan 'Isa were episodic as a result of his isolation. Jock Snell had spent some time there but most of us only visited the place very occasionally. Ralph Daly and John Weakley visited the island in late 1963, with a large group of Mahra tribal leaders, to seek to improve relations between the Sultan and the mainland tribes, who were suspicious that the oil revenues would not be spent on the mainland. The proposal was that the revenues be paid into an account to be opened by the Sultan with the British Resident Adviser as signatory. Expenditure would be in accordance with a budget to be agreed with the Sultan and, implicitly, the mainland tribes. The underlying objective was to prepare the way for setting up an administration on the mainland. This step was taken in late 1963 and was achieved by three companies of the HBL advancing from Jebel Mahrat in the north, via Wadi Murait, and by the landing by sea at al Ghaidha of men and supplies. The expedition, incongruously given the code-name 'Operation Gunboat', was commanded by Colonel Johnson, with Phillip Allfree, a professional soldier himself, as Political Officer and Pat Gray in command of the HBL units. A camp was set up at Murait to guard the landward route and another at al Ghaidha on the coast. Both camps were to become forts over the next few years. This was perhaps the last expansion on the ground of the former British Empire. The operation is well described in Phillip Allfree's book, *Hawks of the Hadhramaut*.[7, 8] The Mahra were schizophrenic about the opening up of their country; they wanted the benefits that oil could offer, but didn't want the controls which a government would exercise; some were totally opposed to the new administration; some very much in favour. An ex-Palestine policeman, Bob Clarke, was posted to al Ghaidha as Political Officer to supervise the selection of the members of a tribal council under the nominal chairmanship of the Sultan, but effectively chaired by a man appointed by him. Clarke then had the task of creating from scratch the rudiments of an administration for the territory. In the main, this required hours and hours of debate and argument, week after week, month after month.

John Shipman recalls that the main burden of keeping the newly formed Mahra Tribal Council (MTC) in play fell on the shoulders of Clarke's assistant, Abdulla Salem bin 'Ashur al Mahri, who had been on the Residency staff for some years. Abdulla's family, although of Mahri origin, were based in Mukalla and acted there as commercial and consular agents for the Sultan. Abdulla was a self-deprecating man of untiring courtesy, high intelligence and extraordinary patience, qualities which uniquely qualified him to assist the kindly, but elderly and phlegmatic Clarke in managing the personal and tribal rivalries which ebbed and flowed within the MTC, and which the Sultan's deputy and chairman of the MTC proved powerless to control. Abdulla's moral courage was tested in early 1967 by the NLF's assassination of his brother Omar in Mukalla. Later that year he cabled the United Nations on behalf of the MTC rejecting independence (he was later imprisoned by the South Yemen's Marxist regime and executed in 1972). Meanwhile, the relations between the MTC and its absent Sultan were at breaking point and the MTC invited the head of the mainland branch of the Sultan's clan, Khalifa bin Abdulla bin Afrar, who resided in al-Qishn, to assume chairmanship of the MTC. Sultan Khalifa, then in his 60s, was a man of simple dignity, with a shrewd understanding of local tribal politics; he was respected for his lineage, judgement and experience of the world beyond the borders of Mahra. Khalifa was a convenient and genial figurehead whose position the British tacitly accepted, notwithstanding their treaty relationship with his kinsman across the sea.

By 1967 the MTC had developed several emblems of statehood: it had recruited and was training its own little army; it was issuing its own passports; it was flying its own flag; and it had established its own post office. A weekly Aden Airways flight linked al Ghaidha, Mahra's fledgling capital with Mukalla, Aden and the wider world.

I visited Socotra once, travelling in an RAF DC3, Patricia accompanying me. There had been heavy rain overnight and the plane nearly turned turtle when it landed as its wheels sank into the runway. We assembled a crowd of people who physically lifted the plane out of the ruts on the runway. When the strip had dried out in the hot sun and wind and was hard enough to support the plane, it departed, the pilot saying he would not return to that strip – we had better find a more reliable one! There was in fact a good, long gravel strip at Qathub, west of Hadibu, which had been used for anti-submarine reconnaissance patrols in the Second World War; I visited it to check its condition, which was pretty good, and found an old aircraft abandoned by the RAF at the end of the war, its doors blowing in the wind, and half filled with sand and dust. The Sultan had in his Council chamber at Hadibu a fine Axminster carpet and a large table and chairs. The chairs had chains hanging down beneath them – the whole suite had been salvaged from a freighter which had gone aground on the Abd-al-Kuri islands, west of Socotra. Lloyds had written off the ship. The sultan had been informed and he had agreed with the Somali fishermen that they could have the liquor if he had the furnishings and the cars being carried on board! The latter were parked around his fort and whenever he wanted cash, he would send one to Aden to sell it.

In 1966, George Hilton-Brown was sent to Socotra to carry out a survey of the social and economic conditions and to identify possible projects for funding by CD&W. He spent four months on the survey and visited much of the island on foot or camel. His report is dated 16 July 1966,[9] and in the 15 months remaining before independence, it was not possible to follow up any of his recommendations. It shows how few resources the British administration of the EAP had at its disposal that nothing had been done earlier. Like earlier visitors, Hilton-Brown found that no one carried arms and there appeared to be virtually no crime. Land rights appeared to be well understood and regulated. The only significant exports, apart from migrant labour, were dried fish, ghee, a few pearls and rugs. Some consumer products and such items as cement were imported. Hilton-Brown paid especial attention to the water resources and wells. He carried a kit for making a chemical analysis of sources of water but also made a pot of tea and mixed it with his whiskey to see how it did!

Occasionally, events beyond the EAP impinged on the local scene. One such occasion was the decision in September 1965 of

Sir Richard Turnbull to dismiss the Aden government and declare a State of Emergency. Rioting occurred in Aden and sympathetic demonstrations occurred in Mukalla and Saiyun. The Kathiri government offices in Saiyun were closed and the Kathiri Armed Constabulary (KAC) were reluctant to confront the crowd. The demonstrators, numbering several hundred came on to the Residency office to protest. Stones were thrown and for a time there was some anxiety. I went down to meet them and invited them to submit petitions and after a short while they dispersed. Jim Ellis in Mukalla felt that in the circumstances a patrol of the HBL should make a visit to Saiyun, an unusual occurrence at that time, to reinforce the authority of the Sultan and the KAC, but soon they were able to return to base.

In December 1965, two years before the announced date of independence, I accompanied Ted Eyre, the Resident Adviser, on a visit to the Saut Bal Obaid, an area of the Southern Jol near to the Federal boundary. The people were familiar with the functioning of the nearby Federal government. We received a most cordial reception, with a 'za'mal' (the inhabitants line up and fire their rifles over the head of the visitors) at every significant village. Petitions were presented, tea and coffee was served and drunk and everything was most cordial. However, they wanted to know what would happen when Britain left South Arabia. Would the street crowds in Aden or Mukalla run the country? Would the Quaiti state enter the Federation? Who would control the HBL and keep the peace? They knew full well the importance of these questions, but they had no representation on any state council and sensed the drift in EAP policy-making. The Resident had nothing to tell them. He could not answer any of the three questions, and could not tell them how they could participate in the consideration of them. For me, it was a deeply dispiriting experience which had a major impact on my own attitude to our role in the country. We were faced with the prospect of just walking away with all the problems of independence unsolved, a betrayal of the trust the people placed in Britain and the Residency.

From the time of the announcement in February 1966 by HMG that Britain would not offer defence assistance to the new state when it became independent, it was quite evident that things could not go on as before. The drift of the last five years in the EAP would come to an end. Arms were beginning to come in and it would be only a matter of time before clashes occurred between those contending for power at independence. The political leaders of the Quaiti state did not know what to do and the Kathiri state could not act independently of the Quaiti state. This is when the narrow membership of the Quaiti state Council, proved a real handicap. Though Turnbull visited the EAP and put the governments under considerable pressure to join the Federation, they remained very reluctant to do so, though no alternatives really existed. Later, the new Quaiti Sultan did wonder about the possibility of some relationship with Saudi Arabia, though this idea was not really pursued.

In the absence of initiatives by the Quaiti state, the tribes began to meet among themselves. The first meeting, organised in June 1966 by Abdulla Said Buqshan, a prosperous Hadhrami trader in the Hedjaz, took place at Jedda in Saudi Arabia.[10] The meeting, which was attended by members of all the major tribes, agreed a five-year truce amongst them, a means for enforcing the truce, insisted that no person or institution could represent their views without prior consultation, agreed to a follow-up meeting and agreed to send copies of the signed agreement to all the Hadhrami tribes. The language describing those committed by the agreement included the phrase 'shaim wa laim', that is it also applied to non-tribesmen for whom the latter felt themselves responsible – mainly sayyids, mashaikh, townsmen and masakeen. The second meeting, which occurred a month later at Qarat Abdul Aziz,[11] actually Kathiri territory and therefore with the approval of the Kathiri Sultan, with stronger representation of important tribal muqadams and a large attendance, confirmed the truce. It also established a tribal 'lujna' or committee to represent the tribes and negotiate with other parties, prohibited any single tribe or muqaddam from negotiating on matters regarding the future of the country without reference to the lujna for approval and rejected the idea of following any foreign authority whatsoever. We learnt that the NLF and the ASP had worked hard to disrupt plans for this meeting, but some stout leaders including Aidha bin Hariz al Minhali, Rabia bin Aishan bin Ajaj and Sultan Hussein had rallied those who were more fearful. Two of those attending represented the SAL.

The Residency sent reports on these meetings to the High Commission in Aden, but neither Ted Eyre, the Resident Adviser nor the High Commissioner thought them worthy of follow-up. In fact they were the only serious attempt made at that time in the EAP to work out an approach to the future of the country. The tribes feared the absence of effective government, which they knew would mean anarchy or revolution. The Quaiti Minister, al Attas, held meetings in the coastal towns to seek opinions of the people, but there was little support for joining the federation and quite a lot of support for the Arab Socialist Party. Though encouraged to visit other parts of the state and attend tribal meetings, he rarely did. Nor did he articulate proposals for the future of the state. It was not until April 1967, nine months later, that Sultan Ghalib called a tribal meeting in Mukalla which was to have been followed by a national meeting. The purpose of this meeting was to have been to establish a National Assembly. Sultan Ghalib postponed the national meeting pending the return of the Minister. He did not return and in the event the national meeting did not occur.

The approach of the Mahra Sultan was extraordinary. As it was reported to the Defence and Overseas Policy (Official) (DOP$_O$) Committee of the Cabinet 'At an unscheduled meeting with Lord Beswick in mid-February 1966, the Sultan gave the impression that he did not want any change and was happy to rely on the Treaty with Queen Victoria'.[12]

In June 1966, there was an attack on the house of Humphrey Friend, one of the British staff in Mukalla. As in the case of the murder of Major Eales the previous year by an HBL soldier under his command, there was a possibility of a personal motive for the attack and it was not clear to what extent the attack represented a new situation in the EAP. Nevertheless, an assessment of the security threat in the EAP prepared at that time[13] concluded that the threat was now substantial and increasing. The political parties were offering large sums to tribal leaders, the SAL was poorly led and organised, the NLF was becoming more organised and arms were flooding into the country. The HBL were the penultimate deterrent, British forces being the ultimate one. But how reliable were the HBL? They had killed their deputy Commandant. Their future was uncertain and no one could tell them what future to expect.

Then, in July 1966, Pat Gray and his wife Edith were shot near their house as they returned from watching a film in the HBL lines.

Gray turned his car round and, although grievously injured, drove his wife to the hospital, where he immediately died. A helicopter from a warship evacuated her the following day. The assailants were HBL soldiers. The evidence of political motivation was more convincing this time. The man principally responsible found his way to Yemen and the Yemenis made use of this fact to say that the revolution had spread to the East. However, interrogation of a probable accomplice, caught by the Federal Guard near Bir Ali, suggested that there may have been a personal element to this incident also, as the principal assailant had been cashiered for striking a junior officer only three days earlier. The investigation[14] did not make a finding on the motivation. The fact remained, however, that the two senior British officers of the HBL had both been killed by their own men. This created real worries for the future of the EAP. If the HBL was becoming unreliable, who was to maintain law and order in the last resort? Major Cotter, Gray's new deputy took over command of the HBL pro tem, and carefully observed the morale of his men, who were shamed by these successive murders. Wakil Qaid Salem Umar al Johi was appointed his deputy. Later, as independence neared, Colonel Johnson took over command, and we began to get reports that some of the company commanders were positioning themselves for the uncertainties of the future. In the absence of a plan for the future of the EAP, no attempt was made to create a single command structure for the armed forces of the EAP or to address the question of pay differentials between the HBL and the state forces, or the budgetary issue.

These concerns also created worries for the first time about the safety of the remaining British staff in the EAP in the period prior to independence. The Residency compound was overlooked from two sides and unless the heights were picketed, was very vulnerable to attack. The staff living away from the compound were even more exposed. Some improvements were made in the communications and some security lighting installed, but basically the housing and office were indefensible against a well-conceived and determined attack. The posts in Saiyun and al Ghaidha were very isolated in security terms. Nevertheless, things returned to something like normality after a while and the EAP drifted further towards the end.

In August 1966, an Aden Airways Dakota en route from the Wahidi State to Aden was blown up in the air, killing the entire complement, including the Wahidi State Secretary and Tim Goschen, the Political Officer in Wahidi. In late 1966, an operation, code-named Operation Waffle[15] was mounted along the Mahra coast, near the border with Oman, to intercept Omani guerillas engaged in training with Egyptian, Soviet and ex-EOKA support. The Irish Guards, accompanied by some marines and a small SAS detachment, operating off HMS Fearless, invested the village of Hauf and captured 25 guerillas and instructors identified by informers. Jim Ellis, who had now taken over from Ted Eyre as Resident Adviser, and Michael Crouch went along as Political Officers.

In anticipation of the independence of Aden, the Foreign and Commonwealth Office began to send staff to Aden so they could become acquainted with the situation. Oliver Miles arrived in Mukalla in January 1967. One of the things which struck him was the absence of serious discussions about the future of the EAP. The Quaiti state Government had failed to broaden representation in its councils, had proved incapable of formulating proposals for the future of the state, the initiatives taken by the tribal leaders had been ignored and the Resident Adviser and the High Commission had allowed the situation to drift. Consultations around the state indicated very little support for joining the Federation, some support for the NLF and other radical groups, and some support for the SAL. As indicated above, Sultan Ghalib had raised the question of a possible link with Saudi Arabia and this possibility was also attractive to some of the tribes. It was not, however, seriously followed up. It was about this time that I had the melancholy duty of delivering to Sultan Ghalib the letter from the High Commissioner giving him one year's notice of HMG's intention to abrogate the protectorate and advisory treaties. Sultan Ghalib felt that HMG's unilateral decision to terminate these treaties was precipitate and not warranted by the situation in the EAP.

During a demonstration in Mukalla, violence broke out and someone threw a hand-grenade into a group of demonstrating schoolboys, killing two and injuring many. The purpose of this barbarity was never clear; the accused, who was said to be a member of the SAL, was eventually sentenced to death. Grenades were also thrown by opposing factions at the minister's house, at the office of a left-wing newspaper and at the newspaper editor's house. Explosives were found and when a parade was held at the Īd ul-Fitr, no one sat next to the British staff – it was rumoured that grenades would be thrown at them.

In the middle of May 1967, the Residency in Mukalla came under attack. The HBL communications office received a rocket attack and some of the housing was engaged with rifles and machine guns. The decision was taken to evacuate women and children. A unit of the SAS under Captain Charles Guthrie (who was later to become the Chief of Staff of the British army) was sent to ensure that the Residency staff could continue to function. In the second half of May, Lord Shackleton visited Mukalla to discuss possibilities for the future with Sultan Ghalib and the Residency staff. He had been appointed by Prime Minister Harold Wilson as Minister without Portfolio to handle the Aden question, which had clearly become a crisis for the government. During the course of the discussions, I mentioned to him that I was leaving the service as I felt our position had become a false one; I had been promoted to be Deputy British Agent in the EAP but was not prepared to take the additional responsibility for what was clearly becoming a fiasco, and had resigned from the service. Though the responsibility of the Advisory staff was to the inhabitants of the territory, we had become principally preoccupied with extracting ourselves from a mess very much of our own making; and had proved unable to resolve the issues of independence effectively. I was due to leave Mukalla soon and he asked that I visit him in Aden to discuss the situation in the EAP. When I did so, he asked what the alternatives might be. I said I thought it was too late to make constructive proposals, that the situation was sliding out of control. The Federal government was totally dependent on HMG, but HMG had repudiated responsibility for its defence after independence. There was no chance of persuading the EAP states to join it and we had not articulated any alternatives.

When, on 3 June, the June war broke out between Israel and Egypt, with the latter being overwhelmed, the NLF asserted themselves in the Federation and the Crater region of Aden was for a few days abandoned by the army after the armed police mutinied. A large crowd gathered at the Residency in Mukalla. Jim Ellis addressed them and tried to persuade them to disperse. The HBL quarter guard had taken up firing positions and in response to provocations in fact fired over the head of the crowd to disperse them. Some of the bullets hit the roof of the palace across the road, at which the palace guard opened fire on the Residency. Sultan Ghalib intervened to stop the shooting on his side and Ellis did the same in the Residency. Fortunately there was only one minor injury which Joanna Ellis was able to patch up. Incidents such as this and the general drift of events led to much concern for the remaining British personnel in scattered, remote stations. In mid-July, the Residency in Mukalla was ordered to plan the evacuation of Saiyun, al Ghaidha and eventually Mukalla. Members of the RAF Regiment were sent to RAF Riyan to ensure that it would be secure until it was evacuated.

Somehow, in the middle of all this, in June 1967, an operation was mounted by the HBL, with RAF support, to arrest a number of Mahra sympathetic to the NLF who had found their way to Socotra. This operation, codenamed 'Snaffle' (who invents these codenames?), and led by Philip Hillman, was completely successful – the entire group was arrested without injury and removed from Socotra. They were tried by the Mahra Tribal Council and sentenced in various ways.[16]

On 16 July 1967, Sir Humphrey Trevelyan, the High Commissioner who succeeded Turnbull, visited the Quaiti and Kathiri Sultans and the HBL. The sultans wanted, belatedly, to move towards a union of the Eastern States; they proposed to treat the HBL as the nucleus of an EAP army, adding elements of the MRA to it; the remainder of the state forces would become a joint armed police. Trevelyan said it was for them to decide; it would take some time to implement, but HMG would not be able to delay its own arrangements for independence. HMG was willing to finance the HBL for two years on the existing basis on certain conditions. These included establishment of a single authority responsible for the HBL; establishment of functioning liaison with the Federal government and their forces; the pay and conditions of service of the HBL would not be amended to their disadvantage; civil aid would only be available if the EAP states joined the federation. Trevelyan clarified that HMG would have no objection to the EAP states seeking civil aid from other sources. After the discussions Trevelyan commented to HMG that in his view the EAP sultans had some justification in not joining Federation in its present condition, before serious negotiations for union had been started and that stopping all aid apart from the HBL payment would place them in an impossible position. They should be given some time. He also reported that the Mahra state wanted to join the Federation now, but advised against this until the other EAP states made such a move.[17]

On 2 August, 1967, Trevelyan again flew to Riyan to meet the sultans, assembled there with some difficulty by Michael Crouch, acting for Jim Ellis, to brief them on the discussions held at the United Nations about recognition of the new state emerging in South Arabia. The UN was intending to hold a further meeting in Geneva, to be attended by Lord Shackleton, at which the nature of the future state would be negotiated. Sultan Ghalib was still not committed to the Federal solution and only reluctantly agreed to go to Geneva; he wanted to establish a Regency Council under his brother, Umar, to govern the state during his absence, but Umar was still in England. Trevelyan urged Ghalib to go anyway to make sure his views were adequately represented to the UN. He left Mukalla on 17 August by RAF transport and transited through Cairo so that he could call on the Arab League for assistance. He arrived in Geneva on 31 August. The same day he heard from Trevelyan that the Residency in Mukalla had been closed down and the key staff moved to RAF Riyan, though he says Trevelyan had assured him that it would remain open until 10 October and that all treaties would remain in effect until 8 January 1968.[18]

The Aden authorities had told Jim Ellis, who was the Resident Adviser, that the Residency would not be closed down until 1968 (this was still the planning date on 16 August[19]), and as he was overdue leave, he should take it in August 1967. Naturally he would have briefed the sultans about this and the expected independence date before he went on leave. Therefore, no one in the EAP would have had an inkling when Trevelyan urged the sultans to go to Geneva that in fact the Residency would have been closed down by the end of the month. For years, Sultan Ghalib believed that Ellis had lied to him regarding HMG's intentions; only within the last ten years did he learn that Jim also had been kept in the dark.[20]

Following the collapse of the Federal government in the federal states adjoining the EAP, Michael Crouch had been ordered to close down the Mukalla Residency and the Saiyun office forthwith. The office in al Ghaidha remained open yet a while under Arab staff, though Sultan Khalifa, accompanied by Abdulla bin Ashur, had travelled to Geneva. Colonel Johnson had been prevented from leaving the HBL compound as the officers did not know what their future was. Crouch had been authorised to inform the HBL officers 'that HMG guaranteed their pensions and all rights'. Evidently, however, the High Commissioner did not want to continue to run the risk of leaving the British staff there, and was moving to evacuate the more remote stations. The Residency was abandoned, quietly, in the heat of the post-lunch rest-period, without any notice to any state official or anyone else, to avoid the danger of their being prevented from leaving. Jim Ellis was at Riyan on the arrival of the British staff there. He then had the lamentable and dispiriting task of explaining to the Arab Residency staff and the senior HBL officers, in the absence of the Sultan, that the advisory functions performed by the British Residency were now at an end and that he would do his best to ensure that they received their pensions and other entitlements. (It would take a strenuous and protracted lobbying effort in London on the part of Jim Ellis, Dick Holmes, Colonel Johnson and others to ensure that HMG honoured the undertakings given.) Jim was shattered by the way his good name had been used by HMG to deceive everyone in the EAP and he vowed he would never again work for the British government; nor would he have the face to work for Arabs again.[21]

Hearing of the closure of the Residency, the EAP sultans agitated to return immediately to the EAP, but were reassured that there were no particular troubles in their states which required their immediate return.[22] On his way back to Mukalla, Sultan Ghalib passed through Beirut and Jedda. On 2 September, he was informed that the Residency staff had been withdrawn to Aden, that RAF Riyan had been closed and the airfield handed over to the HBL to guard and maintain. In Jedda, Ghalib sought a meeting with Lord Shackleton, but this was not arranged. In the absence of civil or military aircraft to return to Mukalla, Sultans Ghalib and Hussain were provided with a ship by a Hadhrami ship owner. However, on arrival at Mukalla on 17 September, they were prevented from landing by the NLF, acting with the support of the HBL, though the latter were then still in British pay.[23] Thus the Quaitis and Kathiris never had a chance to implement the union agreed with Trevelyan.

Hearing of this, some of the tribes sought to arrange a return for the sultans overland from Saudi Arabia. They seized a number of police and military posts and besieged several posts, including Al Abr, Zamakh and Minwakh, normally garrisoned by the HBL. The HBL called for air support and the RAF responded, though Sultan Ghalib was still in treaty relationship with HMG and the HBL had assisted the NLF in refusing to allow him to return to Mukalla.[24]

Ghalib feels to this day that he was duped by Trevelyan into leaving Mukalla on a false premise – that his brother Umar would be brought back to act for him as the head of a Regency Council and that the Residency would remain open until after his return – and that while he was out of the country, his state was handed over to the NLF, supported by the HBL, though HMG's treaties with the Quaiti state remained in effect until 1968. Though Ghalib did not adequately take account of the momentum of events, and may not have understood how difficult it now was to forge a consensus on the future of his state, it is difficult to refute the breach of faith he alleges. I've no doubt that many of the rulers of the Indian Native States had the same feeling 20 years earlier.

Thus to the end, the EAP maintained its detachment from Aden and the WAP. Britain's recognition and acceptance of this separate identity was, however, soon swept aside after independence by the intolerant nationalistic ideology clamped onto the 'People's Democratic Republic of Yemen' by the NLF. That fervour has now passed and perhaps some of that distinctive Hadhrami identity which we admired will return and its people prosper under the new dispensation.

CHAPTER FIVE

ROBIN YOUNG'S DIARIES

Peter Hinchcliffe

Robin Young's eleven years service in Aden came to an end on 12 November 1967. He left by East African Airways VC10 at 16.10 for a flight to Nairobi. I, the only other remaining member of the old WAP Office, accompanied him. He was heading for South Africa and then Australia; I was on my way to Ghana to be reunited with my wife and baby daughter. The previous night we had completed the destruction of the remaining WAP office files in the last bonfire of many outside our bleak 'married quarter' in RAF Khormaksar. We had said goodbye to the diminishing group of colleagues still in the Colony, had paid off our domestic staff and Federal Guard soldier escorts and had had our last joyless walk around a British RAF base slowly contracting on itself as the authorities prepared for the final withdrawal on 30 November. Unusually Robin did not write a brief end of tour valedictory on the last page of his diary; his final paragraph recorded the bonfire of classified papers, the 'frantic' packing and the admission that he still had two final letters to write. He never returned to Aden.

Robin Young arrived in Aden in 1956. He was 29. He came from a Colonial service background having spent many years in the Sudan where his father, Clive, had reached the highest echelons of the elite Sudan Political Service (SPS) as Governor of the Blue Nile Province. Robin himself had followed the SPS colours and served there from 1949 before going on to Aden as the Sudan reached independence in 1955. He had previously been educated at Sedbergh and at Pembroke College, Cambridge. He had two years

Figure 5.1 Robin Young and (partially obscured) Sultan Ahmed bin Abdullah, the then Fadhli Sultan, September 1963, shortly before the Sultan defected to Cairo. Robin and Sultan Ahmed are seen touring the Abyan Cotton fields.

in the Royal Navy at the very end of the war, being demobbed in 1947. In the Sudan he had served in Kordofan province as an ADC to the District Commissioner. His time in Khartoum included spells in the Chief Secretary's office and in the Personnel Branch of the Ministry of Interior. Other 'old' Sudan hands in Aden including Arthur (later Sir Arthur) Charles, Ted Eyre, Dr N.L. Corkill and Ralph Daly, all of whom transferred to the Aden Administrative Service.[1] The NLF murdered Sir Arthur Charles in 1965 but the other three survived. Robin went on to Oman serving there for several years as Director of Development, Dhofar. Ralph Daly joined an oil company there before being appointed adviser to the Sultan on wild life conservation and the environment, and in that capacity helped to save the Arabian oryx from extinction.[2] Robin after retiring to his old home in Devon, died from cancer of the liver on 12 August 1990 at the early age of 63.

After the smooth and relatively orderly transfer of power in the Sudan underpinned by a relatively efficient and sophisticated structure of civil government, the Aden Protectorate must have been a severe culture shock to the young Robin Young. His first upcountry posting as a Political Officer was to the chronically turbulent Amirate of Dhala, where a previous Political Officer, Peter Davey, had been murdered in 1947,[3] and where Davey's erstwhile boss (Major Seager) had been the target of an assassination attempt in 1950. The Political Officer's house just outside Dhala town was a major rebel target and remained such until the local NLF leadership forced the last British occupant out in 1967.[4] One of his contemporaries has the impression that Robin did not enjoy his time there, was pinned down in his compound, subjected to a number of attacks by dissidents and did not get around his 'district' as much as he might have done in less fraught times. Certainly his next assignment to the more peaceful Fadhli Sultanate at Zingibar[5] was more to his liking. It was, by Western Aden Protectorate standards, better developed – at least in the fertile cotton growing coastal strip and had a rudimentary administration. Robin Young, perhaps because of his Sudan Political Service background, was fascinated by anything to do with cotton on which both Fadhli and its neighbour the Lower Yafa' Sultanate depended for most of their state income.[6] His diary lovingly records the amount of seasonal water flowing down the twin wadis: the Bana and the Hassan and he waxed lyrical over the rich brown silt-laden floodwater which was the annual life blood of the new cotton crop. Diary entries from the 2 to 8 August 1962 were almost entirely devoted to the progress of the waters. The extent of the flooding varied from year to year and in good years Robin loved to speculate on whether records would be broken and more acreage would be under irrigated cotton then ever before. When I was Robin's 'cadet' assistant as a newly arrived Political Officer in 1962 I was frequently summoned to accompany him on long walks along the banks ('bunds') of flooded cotton fields. This could be quite frightening with a big 'sayl'[7] coming down one of the wadis and sometimes bursting the bunds and cutting us off from our start point. On those occasions we had to wade through the newly created channels waist high in a strong and swirling chocolate torrent and I remain astonished as to why neither of us was swept away.

Robin Young kept his diary for as long as I knew him, and he had certainly started it some time before my arrival. It is a classic chronicle of colonial history in the making. The first volume probably began in 1959 but I have no starting point except that volume V (the earliest I have seen) began on 1 January 1961 and he generally had a new volume of A4 (green hardback folder) covering four months. (There are, however, gaps when he was on annual leave.) Every evening, if possible, he would retire to his study and type noisily, rarely less than one page and never more than two. This activity may well have been inspired by the habit and discipline of maintaining an official diary in the Sudan for the Provincial Governor who used the material sent in by his subordinates for the Province Diary which went direct to the Governor-general.

His sister Buff Goodbody recounts how on a visit to Mukeiras in 1965 on the upper Audhali plateau, adjacent to the frontier with then (North) Yemen she and her husband were sitting on the balcony of the guesthouse while Robin was typing away inside. Suddenly two shots whistled over the balcony – Buff jumped up and her husband Desmond, perhaps more sensibly, flung himself to the floor. The clatter of the typewriter stopped and Robin's deep husky voice boomed out 'Are you two still with us?', and the typing went on! Happily this was no assassination attempt, merely a local, shooting birds. Robin hated any disturbance during this evening ritual but when, because of unavoidable social engagements or having to work very late, some entries were delayed by a day or two, they are still written with a compelling freshness and immediacy.

Although his diary is a very personal document it tells the reader little about the author's inner feelings whilst saying quite a lot about his views on the situation on Aden and the wider world, as I discuss later in this chapter. There is nothing about relationships apart from references to his parents, his sister Buff and his nephew and nieces; he never married.[8] He had strong views about many of his colleagues (and their wives) but these were usually made in the context of his professional life. Some of his comments were warm and complimentary, others remarks were waspish at times and highly unflattering. He had a very intense interest in the wellbeing of his juniors; many of us called him 'Uncle' Robin (Kennedy Trevaskis was 'Uncle Ken' to him) and that was affectionate and generally respectful. He agonised over political officers' health, the wellbeing (safety) of their families, and their state of mind and how best they might be supported. One personal example. My wife and I underwent a particularly serious attack on our house in Dhala in October 1966 when I was very lucky not to have been killed. Robin's diary entry for 12 October read: 'Peter and Archie Hinchcliffe had a narrow escape in Dhala. They will sleep in that bedroom at the top of the house. I have a feeling that I should order Archie away but I know she loves the place'. Typical of Robin's sensitive and thoughtful staff management. And the more remarkably so as he was aware that Archie was pregnant with our first child. He also agonised about another married couple and about the effect of separation on their relationship with the husband being upcountry and his wife living in Aden. When the husband was ill with a bad flu, Robin insisted on his moving into his own bedroom, the only room with air-conditioning. He did, however, confide to his dairy that he hoped that he would not have to put up with hot nights for too long.[9]

Whatever he thought of his colleagues – whether he liked them or merely put up with them – he would support them through thick and thin. As his diaries make abundantly clear, he was quick to forgive those whom he liked and respected even after the fiercest of disagreements, but slow to change his mind about people whom he found wanting.[10]

The chapters on the Political Officers and on the Eastern Aden Protectorate have a wealth of detail on what kind of activities were a feature of the daily life of 'frontline' Assistant Advisers in both WAP and EAP. Robin's view was a loftier one. By the time of my arrival in December 1961 he was already a very senior Political Officer in charge of the central area of WAP and had three British Political Officers in Abyan and in Lodar working to him. His designation was shortly to be changed to Senior Adviser (West), adding another three British upcountry officials to his charge, and he was thereafter to be based at the British Agency (or WAP Office) at Hiswa on the road between Aden proper and Little Aden. With the formation of the Federation, Hiswa was transformed into the Federal capital; Al Ittihad[11] and the British Agent was to add the title 'Assistant High Commissioner (BA&AHC) (Federation)' to his job description.[12] The incumbent on my arrival was Kennedy Trevaskis – later High Commissioner. The Senior Adviser (East), Ralph Daly, was in charge of the Aulaqis, Beihan and later Wahidi. Robin, in his capacity as Senior Adviser (West), and more especially after becoming BA&AHC in 1966 was increasingly able to influence policy towards the embryonic Federation. So it is for the later years 1965–7 that the diary is a particularly valuable primary source document and I am concentrating on this period, albeit in a highly selective manner, given the constraints of space.

That is not to say that the volumes for 1961–4 are without interest. They include insights into important events as recorded by a significant, if not yet, dominant player. The process of Federation-forming as seen from Al Ittihad, Robin's involvement in tribal politics (Keeni Meeni[13] *par excellence* as he once put it), seeking to curb the activities of a major dissident leader: Mohamed Aidrus,[14] in the highlands of Yafa. On the pan-Arab stage there were various military incidents, culminating in the deployment of a significant number of British troops in support of Federal forces in the Radfan campaign of 1964.

It is quite hard to be sure of Robin Young's real feelings about HMG's policy towards Aden if you rely purely on his diary entries in this earlier period. As an instinctive Tory he was not wont openly to criticise the actions of the Conservative government. I think generally he was strongly supportive. Once Labour came into power in 1964 there was no doubt that Robin feared the worst. Not just because Labour Ministers were not his kind of people, as politicians like Duncan Sandys, the Tory Secretary of State for the Colonies, clearly were, but because of Labour contacts when in opposition with Aden nationalists including the local Trades Union Congress (TUC). Robin was quick to suspect that Labour would instinctively favour Aden politicians over his Protectorate friends, the 'Sultans', whose baby the Federation was perceived to be and for which the latter believed that they had the full support of the Conservative government. He also was easily convinced that a Labour government would be uncomfortable with con-tinuing colonial responsibilities and would want to be shot of them as soon as possible. These suspicions were fed by corres-pondence with (Sir) Kennedy Trevaskis who was replaced as High Commissioner by Sir Richard Turnbull in early 1965. Trevaskis had been well regarded by the former Conservative administration and he maintained close personal links with Tory opposition figures after the 1964 elections, such as Julian Amery, Duncan Sandys and Nigel Fisher. Trevaskis also maintained more or less covert contact with a number of Federal Ministers and continued to advise them on how they should deal with HMG long after his departure from Aden. As Robin Young noted in his entry for 12 April 1965: 'More Keeni Meeni today but I suppose never a day passes without a little of that'. This was a reference to a private channel between Mohamed Farid then Federal Minister for external affairs and 'Marabah' the code word for 'Uncle Ken' which Robin invariably used in referring to the previous High Commissioner. The channel also extended to Sandys and Fisher. Mohamed Farid 'had written (to Uncle Ken) about the woes of Federation in dealing with the nationalist Aden politicians. Whether it will be too late to take action remains to be seen. But a few pointed questions in the House might help.'

Another sympathetic ear was that of Laurie Hobson, a highly effective and well-informed security adviser to the High Commission who was subsequently advised not to return to Aden, being a major terrorist target. (He too had good Tory contacts; his sister Valerie Hobson, the actress, was married to John Profumo, a former Conservative Minister for War – the central figure in the Christine Keeler call-girl scandal.) Hobson, a close friend of Robin's, was a good source of information on the new High Commissioner's thinking and reported to Robin (entry for 10 April 1965): 'Turnbull had told him that there was no policy on Aden at the moment except that both Wilson and Greenwood would give up the base if they could. Review of defence commitments under way.' This was a major piece of grist for Robin's anti-Labour mill, feeding his existing prejudices all too effectively.

Robin's doubts about Labour's attitude towards Aden affairs long predated the General Election of 1964. Especially following the 'rough wooing' of Aden Colony by the Federation culminating in the 'shotgun marriage' forced through the Legislative Assembly in September 1962 it was clear to him that the left-wing members of the Labour Party at least were opposed to the Federal project. To them, not only was it wrong in principle to maintain a military base against the wishes of the local nationalists, but also its viability was highly questionable. One diary entry of 1964 is revealing. Robin was writing a paper countering UK TUC criticism about 'appalling conditions' of cotton workers in Abyan. 'The usual sort of left-wing line, which is taken by Cairo Radio and then followed by the pinks in London.' Indeed the left of the Labour party which had enjoyed good relations with the nationalist Aden TUC had been dubious of the Federal scheme long before the incorporation of Aden State into the structure. Thus members of the opposition who visited the area were not only treated with great suspicion, but also had, on occasion, to be subjected to attempts to have wool pulled well over their eyes. A case in point was the visit by two Labour MPs in June 1962. Robert Edwards and George Thomson had been invited by Abdullah Al Asnag, at that time probably the most prominent nationalist leader in Aden. Robin's entry for 17 June records how he was summoned by Ken Trevaskis, then the British Agent, to discuss the visit and to work out how best to leave the visitors with the impression that there was strong popular support for the Federation. To this end 'spontaneous' demonstrations by crowds carrying pro-Federation banners were organised in Abyan to greet the MPs. The crowds composed of Federal Guard policemen, off-duty members of the FRA in civilian dress, farm workers trucked in by the local authorities and anyone else who could be rounded up for the occasion. I was in charge of the 'popular' welcome in Ja'ar, the administrative capital of the Lower Yafa' Sultanate and was concerned that some of the more enthusiastic (but illiterate) demonstrators had carried their banners (which we had worked hard to manufacture) upside down! As it happened, both Edwards and Thomson, according to Robin were genuinely impressed by the degree of development in Abyan as represented by the Cotton Board and various successful small-scale cooperative schemes. The official view was that the visit had gone well. Nevertheless Robin subsequently (26 June) quoted Ken Trevaskis as saying that the TUC were 'cock-a-hoop about the visit and felt they had successfully torpedoed the proposal that Aden should join the Federation'.

On another occasion in January 1964, three other Labour MPs visited Abyan to see nationalist detainees suspected of involvement in the grenade attack at Aden airport, which had targeted Trevaskis (and fatally wounded George Henderson.[15]) They were jostled by a 'mob' involved in another 'spontaneous demonstration'. The crowd was protesting against the perpetrators of the bomb outrage (a number of Fadhlis, including a member of the ruling family were injured by the grenade). They were apparently 'rescued' from the crowd by Stephen Day, the local

Assistant Adviser, who had played a major part in organising the 'riot'! To Robin's glee, on their return to London the MPs visited the Colonial Secretary and were full of praise about Stephen Day's courageous conduct during the riot. 'Little do they know' was Robin's diary comment on 12 January. Actually Robin's account was not altogether accurate – see Day's own version in Chapter 3, but the point is that Robin wanted to believe his version because of how he felt about the Labour party.

Robin Young's attitude towards the Labour party and later the government it formed in 1964 was probably shared by many of his colleagues and a number of senior military figures. This was partly due to the natural class conditioning of someone from his kind of family and educational background. Certainly his boss Kennedy Trevaskis was also an instinctive Tory and Robin, who had an enormous admiration for 'Uncle Ken, willingly absorbed Trevaskis' prejudices and suspicions of what they believed were Labour's real agenda. And Robin, like so many other British 'Arabists' of that period, equally instinctively favoured the upcountry Arab, the true tribesman. This reflected his Sudanese experience. The upcountry 'Bedou' (few were actually nomadic), with his warmth and simple dignity, keen sense of humour, colourfully costumed, arms-bearing as part of their daily dress code, wiry and warlike and with an apparently chivalrous code of conduct, was usually appealing to the average Colonial administrator. This was so, especially in comparison with the detribalised, suit-clad Adeni who was likely to be encouraged in his 'anti-Western' nationalism, brainwashed indeed, by the vitriol of Cairo Radio and the beguiling 'Arab Nationalist' rhetoric of the Egyptian President Gemal Abdul Nasser. 'Loafers' and 'Suk Rats' were epithets commonly used by Robin (and other political officers including myself) in describing Adenis (with whom we had little contact) and especially demonstrators or strikers. He was also contemptuous of most of the Aden politicians and felt that their attitude to their Federal colleagues was born out of unthinking nationalist prejudice and ignorance of what conditions in the Federation outside Aden State were really like.

Attitudes cut both ways. Labour politicians had their own gut instincts. They felt ties of sympathy and common interest with some of the (perhaps more moderate) Aden nationalists: politicians and Union leaders. By the same token they were uneasy with many of the traditional rulers. Denis Healey recorded his impressions of a visit when in opposition to the 'misbegotten Federation . . . controlled by the backward sheikhs from the protectorates . . . whose main occupation was fighting each other' (*The Time of my Life*, p. 231).[16] Robin recorded in his diary entry for 3 April 1965 that Sir Richard Turnbull (who succeeded Trevaskis) told him that on a recent visit to London accompanying a Federal delegation: 'Labour people still had their prejudices over the cloth cap *vis-à-vis* the top hat. Tall distinguished men in turbans caused instant dislike.'

And as for these 'tall distinguished men' one gets the impression from Robin that they never had much time for the Labour government, nor indeed for High Commissioner Sir Richard Turnbull, whom they saw not only as a Labour appointee but also as a very poor substitute for their beloved Kennedy Trevaskis (whom Labour had replaced not long after their election victory) and through him the former Conservative administration.

It is therefore perhaps not surprising that once the Labour government had announced in its 1966 Defence White Paper that the Federation was going to be given independence 'in 1968' without benefit of a defence treaty and that the base was being given up, Robin Young, supported by some other senior British officials involved in the Federation, worked actively to modify UK policy on Aden and indeed to oppose some of its features perceived to be damaging to the viability of the Federal project. This was not the action of a disloyal and disaffected public servant but the instinctive reaction of someone who cared passionately about t he future of South Arabia and its peoples – someone convinced that the Federal idea, with all its imperfections was the correct road to take. It was the action of someone who felt strongly that the failure of the Federation would open the door to Egyptian hegemony in the region and all the damaging consequences for British and Western interests.

Robin Young heard about the outcome of the Defence Review from Ian Baillie who had been previously briefed in confidence by the High Commissioner. (Ian was the senior British civil servant working with the Federal government at that time.)[17] In his diary for 2 February 1966 Robin writes: 'We are clearing out lock stock and barrel leaving our friends high and dry and apparently London does not care a hoot what happens thereafter. I was hit for six. I felt as if my tummy had suddenly been removed.' He even contemplated 'putting a Federal Guard or FRA officer up to doing a coup'. Robin records that Ian Baillie's reaction was also one of dismay and of despair. 'IB feels Sultans should retire to their country estates and let the Federation go hang. Rulers should be told to make what terms they can with the Egyptians. Do we' asked Robin rhetorically 'really intend to leave the Egyptians in charge of South Arabia?' Having obviously cooled down he added more reflectively that the base could go but we should give the Federation more funds to expand their own forces and keep some kind of defence treaty after independence. Two days later he told Ian Baillie 'we should enlist [the] help of senior military and political friends to fight [the] Labour Government: Sandys and Amery in particular.' He records, however, that 'Ian Baillie sticks to view that Rulers should make what terms they can with the opposition.' The previous day he had written to Ken Trevaskis: 'I cannot believe that we should advise the rulers that they should throw in the sponge and seek best terms possible from the Egyptians.'

I believe that from that moment Ian Baillie felt that we had betrayed the Federation, that it was accordingly doomed and that he was therefore determined to leave as soon as he decently could. By contrast Robin, despite periods of pessimism, self doubt and even downright despair, believed that enough could be salvaged from a seemingly foundering wreck to erect a viable and enduring structure for an independent South Arabia. And that he would soldier on to see it through. This fortitude and commitment demonstrates how Robin lived partly if not largely by the causes, which he adopted. The first (and probably the more fulfilling) was the Sudan;[18] then Aden and the Federation. A striking testimonial to a breed of public servant of which Robin was an outstanding example.

A Labour Minister, Lord Beswick was shortly due in Aden to break the news formally to the Federal government. Surely an uncomfortable mission given the contrast with avowals of virtually open-ended commitment which had been his message on his previous visit a few months earlier. Before Beswick's arrival, Robin, on a visit to Dathina on 5 February, had obliquely warned Naib Hussein Mansour about coping in the absence of the British: 'Friends might be slaughtered in the streets when that time came.' But 'Hussein Mansour [was] very confident that nothing would happen to him in Dathina.' Looking round Dathina, its gardens and the wells that serviced them, Robin wished to have another ten years in South Arabia to 'finish what had started only a few years ago. In 4 years 30 pumps and wells have been created in the Hassani area. Dathina has become a Vale of Evesham. All this probably cost not more than £40,000 plus rifles and ammunition.'

Robin Young had very little confidence that the High Commissioner would stand up to the Labour government either in the interests of the Federation or to protect the British position in the Middle East. He had had a generally poor opinion of Sir Richard Turnbull since his arrival as 'Uncle Ken's' replacement. His diary entries often refer to Turnbull as 'crumble'! He attended a meeting at Government House on 8 February to discuss the Defence Review and Lord Beswick's imminent arrival. 'HE at his most muddled. I do not think that I have met anyone less capable of leadership than Excellency' wrote Robin that evening.[19] It was partly because of a doubt about the High Commissioner's effectiveness, that senior British officials working in the federal capital had formed an informal group, categorised by Robin as the 'plotting committee' (referred to in the diary entry for 16 June 1965 as 'the Keeni Meeni Committee'.) The core membership was Robin, Ian Baillie, Ralph Daly (Permanent Secretary in the Ministry of Internal Security) and Charles Chaplin (PS, Ministry of Defence). As Robin's diary records, *ad hoc* expansions to this charmed circle included Dick Holmes, the Attorney General and even senior Federal Ministers, usually Sultan Saleh, the Audhali ruler (Minister of Internal Security) Sultan Fadhl bin Ali, the Lahej ruler (Defence) and Sheikh Mohamed Farid, a senior Aulaqi, the Minister for External Affairs. It was a highly unorthodox arrangement, especially for loyal government servants, but Robin and these colleagues felt strongly that right-minded people needed to work together to salvage something from HMG's apparent determination to pull the plug on the entire Federal project. Indeed, he felt the need to strive to save HMG from itself with regard to possible unwelcome consequences of its policies in the region. The British members of the group did worry about a clash of loyalties – to Britain or to the Federal government – and agreed at a meeting on 14 February 'No solution other than resignation if things get worse'.[20]

The 'plotters' suggested to some of the Federal ministers what line they should take when Lord Beswick came out to present the outcome of the review. One demand was that the Federal forces should be 'made capable of standing on their own feet'. In the event, Beswick on 15 February got a hostile reception at meetings with British civil servants from both Aden and the Federation. In marked contrast, the Supreme Council greeted his dire news calmly: 'Sultan Saleh responded, all smiles and no one else was allowed to speak'. This was the reaction choreographed by the 'plotting committee'. Robin noted, however, that Sultan Saleh was 'too smooth' and Beswick 'might as well have announced £5 million of development aid'. Even in private the rulers took it well, except for Sultan Nasser, the Fadhli Sultan, who talked about 'being murdered in the street'. Robin was particularly taken with Amir Sha'aful's stoicism. 'He impresses me more and more. Shows no sign of fear yet his position is probably the most dangerous of all.'

The angriest reaction came the following day when Lord Beswick met with the assembled Assistant Advisers. 'Stop shaking your head at me' demanded Beswick as Godfrey Meynell 'in fierce form' slated the Review and its implications for the future of South Arabia. Robin felt that Beswick might have been impressed by some of the demands made by Sultan Saleh on behalf of the Federal government at a subsequent meeting, especially the need for some form of defence after independence. But Robin felt that Sultan Saleh's pitch to Beswick was 'read in an unimpressive manner'. The British Minister's reaction was not recorded and he shortly afterwards returned to London, his mission completed. His arrival more or less coincided with a letter from Robin to 'Uncle Ken' conveying the latest thoughts of the 'plotters' confined in this instance to Baillie, Daly and Young. Their feeling was that 'If rulers ask advice suggest hold hard for three months to see if pressure can make HMG change mind, not on base but on continuing defence commitment after independence. If not successful rulers should head for home and come to terms with opposition.' Robin added in a diary aside that Ian Baillie claimed that Denis Healey, the Defence Secretary, was quite cynical. 'The general impression of London not caring seems to be confirmed. It is a wretched outlook.'[21] On 2 March Robin heard from his mother that Ken Trevaskis had been in touch with senior Tories: 'Heath, Douglas

Home, etc.'. All promised support. He had also just seen Trevaskis' letter to *The Times* deploring independence for South Arabia without assurance of defence against aggression as bad faith and cynical irresponsibility.

There is not the space to extract from the Young diaries (covering the rest of 1966 and early 1967) in any detail how he, senior British officials working with the Federation and a handful of key Arab Federal ministers worked both to influence HMG policy and to try and create a cohesive and forward-looking strategy for the Federal government. The bones of what they were trying to do – from Robin's perspective were as follows:

(a) To persuade HMG to reverse the decision on no defence arrangement after independence.

(b) As part of achieving (a), to work on senior Conservatives mostly via Sir K. Trevaskis. Some of the steam (and most of the optimism) went out of this with the Labour 'landslide' victory in the election of 31 March 1966. Robin commented in his dairy of 1 April: 'Regards Aden I am sure there will be no going back on the Defence Review now'.

(c) To broaden the basis of the Federal government whilst working towards a unitary state to be dominated by former Protectorate figures. This involved encouraging the Eastern Aden Sultanates of Quaiti and Kathiri to throw in their lot with the former WAP states and with Wahidi, originally in EAP but by then a member of the Federation. Facilitate the return of exiles like the Al Jiffris, of the South Arabian League, former dissidents such as the Aulaqi Bubakr bin Farid[22] and the two senior Protectorate members of ruling families who had defected in 1964: Ahmed bin Abdullah, the former Fadhli Sultan and Naib Ja'abil bin Hussein, the Audhali Sultan's younger brother. Also try and come to terms with some of the less radical political opponents in Aden and in exile. Even the firebrand Abdullah al Asnag originally of the People's Socialist Party was thought to be a possibility.[23]

(d) To put the Federation's house in order especially through the adoption of a credible and workable constitution. The proposals produced in the Hone and Bell report formed the core of this, although not all of that document was acceptable to the Federal Supreme Council. Much of the discussion centred on who should be President and who Prime Minister. (Sherif Hussein of Beihan was thought to be the prime candidate for the President, to be balanced by an Adeni Prime Minister with a third of ministers coming from the colony.) The system of a rotating monthly chairman of the Supreme Council was not working nor was there any consistent leadership from the centre. Part of this discussion was the persistent and long-standing demands by the 'Federalis' to be given more control of internal security in Aden State. This (by the end of 1966) became a debate on at what point before independence would the indigenous government take over full control of the former colony. The best offer the High Commissioner could come up with was one month, which the 'Federalis' thought unacceptable.

(e)   To elicit the help of the Saudis. Especially the King: Feisal bin Abdul Aziz. Sultan Saleh's first comment on hearing about the Defence Review was that the 'Federalis' needed to 'find a protector fast' and 'should approach King Feisal' (*Young Diaries*, 14 February 1966). He was known to be unhappy with President Nasser's policies, wanted him out of the Yemen and had strongly supported the Yemeni royalists. The Saudis were also felt to be crucial in delivering EAP and as a source of development aid. (At one point they offered £6 million for road building and 150 scholarships.) Curiously one important intermediary close to the King was a wealthy building contractor of Hadhrami origin: a certain Bin Ladhin one of whose (many) sons Usama (about 12 years old in 1966), later founded Al Qa'ida.

(f)   To strengthen the international reputation of the Federation and to work, where possible, with the UN. The acceptable face of the Federal authorities in international bodies was deemed to be the very articulate Sheikh Mohamed Farid. He made a number of visits to New York to put the Federal case, which was otherwise in danger of going by default. This debate also focused on whether or not, for tactical reasons formally to accept the UN resolutions about the future of the territory and to cooperate with a UN visiting mission from the stridently anti-Colonial Committee of 24.

Not all of this was by any means contrary to HMG policy and in some instances enjoyed the active support of the High Commissioner. It all ended in tears, however, as John Ducker's chapters describe. Despite the many disappointments and setbacks, though, Robin never lost hope (even as late as his departure on his last leave in April 1967) that something workable might, against all the odds, be salvaged from the Federal project. Despite a growing conviction that HMG was not going to change course and would abandon a leaking ship to an inevitable watery grave he encouraged his Federal colleagues, Arab and British, to stay the course and make the best of an increasingly bad job. Many of his British colleagues lacked his staying power. Those Federal leaders who were also prepared to stick it out became a dwindling band, having made the realistic assumption that they no longer had the wholehearted support of the British government which regarded Aden as an increasingly heavy burden to be shed as soon as possible.

Robin Young confided to his dairy on 24 March 1964:

> Many and varied are the roads travelled by a Political Officer ... four in the afternoon learning or teaching how to lay mines on the other side of the frontier. At five discussing the appointment of a Director of Agriculture; at six discussing Radfan and Quteibi problems. At eight dining with two lawyers.

In addition he would probably have had a full morning seeing a stream of visitors all demanding something, plus the inescapable round of meetings mostly to do with some aspect of security. (Late March 1964 was just before the major Radfan operation got under way in earnest.)

Much more now is in the public domain over the once highly secret operations to counter the activities of terrorists based across the Federal/Yemeni border.[24] Part of this was wrapped up in the policy to assist the Yemeni royalists to fight the Egyptian-supported Republican regime, which came to power in 1962 having overthrown the Imam. This was a proxy war against the Egyptians who were increasingly seen as paymasters of the nationalist liberation movements, their trainers and weapon suppliers. They had made no secret of their intention to drive the British out of South Arabia and to destroy the 'puppet' Federal regime. Robin was peripherally involved in assistance to the royalists but his diary records their fluctuating fortunes as seen from Aden and frequently gleaned from 'Sigint': intercepts of Republican and Egyptian radio messages. Much of the materiel for the royalist forces under the command of Al Hassan, uncle of the former Imam Mohamed, whether from Saudi Arabia or from HMG, was channelled via Sherif Hussein of Beihan whose state was contiguous to Yemeni territory in royalist hands. Beihan was outside Robin's area as he was Senior Adviser (West) at the time of the revolution. Some operations were channelled through Mukeiras on the Audhali Plateau with the active involvement of Naib Ja'abil Hussein, within WAP, but not on the same scale as the Beihan sector.

Robin did not doubt the necessity for anti-Republican/Egyptian operations. On 17 October 1962 he noted that 'Working on a paper with the British Agent (Trevaskis) on the threat to our position should the republicans establish themselves. It makes gloomy reading.' Previously he had noted (6 October) 'HMG agreed to £20,000 for Al Hassan'. This was in addition to £7000 authorised by Trevaskis on 4 October plus 40,000 rounds of ammunition to go 'north' via Sherif Hussein. A few days later London approved 'substantial help for Al Hassan. Said to be 2000 rifles, lots of ammo and £20,000.' Robin was obviously enjoying all this: 'Another busy day spent in a good cause, that of organising revolution in the Yemen. Great fun I am sure.' In all this excitement Robin was aware that not all this assistance in support of a worthy cause would reach its intended recipients. Sticky fingers lay in wait. He commented on 8 October:

> Sherif Hussein to receive from the Keeni Meeni boys [a reference to the local MI6 operation] 500 rifles, £20,000 in cash, 300,000 rounds (.303) and 80,000 rounds of Mauser ammo to be delivered to a desert airstrip near Beihan. Total received to date 540,000 and £27,000. [He added] Not bad going. After it is all over, the Sherif, I dare say, will not have one Rolls Royce but a stable of them!

The whole question of 'Keeni Meeni' as a tool of official policy was highly controversial and especially the use, for political purposes, of arms and ammunition. Several of my colleagues were very opposed to the principle and the practice; this clearly emerges from the chapter on the Political Officers in WAP. A colleague from EAP (where these activities were unknown) wrote to me: 'Gifts of rifles and ammunition to rulers *et al.* tended to undermine all attempts to create a responsible system of government.' Another who served in both Protectorates puts this practice in a more modern context: 'As an instrument of covert Government policy, to pour arms and ammunition into the area is almost – on a much smaller scale of course – as culpable as the US with its pro-mujahadeen anti-Russian policy in Afghanistan.' Most army officers were highly dubious fearing that these weapons so freely handed out would end up being used against their troops. Robin was a stout defender of the use of arms and ammunition – whether as an anti-terrorist tool, a reward for services received or anticipated or as a means of raising the resources for much-needed development. There was little evidence that the rifles handed out so liberally were actually used as weapons by the opposition – rather they were a means of exchange. And it was a cheap way of raising cash. A .303 Lee Enfield rifle bought through the Crown Agents, HMG's official arms dealer, cost about £4.10.0. Its 'street value in the Federation varied between £50 and £100 depending on its mark'.[25] A round of .303 ammunition was worth about one shilling. Robin's diaries are full of references to development projects – digging wells, buying pumps, agricultural machinery the wherewithal for which came from the sale of this weaponry. The reference to a Vale of Evesham in Dathina is a case in point. The amazing development that Godfrey Meynell achieved in the Radfan after the 1964/5 campaign is another. Robin's diary entry for 17 August 1964 refers to finishing off a development proposal for Haushabi involving £20,000 for 50 pumps and £11,000 for two D4 Tractors. Some of this money was to come from sales of rifles and some from 'Bolster' (see below). Such diversion from political for developmental purposes was, Robin records, much to the disapproval of his boss in WAP office in 1962–3: Kennedy Trevaskis.

If Robin rather relished his involvement in 'keeni-meeni', it is clear from his diary that he agonised over some of its consequences, especially those rising from the policy of retaliating within the Yemen for terrorist activity, such as mine laying sponsored by the Egyptians inside Federal territory. His first reference to 'Operation Stirrup' – the distribution of arms and ammunition to frontier tribesmen – appears in his diary entry for 13 January 1964. The local MI6 director had told Robin that

> we can use Yemeni tribes to cause trouble in the Yemen as retaliation for trouble in Radfan or elsewhere. 700 [rifles] and 700 [boxes of 1000 rounds of ammunition] approved. This plus £50,000 for Bolster we should be able to make quite an impression both in frontier areas and inside our own frontier. Mines also available for retaliatory mine laying.

In addition to Stirrup there were several other covert operations whose aim was to retaliate against or to deter subversive activity organised from Yemen, including Egyptian support for liberation movements such as the NLF and FLOSY:

Operation 'Eggshell' – mine-laying
Operation 'Bangle' – sabotage and subversion
Operation 'Rancour' – the provision of arms, ammunition and money to induce Yemeni tribes to neutralise mainly Egyptian Intelligence Service (EIS) centres of cross-border subversion against the Federation, especially in Beidha and Qa'ataba

There was also Bolster, a covert fund to prop up friends and support other political objectives within the Federation.

Robin's entry for 21 January spelled out the ground rules as laid down by the High Commissioner, (by now) Kennedy Trevaskis.

> We should not start anything until the other side begins or looks like beginning ... We must confine activity to near frontier areas so Ibb is out. London to be given a list of tit for tat targets. Purpose is to inflict twice as much damage as inflicted on us but on similar targets to those attacked by the Yemenis.

Some of the money was to be given to the 'rulers concerned but not to Sherif Hussein'. It was obviously felt that he had done well enough so, in practice, it was the Audhalis and Amir Sha'aful of Dhala who were to be at the other sharp ends of these operations.

All this was fine in theory but in practice could have painful and serious personal ramifications. On 9 February a mine exploded under a civilian lorry in the Wadi Hardaba. Robin drafted a signal to London outlining the retaliatory action, which was to be carried out in accordance with the policy as agreed by the High Commissioner. For one mine in the Federation, two in the Yemen. On 12 February the MI6 representative had delivered two 'infernal machines' to Robin's house at Al Ittihad. Three days later the diary records a meeting with an unnamed Royal Engineer Major and 'some Audhalis' Robin noted: 'fruits of meeting should be apparent day after tomorrow . . . I had no idea that mines could be primed so easily'. The entry for 17 February records a mine exploding on the Dhala/Qataba road under a Yemeni lorry inflicting casualties. 'Sometimes it is hell being a political officer' was Robin's anguished comment but he added 'if people play with fire I suppose they are almost certain to get their fingers burnt'. Robin was never happy with the tragic consequences of such actions but he felt that in war there was no practical and effective alternative to such tough and ruthless measures. This particular incident continued to weigh heavily on his conscience and he referred to it again on a number of occasions in his diary.[26]

Unlike many Political Officers such as Rex Smith, Hugh Walker, Roy Somerset, John Harding and Michael Crouch, Robin had no serious doubts about the use of arms and ammunition (and the various secret funds) as an instrument of policy. Or if he did he did not confide his worries to his diaries except when, as mentioned above, an operation went wrong, leading to civilian casualties. It was, by the time of his arrival, such a feature of the WAP (in particular) landscape that it would have been very difficult to carry on without these sweeteners and (later) sources of desperately-needed developmental funding. And the figures could be high. Regime change in Dathina in 1964, the appointment of Hussein Mansour and the acquiescence of the 'Lugna' (State Council) involved '100 (rifles) and 100 (boxes of ammunition)' for Hussein and '75 and 75 to bribe the Lugna' (Diary 23 February). When Sultan Nasser of Fadhli was installed as ruler following his brother Ahmed's defection to Egypt he was generously supplied with the wherewithal to ensure the loyalty of his subjects. As the threat of violence increased upcountry Robin agonised on 14 July: 'Unless we can give out rifles on a large scale we shall find ourselves in the soup. Things are getting more complicated as the dissident campaign mounts.' That same day Hussein Mansour had asked for 500 and 500 to deal with trouble in Dathina where the NLF, frustrated in Radfan, were opening a second front. I return to this topic when writing about the Political Officers.

It seems remarkable, in retrospect, how Robin Young was allowed to take five and a half months' leave in the spring of 1967. But perhaps there was no alternative. His leave had been twice postponed by staffing changes and was prolonged by two operations on his throat for a benign but uncomfortably large growth. His voice had long been noticeably husky and gravelly, blamed by him on excessive pipe smoking. During his absence, as recorded elsewhere, the Federation collapsed. His diary entry for 1 September noted 'I arrived to a very strange and if not chaotic world. The blinds are very rapidly coming down on the little WAP world we knew.' Indeed they were. The old WAP office had been closed a week before and all Europeans living in Al Ittihad evacuated to the comparative safety of the colony. Its rump was in Jean Randall's house, a former married officer's quarter in RAF Khormaksar. Jean, the other secretary, Margaret Brennan, now joined by Robin, lived upstairs. Bill Heber Percy and I on the ground floor. As Robin arrived at the airport he was 'faced by another sign of the changed world': Sultan Fadhl bin Ali and several hundred supporters and retainers from Lahej were leaving for exile in Saudi Arabia. The ruling families of Audhali, Shaib and Dhala had already gone. The NLF had overrun most of the old Western Area with the young Lower Yafa' Sultan Mahmud being held prisoner in Zingibar. Al Ittihad was a vacuum but Robin believed that the High Commissioner (another change since he went on leave) Sir Humphrey Trevelyan would like the NLF to take over there as well. In these circumstances 'it is difficult to see what sort of role the rump of WAP office can play. In fact I am not at all sure whether we shall not be a bit of an embarrassment.'

This role was to be a steadily decreasing one. As the NLF and FLOSY rolled up state after state and prepared to square up to each other in the final battle, to be fought out in the streets of Aden, to become the successor regime to the British, Robin Young and his small band became increasingly marginalised. Former friends and contacts were either lying low or making what peace they could with the rampant nationalists. Very few were prepared to make the trip to behind the wire in Khormaksar to let the beleaguered British have any insight into what was now happening upcountry. The only regular source of information was from South Arabian Army (SAA) units who were mostly operating in a static role as observers and on the whole keeping their head down as FLOSY and the NLF slugged it out. Much of this information was highly selective as the army was obviously positioning itself for the post-withdrawal situation of having to live with a nationalist regime and it increasingly wished to avoid accusations of close collaboration with the retreating Colonial power. And as the Federal government had ceased to function they were themselves in something of a limbo. Robin regularly attended meetings at Government House chaired by the High Commissioner but the informed contributions that he could make became increasingly rare. His diary reveals that he was soon aware that he was no longer a member of the magic circle around the High Commissioner, which influenced policy and his advice was only occasionally solicited. When it was, it was mostly about preparing briefing on such topics as prominent Federal personalities, the tribes, frontier disputes and other matters of possible interest to the embryonic Embassy, which would represent HMG's interests after a post-independence indigenous government had been formed. Robin once had hopes of being offered a contract by the Foreign Office to stay on for a period to see the new regime in, but that was in the days that an orderly transfer of power to a more friendly government had seemed possible. Certainly the subject was not raised again after Robin's return from leave, but as late as 10 November, two days before he left, he wrote 'in my heart of hearts I would be pleased to be asked to remain on for the last ten days or so.' But in the same breath he acknowledged that as he was so far out of the loop (he had not attended a high level meeting for six weeks), that such a request was not likely.

Robin had mixed feelings about Sir Humphrey Trevelyan. He noted in his entry for 2 September that he was impressed with his 'charm, quick wit and very high mental ability'. But 'I should say that he is absolutely ruthless and should anyone oppose him that I think would be that.' Robin was convinced that somehow Trevelyan had engineered the collapse of the Federal government over the past two months. He believed that the root of the final collapse was the events of 20 June and the failure of the Federal government to deal with them but 'the fact that he got all the ministers to go away to Geneva when there was trouble brewing in more than half the states was the *coup de grace*'. After the failure by Bayoumi to form a government 'H.E. went all out against the Federalis and within a period of four weeks he has secured the crumbling of the government.' Robin also fingered the Commander of the SAA, Brigadier Jack Dye,[27] as being an important party to this process. 'When it became clear that that the (South Arabian) Army with the withdrawal of British units from up-country was not prepared to take a part in dealing with the internal troubles in the states then the rulers started packing their bags.' In Robin's view, once the toughest pillar of the Federation – the Audhali ruling family, had fled the country then 'the tide already moving against the rulers became a flood'. A decisive factor in this was the refusal by the High Commissioner to authorise air strikes against troublesome villages as requested by the Audhali authorities. At that point he made it clear that any future air action would require the endorsement of the SAA, by that time (after 20 June) in passive mode. This was a clear signal to the rulers that as far as the British were concerned they were on their own and could expect no further practical support.

These closing pages of Robin Young's diaries chronicle, with surprisingly little apparent emotion, the last days of British Aden as seen from the perspective of a predominantly military stronghold steadily shrinking behind more and more barbed wire as chunks of the colony was handed over to SAA and Aden police control. As after bloody street fighting, the NLF finally triumphed over FLOSY thanks partly to support from the SAA who had decided to which mast their colours should be nailed.

Apart from putting personal affairs in order, including paying off staff, the major preoccupation was the old WAP office files. These had been rescued from Al Ittihad a few days before Robin's return from leave by Bill Heber Percy and myself to stop them falling into unfriendly hands after our withdrawal from the Federal capital. We also used this opportunity to rescue a number of Elizabeth Daly's cats, 15 at least and although this was not a f ull complement it was enough to inject a major new breed into the Sardinian feline gene pool. The moggies were sent off to the Mediterranean island where the Dalys had purchased a holiday home a couple of years before.

Robin described how the files were disposed of in an orgy of burning over several days in Khormaksar. One bonfire of blazing paper attracted the attention of a patrolling military helicopter. I have movie footage I took on my 8 mm camera of the letters 'WAP' spelt out in burning files on the sandy soil of RAF Khormaksar Married Quarters![28] Robin was instructed to hand over the more important files to the future Embassy in Steamer Point. Some had been sent home and are now in the British Library. These files were severely 'weeded' before being passed on, Robin being instructed to destroy the more 'embarrassing' (his word – not explained further) papers before they were handed on. It is of course a pity that these accounts of day-to-day life in the Federation and other primary source material had to go up in smoke, but the more important policy documents have survived from those folders. Details of tribal affrays, secret counter-insurgency operations funded out of the code-worded money bags, some of the State 'handbooks', notes on hundreds of local personalities, raw intelligence gleaned from a variety of (often dodgy) sources, voluminous reports from upcountry Political Officers and many examples of less sensitive 'keeni meeni' are all gone and are not duplicated elsewhere.

And so to the final departure as described at the start of the chapter. The NLF kept up attacks against expatriate targets if only to be seen maintaining the momentum of the revolution. Amongst the last British civilian casualties was Derek Rose, a young information officer, shot in the back in Steamer Point. 'The whole thing is a frantic waste. To die now in Aden, and for a young man to die is a criminal waste. Derek was so full of life. I shall never forget his deep chuckle.' He was buried at sea a few days later. The High Commissioner agreed that WAP office could close on 12 November.[29]

CHAPTER SIX

THE MILITARY

Peter Hinchcliffe

INTRODUCTION

This is an account of how some servicemen (and one service-woman!) saw life in Aden and upcountry, mostly in their own words. They are all British although a number served on second-ment to the Federal Regular Army (FRA) or its predecessor the Aden Protectorate Levies (APL). The main campaign, outside Aden, in which British and Arab soldiers served was the Radfan operation which in two phases lasted from early 1964 until late summer that year. A considerable number of British units were committed to phase two after it was clear that the FRA could not cope on its own. Both British and Arab units were also involved in counter-insurgency operations from 1963 until 1967 in Dhala to the north of the Radfan. The FRA bore the brunt of similar operations elsewhere in the Federation notably in Dathina, Beihan, the Audhali plateau and the Aulaqis. The other major campaign was counter-insurgency in Aden itself. This was predominantly a British undertaking – the FRA had no writ to operate in Aden State, local Arab forces were increasingly ineffective – and the intensity of the conflict steadily increased from late 1964 until the eve of British withdrawal. Once British withdrawal was formally announced in early 1966 in the Defence White Paper it was clear that this was not a contest that the security forces were going to win in the absence of a viable political solution. The nadir was the 'Mutiny' of June 1967 described by John Ducker in the first chapter.

Heavy British casualties at the hands of their Arab comrades and the enforced temporary abandonment of Crater ensured that the British, at least, would never fully trust the Arab forces again. The impotence of the Federal government at this juncture was the final nail in its coffin. As the South Arabian Army threw its weight behind the NLF, the British forces mainly disengaged from all but the most peripheral of peace-keeping duties, being concerned with their own security and allowing the nationalist forces to slug it out without interference.

THE ARMED FORCES

The Aden government's publication 'Welcome to Aden', second edition, printed in 1963[1] had newly-arrived servicemen's families as its main target readership. Containing hints on tropical hygiene, 'civilian' dress, sports clubs, other recreational activities and how to make the most of day-to-day life. Having warned that life in Aden is rather restricted 'both spatially and socially' with chances to make upcountry trips into the Protectorate 'rare', it goes on:

> Yet most families find their tour in Aden pleasant, especially in these days when air-conditioning and import of frozen foods, or fresh food by air, have transformed the difficulties of life here in the hot season. For those who have a special hobby or interest there is no lack of opportunity to pursue it, and while life in a highly cosmopolitan and rapidly developing country where the customs, traditions and hopes of East or West meet may sometimes be irritating, it can never be dull.'

Nowhere in the entire guide is there any reference to possible terrorism or much discussion on political issues; there is a throw-away line on the formation of the original Federation in 1959 and a reference to relations with the Yemen being 'strained', but this is put in the context of the Yemen's claim to Aden and the Protectorates rather than to any ongoing dissident activity sponsored or encouraged by the Yemen. Nor is there any reference to the overthrow of the Imam and a new revolutionary regime in Sana'a. The presence of the base and the military generally is explained by the strategic necessity of keeping troops 'permanently' East of Suez as a 'spring board for operations in the Middle East area ... without its base facilities and the forces stationed in Aden, it would not be possible for Her Majesty's Government to carry out its obligations'.

Colin Noyce[2] served in Aden in 1964–5 as a Leading Hand, a member of the crew of HMS Anzio, a tank landing ship. She was mostly involved in exercises in the Gulf or on patrol searching vessels (mostly dhows) suspected of running slaves or gold. When ashore Colin enjoyed

> the facilities at the NAAFI[3] Mermaid Club[4] where we swam, ate and drank with members of the other services based in Aden. My impression was that for those of us who came and went Aden was a good place, but for those who were posted there permanently it was a less attractive prospect! Those of us who wanted to buy our 'rabbits' (presents for those at home) found Aden to be a paradise of the latest electronic goods, watches, and other attractive goods at very cheap prices – even better than Singapore at that time.

Noyce was aware of restrictions imposed by a deteriorating security situation. 'As the situation in the Radfan worsened we were forbidden to go to Crater City (as it was known by the lads) but that did not stop us.' His only security-related incident was in 1965 when the Anzio received a signal to 'make all haste to Aden where rebels had revolted and attacked Broadcasting House. We were to steam back and put landing parties ashore. There was much apprehension as we made full speed (10 knots at most!) toward Aden.' To no avail, however, as the assault carrier HMS Hermes was closer and the Anzio was stood down.[5]

Tim Toyne Sewell,[6] then a young subaltern in the King's Own Scottish Borderers (KOSB),[7] arrived in Aden in February 1962 with his battalion on board the troopship Oxfordshire. Despite being early in the year some of the 'Jocks'[8] were already suffering from the first signs of prickly heat.[9] According to Toyne Sewell the 'old soldiers'' perception of 'the Red Sea was "the arsehole of the British Empire, with Aden half way up it"'. It was certainly not a popular posting for the average serviceman, nor was the daily routine in a then mostly peaceful colony either demanding or particularly exciting.

The KOSB working day was from 6.30 to 1. Most training was pretty low level, reflecting the fact that a considerable part of the battalion was made up of National Servicemen. There were few facilities in the camp apart from a 25-yard range, a confidence area, a swimming pool and a squash court. Much time was spent square-bashing, weapon training and anti-riot training.

The anti-riot training was, says Tim, in a format unchanged from the Raj.

> The drill was simple; march towards the crowd as if on parade, halt, soldiers on flanks turn alternatively inwards and outwards to guard against snipers on the neighbouring roofs, front rank kneel with rifles at the ready, unfurl a banner saying 'Disperse or we fire' in English and Arabic, and wait for the crowd to attack. Fire one shot at the ringleader, collect his body and watch the crowd disperse. It all sounded too easy, and indeed it was until there was rioting in Crater, the Arabs refused to play by our rules and broke up into small, mobile groups and attacked from all directions. A foretaste of Belfast street violence!

Colonel Alistair Thorburn,[10] who commanded the KOSBs in Aden, had a slightly different take on his soldiers from that of one of his subalterns!

> The presence of National Servicemen did not make for low-level training. They came to us after strenuous basic training at the depot and soon adjusted to more advanced training in the battalion. They were intelligent first-rate soldiers – many getting rank stripes, occasionally three. Square bashing was cut down to a minimum. There often were special ceremonial occasions for which drill had to be practiced.

Nor did Colonel Thorburn see prickly heat as much of a problem and regarded the sporting facilities in Aden as first rate plus excellent opportunities for upcountry training with one KOSB company always in Mukeiras on the Audhali plateau. But

'I have to admit however that Aden was a better officer station than an "other – rank" one'.

Brenda Hannigan,[11] a member of the Women's Royal Army Corps (WRAC),[12] arrived in Aden in November 1963.

My first recollection was of arriving at Khormaksar Airport – getting off the plane and the heat hitting you like it does when you open an oven door, and the smell! I thought it was something that would go away but on asking the driver taking me to my billet what the smell was she said, 'It's Aden – you'll get used to it.'

The WRAC billet, which was originally Officers' Married Quarters, was facing the parade ground which was used for helicopter landing. There would be a call on the radio informing us that casualties were being brought to Steamer Point from upcountry and we would watch them land on the parade ground to be taken to the military hospital by ambulance, then a short while after there would be another call on the radio asking for blood donors to go up to the hospital to give blood, as there was no blood bank.

(She was in Aden for 18 months, until May 1965.) I worked as a clerk at HQ Middle East Command in the General Staff Department, next to the Ops Room and I worked for an Officer who organised travel arrangements, accommodation and itineraries for visiting VIPs. Our working day was from 7 a.m. to 1 p.m. without a break, our meals were taken in the RAF Mess, and then we usually spent the rest of the afternoon on the beach – what a life! As the trouble became more serious we weren't allowed to walk to our place of work and had to go by army bus, the outside of which was covered with mesh panels so that if a grenade was thrown at the bus it would bounce off (hopefully!) and with an armed soldier at the doorway of the bus in case of snipers. For some reason we were never afraid, just carried on regardless, all part of the job, so to speak.

I remember being without water for a few days, cut off by the Arabs, I think, no showers in all that heat! We had to go for a dip in the sea, and I have never drunk so much lemonade, 7-up, etc. Also when the Arabs went on strike for a few days, the WRAC were sent to help out at the hospital to cover the jobs such as cleaning, making tea, etc. that the Arabs did – I was in the maternity and children's wards.

[Brenda's memories are mostly positive.] We had a good social scene – lots of parties for birthdays, anniversaries, engagements, etc. – any excuse would do. Also we used to get invited to Regimental Dinners, which were always held at Little Aden, and transport would be provided, mostly 3-ton trucks! There we were in all our finery being bounced along in a 3-ton truck, rather took the edge off the occasion but when we arrived we were treated like VIPs. These were usually in the open air with armed soldiers around the perimeter for protection against snipers and grenade throwers.

WRACs did not serve upcountry. Many male servicemen also never made it out of the confines of Aden Colony especially after the security situation in the Federation deteriorated from late 1963 onwards. Judging from the many entries on the Aden Veterans' website[13] it was mostly those people, mainly in the support units, who did not have this opportunity to escape, who disliked the place so much. 'My worst posting', 'Never want to go back' are common comments! Two others from the website are worth recording to give the flavour of what was probably a widespread, if minority, view:

> I served for two years in Aden, 1965–7. I was on duty when the mutiny took place. To me Aden was the worst two years of my life although I do have some fond memories of Steamer Point and Little Aden.

> Based in Falaise Camp in Little Aden for the whole of 1964. It was the a**e-end of Empire. Only God knows why the government of the day thought it was worth a single one of our friends' lives. Loathed every minute of it.

Not so for David Lawrence.[14] As a Royal Signaller, he had a very brief spell in Mudia in mid-1964, but otherwise spent all his time in Aden itself. He did not find the posting (from December 1963 until May 1965) boring:

Perhaps I have a high boredom threshold! Barrack life was little different from any other garrison but it was enlivened by the fact that we were in an exotic location that had many echoes of British India about it. The language was spiced with Hindi expressions – vehicles were called gharries, the parade ground at Steamer Point was known as the Maidan and Arab night watchmen were chowkidars. [Most of the shopkeepers were Indians.]

Social life, however, had its problems and was

handicapped by a lack of available ladies, but a number of soldiers made friends with the servicewomen stationed at Steamer Point or the daughters of service families. The high-point of the social scene were the weekly dances at the Mermaid club run by the NAAFI at Steamer Point. Coming down the scale there were Forces cinemas at Waterloo Lines, RAF Khormaksar and Steamer Point. There were also the unit NAAFI and canteens run by religious organisations, typically, at Singapore Lines, the MMG [though distanced from its origins, Mission to Mediterranean Garrisons]. For some reason, drinking never seemed to be the problem that it was in, say, German garrison towns.

Roy Venables,[15] a newly promoted Sergeant (aged 23) in the Royal Army Ordnance Corps (RAOC) arrived in Aden in August 1964. He worked in HQ Middle East, Command:

I liked the camaraderie of our little community at Fort Gold Mohur. I got a Fiat 500 eventually and this allowed me to get out a bit. I liked being only responsible for my job which was quite interesting and worthwhile. I was pitch-forked into placing local contracts so got to meet some strange characters and learned a lot. I liked being waited on hand and foot; all the more novel because I was just promoted from Cpl and this was my first experience as a senior NCO. Our waiters and cooks, etc. were Somalis, quite likeable and amiable. Our cook was called Mo and he had served on American ships at some time. He had very little English and what he had was rude and American in style. So, when serving up the super lunch to the female guests as they filed by he would come out with what he thought were blinding compliments like 'Hello, you c**k-s**king Limey!!!!'

I disliked the fact that you could not meet anyone outside the military. I disliked the long and increasingly frequent guard duties and I used to worry in case I got engulfed in a serious security incident. Guys who we felt had opened fire for the right reasons but mistakenly, had to go before the civil courts. I knew a guy who passed from being regarded as something of a hero to being vilified in the course of one morning.

European civil servants and business people would have nothing to do with us, which I felt was unfair, as I believed then that the Army was actually looking after them. Having become a civil servant in later life I modified this view.

Unlike Roy Venables, David Lawrence had some excitement outside Aden.

The most interesting was a spell at Mudia, where the town was coming under attack from insurgents; I was slightly wounded when a rocket-launched projectile hit the building in which we were staying. This would have been mid-64.

He remembered the Political Officer at the scene: 'turning up in civvies but carrying a Sterling SMG'.[16] Aden itself became increasingly hazardous during his tour. His arrival had coincided with the attack on the High Commissioner at Aden Airport and then just before he left on 10 November, 1964:

a grenade was thrown at a group of servicemen outside a restaurant in Steamer Point, six of the servicemen were wounded. This was followed on the 28th of November by a second incident when a bar frequented by off-duty married servicemen The Oasis, in Ma'alla was the target of a grenade throwing. A Royal Signals corporal, George Slater was killed. His companion was awarded a CinC's Commendation for alerting the patrons and attempting to shield someone with his own body. I certainly see these two incidents as the start of the troubles in Aden Colony. The next major incident, as

I recall, was on 24 December when a grenade thrown into a children's Christmas party at RAF Khormaksar killed Gillian, the daughter of Air Commodore Sidey, the RAF's Principal Medical Officer for Middle East Command.

Former Lance Corporal R.M. de B.M.G. Von A. Fitzgerald[17] with The Prince of Wales' Own Regiment of Yorkshire (PWO) also experienced how dangerous life could be in Aden for the off-duty soldier. It was Christmas Eve 1965.

I was peacefully enjoying an ice-cold beer with a friend at a bar in the Crescent – the main shopping area of Steamer Point. The chatter of bargaining tourists and shopkeepers was suddenly shattered by the fierce report of a hand-grenade exploding. This was directed at British people in the bar. Within seconds the area swarmed with armed British troops. Then came the 'ping' of the striking mechanism of a second grenade, followed by the warning shout 'Grenade!' – which sent everyone plunging to the ground. Immediately a second explosion took place. The two-grenade trick had recently been introduced. The first was thrown to kill if possible, but primarily to attract troops to the area. The second was intended to cause more casualties. [In this case there were no injuries but the tactic did take a toll until soldiers learned not to 'bunch' in the area of a terrorist incident.]

George Hutchinson's[18] service in Aden was during a slightly earlier period than most of the other contributors to this chapter.[19] He arrived with sixty others on his nineteenth birthday in October 1957 to serve on secondment with the Aden Protectorate Levies (APL), later to metamorphose into the Federal Regular Army (FRA). As a trooper from the 15/19 Royal Hussars he had the task of training the Levies on how to operate Ferret armoured cars. It was all very strange.

The culture shock was an underestimation of our arrival. None of us was informed as to what to expect. An Arab, to us, was something we saw on old movie screens. As anyone who has spent any time in Aden will tell you, it's commonly known as a punishment posting for most of the British army. A combination of the weather, the sun, flies and disease. [On-the-spot briefing was minimal, two hours in George's case.] We were going 'upcountry'. And that was the place to be if you wanted some action. We arrived with armoured cars – Ferrets. Each of us was given an Arab – literally given an Arab – who we were to teach about Ferrets. Mine was called Mustapha – I believe every Arab was called Mustapha at the time, or, if not, Ali! I was lucky. I got a lad about 22 years old – I was only 19 so he was older than me. He could speak English better than me – considering I come from the Newcastle area!

George records that Mustapha and some of his friends defected to the Yemen during a firefight upcountry.

At the time we thought that this was very funny and then we realised that Mustapha, and several of the guys in the Levies were actually Yemeni and not the Adenis that we expected them to be. This was a constant problem in the Levies. We didn't realise who we were teaching or who we were serving with, because, we were told, Aden was British and the Yemen was of course the enemy, and we were at war with them.[20]

Micky Tillotson[21] was a company commander with the Prince of Wales's Own (PWO) Regiment of Yorkshire. The regiment had three tours of duty in Aden between 1958 and 1967. The 'hottest' were when the Regiment returned to serve almost continuously for most of the last three years.[22] Tillotson arrived in November 1965 'direct from Malaysia where we were winning the campaign against Indonesian "confrontation"'. The PWO were operating in the colony using the tactics practised by the Royal Anglian regiment, which they replaced. This was known as 'coat-trailing'.

The famous tactic of 'showing an armed presence' was the order of the day, with British troops becoming targets for grenade and sniping attacks in Crater, for no discernible bene-fit. In my company, I introduced a series of minor tactical tricks to give the soldiers a feeling they held the initiative. My own coat-trailing was totally ineffective, but the system of having an obvious road block, with 'cut-offs' behind and down side streets to catch those deliberately avoiding them proved useful. More importantly, this whole variety of 'tricks', some of sheer pantomime, amused the soldiers and made them feel they were on top. (They also knew that I would not risk a single life for an obviously lost cause and my company did not lose one.)[23]

Coincidentally Micky Tillotson and I were together in Dhala in 1966 where he commanded C Company, PWO, and I was the Political Officer. He describes in *With the Prince of Wales' Own* (see note 22) a 'dissident' attack on government targets in Dhala (including my house) on 29 July. This was a typical upcountry incident, perhaps more frequent in Dhala than elsewhere and merits inclusion:

> At 0220 hours a group of dissidents of unknown strength attacked the Emir of Dhala's palace and the local Political Officer's house with blindicide [Czech anti-tank] rockets[24] and mortar fire. The PO's house, with walls two feet thick, was built to withstand attack but the PO very reasonably called for fire support. This was not easy to provide, as both his house and the Emir's palace lay to the south of C Company's position with the Dhala souk between them. Mortar defensive fire tasks near the Political Officer's house were fired and 11 Platoon (2Lt Michael Garside) was despatched to ambush what was judged to be the dissidents' likely withdrawal route to the hills.

Tillotson's account continues:

> A possibly unique feature of this action was its direction by the commander of C Company (the author) sitting on a bucket. He had been an active casualty to gastro-enteritis throughout the previous 24 hours, a condition, which the dissident attack did nothing to calm. The mortar defensive fire (DF) tasks drew small arms fire and two mortar bombs from the attackers but no casualties or damage were sustained. The action ended at 0315 hours when, according to intelligence later received, the dissidents withdrew southwards – away from Garside's ambush waiting near the foot hills – taking two of their wounded with them, one of whom died the next day.[25]

Trooper Paddy Lynch[26] had mixed feelings about his time in Aden with the 9/12th Lancers. He arrived in Aden in 1963 and was sent to join his squadron upcountry. First impressions were not favourable.

I was assigned to A Squadron 1st Troop; they were out at Dhala, so pretty soon I was on the first transport going out there. It wasn't exactly a comfortable journey. I was sat in the back of a three-tonner with a FRA escort. They were the troops we were to be working with. It was also my first experience of Sheikh Othman. Not exactly the friendliest of places to drive through, as at this particular time there was a student demonstration and they hurled anything they could at us. I was armed with a Sterling sub-machine gun and three magazines of ammo and the escort was armed with an old rifle. At one point someone tried to climb onto the back of the wagon and the Arab fired at the intruder. After a long drive, or so it seemed, we arrived at Thumeir, which was a FRA fort on the Radfan. We stretched our legs and found some water to drink; it tasted a bit brackish but at that time I would have drunk anything. My next big shock was the Dhala Pass. The rule here was passengers walked just in case there were mines. We were met by a squad of 45 Commando who led us up the most precipitous path I had ever been up. I daren't look down in case I shat myself so I kept on going until we rounded a rocky outcrop and found ourselves at the top. We sat around with 45 Commando till our vehicle reached the top. Back on board we headed out towards Dhala. It was starting to get dark by the time we reached Dhala and I was getting to feel tired, and our driver said it was the altitude.

We reached the camp at Dhala, which was situated on a smallish plateau approached by a rocky road. Opposite our camp was 45 Commando's camp, similar in style. I was met by 1st Troop's Sergeant Wilson, and with him was a corporal, 'Darky Night' as I got to know him. First thing was to get a bed then some equipment was issued to me. I found the rest of the Troop sitting around in the marquee that was to be my home for the next few months. The Troop Commander was Lt. St. John Airey. Wally offered me my first Dhala beer and it was warm. I sank back on my bed, none too comfortable either, and lit a cigarette up. Soon I was being told what the place was like.

Within minutes found out for myself. I had to go to the toilet. I wasn't expecting all modern conditions but I didn't expect to have to crap into a long drop. I could hear scuttling noises from below me. Later I was told that rats lived in amongst the crap and they were known to have taken a bite out of someone's arse. Also you didn't stroll out smoking a ciggy, as there were snipers out in the hills. Soon I was falling asleep, my thoughts so far, 'What a f**king dump!'

Chris Norris[27] was a Royal Marine driver in Little Aden in 1961. He described Aden as a magical country; but not Aden itself.

I had a yearning to go up to the hills (Radfan). I thought it immensely exciting, so I volunteered. I loved it, maybe because it wasn't so disciplined as Little Aden was. Maybe the nearest I can equate it to, is the Long Range Desert Group;[28] we just wore chukka boots and had an assortment of odd headgear, driving around in Austin Champs with goggles round our necks and water choggles[29] hanging off the wing mirrors. Everyone covered in dust from head to foot. I know we were there to do a job, but there was just this hint of 'Boy's Own' about it.

Chris had an ingenious way of exploiting local wildlife:

Living in tents with mosquito nets that had more holes than a lorry load of Polo Mints, we did have a backup system, chameleons. Tie a piece of thin string of about two meters long just above their hind legs, the other end is attached to your metal bed frame, give them complete freedom of your bed space and they will catch all approaching mosquitoes.

Certainly he enjoyed his time in Aden.

Driving was I suppose what I really liked doing. Every so often we drive down to Little Aden for a day or two, load more stores and petrol, have a swim, do some shopping for yourself and the other lads and return to Dhala. This was always done in convoy with the 'Cherry Pickers'[30] driving their Ferrets at the head and rear of the convoy, in case of an ambush. I'd heard rumours down below that you were not a Dhala Driver until you can 'do' the pass[31] in one, which basically meant taking a three-ton Bedford RL around a very sharp bend in one – it was possible, just not turning the steering wheel until the right moment, and then swinging it round really fast, you would just scrape round. If you didn't you would end up shunting the vehicle backwards and forwards, and of course everyone down the convoy could see you. These convoys were normally without incident, but occasionally some Yemenis would have had a session on the 'hashish'[32] and start using us as a fairground shooting gallery. I had a passenger on one convoy that was ambushed, a vehicle fitter who leapt out of the vehicle, dived under it. I was still getting out of the cab of the vehicle as bullets were flying around all over the place and I heard these pumping noises as I was climbing down. When I looked, my passenger was pumping up the Primus we always carried, making a cup of tea for both of us, and all you could hear were bullets ricocheting around the area.

I never had the same relaxed attitude towards ambushes! I was personally beholden to RAF fighter pilots for helping to extricate a company of FRA escorting a Federal government Court of Enquiry led by Jim Ellis (Permanent Secretary, Ministry of Interior), Colonel Chaplin (PS, Ministry of Defence) and Dick Holmes (Federal Attorney General) from a very frightening experience. I was in attendance as the local political officer and we were ambushed in the Radfan Mountains on 3 March 1964 by a large party of well-armed 'dissidents' on our way to investigate the circumstances of a previous ambush which had led to FRA casualties! Under fire from high ground and on terrain which afforded very little shelter we extricated ourselves thanks to covering fire from Hawker Hunters with two FRA soldiers killed and a number wounded. Without the prompt arrival of the RAF and their accurate fire on rebel positions, casualties would certainly have been much heavier. (As it was a bullet ruined my packed lunch!) Incidentally this was the incident which was the catalyst for phase two of the Radfan campaign involving considerable British troop reinforcements.

The use of aircraft (fighters and bombers) for strikes against hostile targets, punitive bombing of insurgents' houses, close air support for troops on the ground or for 'flag waves' (to demonstrate

Figure 6.1 A Federal Government court of enquiry with senior officials including Peter Hinchcliffe (as Political Officer, Radfan) just before they came under heavy fire from dissident tribesman (March 1964). Ironically the court was investigating a previous ambush in the same place a few months previously.

the long and muscular arm of HMG) were a prominent feature of our military activities.[33] Tim Toyne Sewell was a great fan:

> Spectator sport was watching the RAF Hunter (successor to the Venom) pilots attacking rebel positions deep in the valleys between the mountains. They flew at the limits, heading down the between the rock walls until it seemed that they must crash into the mountainside, firing into forts or sangars with long bursts of fire, before hauling back the stick and going vertically up over the mountain lip. It was real Biggles stuff and the RAF won plenty of plaudits from the Jocks, who knew that they would be well served if they needed help in an emergency.

Colin Richardson[34] was a RAF Venom Mark 4, ground attack aircraft, pilot based at RAF Khormaksar from 1957 to 1959 with RAF Eight Squadron. He had a busy time:

about a third of my time was actually flying from Aden. Another third of my time spent upcountry with the army – the Aden Protectorate Levies – doing ALO, Air Liaison Officer duties. Now, what that meant was forward air control of the aircraft for the army – in other words, the ground attack aircraft – and about another third of the time up at Sharjah for the Jebel Akhdar War.[35]

In June 1958 he was engaged in an operation typical of many at that time.

There was a bomb outrage in one of the restaurants in Steamer Point frequented by HM forces. The intelligence guys got onto this and found out who was responsible. It was a guy called Mohamed Aidrus,[36] who lived upcountry near Al Qara', in the Lower Yafa' Sultanate. The town itself was on a kind of slab, with cliffs all the way around, and then scree underneath that. So you could never get an army up there. And the guy, himself, had a magnificent house, a few hundred yards north of the town itself – kind of manor house – it really was rather splendid. And so, one afternoon, leaflets were dropped on it, by the Venoms warning everybody to leave the house by tomorrow morning, because it was going to be knocked down. The first aircraft was there about 7 a.m., and we kept on firing rockets at this house until about lunchtime, with the idea of reducing it to knee-height. It was assisted by all the ammunition they had in the house blowing up as well. And then on subsequent days, we went round and knocked down the houses of his friends who had helped him.

In total six houses were destroyed at Al Qara and neighbouring villages as the result of 18 Venom sorties.

Colin Richardson took part in other operations including lifting the siege on Roy Somerset and the APL detachment on Jebel Jihaf, also in 1958 – as described by Roy in Chapter 2. On an earlier occasion his squadron carried out airstrikes on Qa'taba town, just across the Yemen frontier from the Emirate of Dhala, from where it was suspected 'dissident' activities within adjacent areas of WAP were being organised. This was something of a 'sting' operation according to Colin:

the Yemenis were building up strength in Qa'taba. The Eight Squadron pilots were flown up to Dhala airstrip and we all drove up to the border, and got into a slit trench with one of those huge naval telescopes, and the Yemeni artillery positions were pointed out to us. On the following morning, some lorry was driven close to the border, and the Yemenis rose to the bait and fired on it. If they fired across the border, we were allowed to fire across the border.[37] They didn't realise, when they opened fire on this lorry that there were a whole load of Venoms – out of earshot quite close by – and they came in and they knocked out the artillery there.

Most of the military people whom we have interviewed or have had accounts of their experiences from, especially the more senior ones, agree that service in Aden afforded them considerable professional satisfaction. Operations in Aden itself were challenging enough and many of those who served upcountry and above all in the Radfan campaign in 1964/65 relished the opportunity for active service in exotic surroundings.[38] Toyne Sewell:

to those involved in it the adventure and excitement was to remain highlights of our lives. [As he saw it:] The nearest I can equate it to is one of the pre-war Northwest Frontier campaigns in India. The country was rough, barren and mountainous, the maps inaccurate or non-existent, roads were few and far between and therefore few if any vehicles could get up to support the troops. Kit was carried or strapped on the backs of camels or donkeys. It was basic soldiering in the truest sense. Yet the simplicity of it all allowed young officers, in particular, enormous freedom of operation. It was not unusual to be sat down by one's company commander, have a distant hilltop pointed out and be told to take it and hold it until further notice. Or one would march with thirty Jocks in tow, edging a thousand feet or so up the hillside to a small fort, with which most hills were crowned, and then, having chased off any rebels remaining, and few of them stayed around to wait for us, set up camp. For the next week or so one patrolled or ambushed the nearby tracks and wadis until being told to move on to another hill.

Eric Grounds[39] was a young subaltern (2/Lt.) based in Aden with the Queen's Dragoon Guards from November 1966 until August 1967. He celebrated his nineteenth birthday in Habilayn in spring 1967. He saw active service upcountry and in Aden. 'The first time I was under fire was in Habilayn (mortar fire in the small hours of the morning) and subsequently on occasion when escorting convoys (with armoured cars).' It was apparently exciting rather than frightening.

At 19 the notion of violent death was pretty remote. I guess I was under fire 40–60 times during the period and simply cannot recall any sense of fear. Excitement, determination to win, the thrill of the chase – those were the immediate sensations.

It was in Aden, Sheikh Othman and Crater, rather than upcountry that Eric Grounds experienced serious action.

Figure 6.2 The British army camp at Habilayn, Radfan, in April 1964. British troops were there in support of the Federal Regular Army (FRA) as the build-up to large-scale military operations gathered pace.

One night we had moved to the north of Sheikh Othman to wave the flag at the police checkpoint. We stopped briefly, facing north and come under fire from the town behind us. The troop swiftly splintered into its individual parts, with vehicles following a practised routine to identify whence the fire came. For the first and only time I told my driver Trooper Paul Ivin, to close down. He remonstrated: I insisted. Heavens only know why I did; it was an inspiration. Five minutes later, as my vehicle turned off the tarmac to coast towards some dwellings on the western edge of the town, we were hit on the glacis plate (protecting the driver's window) by a blindicide [Czech anti-tank rocket]. Had we not closed down, it would have almost certainly killed Ivin, and may well have done for the remainder of the crew, too. Ears ringing and slightly dazed by the explosion, I remember thinking 'Wow!' It was a good ambush, and we were under sustained machinegun fire; an extended mobile battle followed, during which we caused a number of casualties.

Eric subsequently returned to the site of the attack and found the remnants of the rocket, which is now in the regimental museum in Cardiff.

L/Cpl Fitzgerald was also almost euphoric in battle:

When I first came under fire I experienced a great thrill. The drama of life and death was enacted before me and I was playing a part in it. Bullets ricocheted off the rocks and whined through the air. Mortar bombs and anti-tank missiles exploded frighteningly close. The air was filled with dust and the smell of cordite, which irritated the lungs and brought tears to the eyes. Officers and NCOs shouted orders and the din increased. When the skirmish ended came the realisation of how close one had been to death. [On that occasion there had been no casualties but] for days afterwards those of us who, for the first time, had experienced a minor battle discussed the fight. We somehow felt like different men. I gained an increased respect for the preciousness of life.

Many of the accounts of the Aden military experience are from British people serving with British units. Outside Aden most of the burden of day-to-day soldiering was borne by Arab forces, which in the case of the FRA[40] had a handful of British officers. Throughout the mid-1960s 'Arabisation' ensured that apart from a few specialists, only the highest ranks (by 1966, the Brigadier commanding and his two area commanders (full colonels)) had British incumbents. John Agar[41] commanded the FRA's Signal Squadron from 1963 until 1966. He had the task of training up local soldiers to take over from signallers on secondment from the British army. His British team suffered a casualty during the Radfan campaign: Cpl. R. Davies, who was blown up by a mine in April 1964. John Agar recalls:

> Mining of Wadi beds – there were no tarmac roads beyond Lahej – was a constant peril. The British had conveniently left large quantities of mines in Egypt when they withdrew from the Canal Zone, and they found their way to South Arabia.[42] British troops serving with the FRA were volunteers; they were seen at their best when facing continuing personal attacks;[43] grenades lobbed into canteens, tents and messes, and the ever-present fear of mines. The British Signaller proved himself to be courageous, steady, restrained and good-natured. His unfailing sense of humour was a cardinal quality. He also noted the local soldiers were fun to serve with and had their own brand of humour.

Logan Brown[44] served with both the APL and the FRA from 1956 until 1963. At an early stage he had the task of recruiting new soldiers and was asked to select 30 in Lodar in the Audhahl Sultanate. Over 400 turned up in front of the local Government Guard Fort but how to select them?

> I devised what I thought was a sensible solution. I would point at someone in the crowd and say 'the chap with the blue mishedda'. He then would have to fight his way through the mob, to the bottom of fort – if he could do that, we reckoned he was fairly tough. He then had to see the medical officer, and then the Intelligence Officer (IO) to see that he wasn't a local dissident. He then met me at the top of the fort and if he passed all the others and he could understand my Arabic he was good enough to come in. [They got 29 new recruits this way but the

thirtieth, of the right quality, proved elusive.] Just at that moment a couple more, carrying rifles over their shoulders, turned up. I said 'the one on the right, let's see if he is any good.' He fought his way through the mob. He saw the IO who was a bit concerned as he had a bullet wound, and he thought he might well be a dissident anyway. And then he saw the doctor who was very worried. He said to me 'This chap's got a funny, a very funny arm and I don't know if he is going to be any good.' Then the Mulazim (APL Lieutenant) had a brilliant idea. He said 'Sahib, he has a rifle – give him two rounds and see if he can shoot.' So we pointed out a white rock about a quarter of a mile away and said 'Fire at that.' And he did, hit it both times, so he was in.

Adrian Donaldson[45] was sent in 1961 to 'Ataq in the 'Aulaqis to raise and train a new FRA battalion – the Fifth. This had been a particular hot spot in the late 1950s and one local tribe, the Rabizis, was giving the government some problems. The newly-raised battalion acted as local peacekeeper in a troublesome area and had

a policy of making sure the only water resource we controlled was shared with the locals. We also treated the sick (mostly children with measles) over a wide area around us by sending out RAF medical NCOs, duly escorted, to many villages in the neighbourhood. So successful was this that mortar attacks and sniping which plagued us when we first arrived stopped completely after a month or two. A Rabizi chief (complete with spear and blue paint)[46] contacted me personally in my HQ one night and told me that my men and I could 'walk in peace over their land and that our enemies would be theirs'.

He felt that one of the problems that the FRA had was that there was

no operational plan or if there was one we were not told of it. Our tasks were routine ones of local patrolling and picketing routes when British forces or VIPs were moving. This despite the fact that our soldiers were fit and well-trained for action in conflict. [But having said that he describes a major FRA operation] to cross the Yemen frontier to recover the body of an SAS trooper who had been killed on our side of the border but taken over there for delivery to an Egyptian intelligence officer for reward. The body was dumped (bound from head to foot like a Michelin tyre advert) and dumped in a dry well close to a Yemeni village. We had to fight our way there and back against local opposition.

Adrian later served as an Area Commander (Full Colonel appointment) in Radfan with British and Arab troops under his command. He was not impressed with some of the British units: 'I was most disconcerted to find the apathy and fortress mentality that prevailed. I had to really exert myself to the full to get them out of their camps to patrol day and night and make their presence felt.' One exception was Admiral Sir Michael Le Fanu, the Commander in Chief, British forces.[47] He asked to come on a night patrol with 5 FRA under Donaldson's command! The other top brass in Aden made so much fuss that the idea had to be abandoned with Le Fanu gracefully withdrawing to save Adrian embarrassment with other senior officers.

Although many British servicemen were impressed by the professionalism of the FRA there were doubts about the force's commitment and loyalty to the Federal government and their British allies. There was an oft-repeated jibe that rebels often were FRA soldiers on leave. There was an undoubted racist tinge to some comments. As a British officer who served with an APL unit in Beihan in 1959 observed: 'This was at a time when Arabs were "Wogs" to the army as a result of the activities in Egypt.' And I remember one British unit, in particular, notorious for their rough and ill-tempered treatment of local people at security checkpoints or during house-to-house searches made a practice of referring to Adenis as 'Gollies', being expressly forbidden to use the W-word.[48] This kind of attitude seemed at times to colour the relationship with Arab military colleagues.

Micky Tillotson: 'I had no confidence in the loyalty of any of them (FRA, Federal Guard, Aden Police), finding it safer to consider [that] they were hostile or potentially so, as I would have been in their shoes.' Tony Besse,[49] a member of Aden's leading trading company was scathing about the FRA in particular: 'a piece of costly decorum devised to bolster up the Federation but totally ineffectual in dealing with tribal rebellion. Its main troubles: corruption in the ranks and the predominance of tribal loyalties over regimental discipline.' Frank Edwards,[50] who served as an intelligence officer with the FRA from 1963–6 also perceived tribalism as a fundamental difficulty:

> It had taken forty years to establish the FRA as a mixed-tribal force. I always felt that a soldier's first loyalty was still to his tribe. To that extent, I was of the opinion that there was no natural loyalty to the Federation as such. It was seen as a largely meaningless structure, debased by the inclusion of Adenis (there were few Adenis in the FRA itself). In so far as any one tribal leader gave overt support, then members of that tribe would also declare loyalty to the Federation, but no more.

As far as anti-Federation political influence on the military was concerned: 'as for support for FLOSY or other subversive organ-isations, despite the daily propaganda war, I held no suspicion that any of the Arab officers, especially those senior to me (I was a Major) were active supporters.' And (the Tillotson point) after the Defence White Paper of February 1966:

> officers would naturally be looking how best to secure their personal futures. I anticipated that loyalty to the FRA would play a less dominant part and tribal loyalty resume its old dominance. I did not anticipate a large-scale defection to any organisation or government based in and on Aden.

Adrian Donaldson also had doubts about the loyalty of some of the FRA soldiers to

> either the British or the Federal government. But, if anything, I would say they were more loyal to the British and felt more than a little betrayed as a result. Though they seldom mentioned it to me they certainly felt that they were not trusted by either by the Federal government or HQ FRA.

Ashley Tinson,[51] a company commander with 1 APL had his moments of anxiety.

My company staged in Lodar on the way [from an operation further east.] Most of my soldiers came from that area so I said anyone who lived locally could go home for the night, so long as they were back ready to move at eight next morning. I had a very worrying night. Everyone except Mohamed Siari, my 2ic, and a couple more, disappeared. Our small party sat around a fire when a blue[52] figure arrived whom Mohamed introduced as his uncle. Chatting around the fire, with me worrying if I would have a company in the morning, we talked of Sputniks. The old man, bare apart from his loincloth, blue all over with a blue rifle, had a (blue) transistor radio on which he listened to *Saut al Arab* from Cairo. He knew more than I did about space rockets. At eight next morning the entire company was on parade ready to go. I was very relieved and very heartened by their response to my concession.

Robin McGarell-Groves,[53] a Royal Marine officer who had two tours in Aden as 2ic 45 Commando and later as CO, worked a lot with the FRA when based in Dhala helping with escort work on the periodic Dhala Convoy, which was an FRA regular responsibility.

Upcountry we developed good relations with the local Political Officer and the Emir but never got really close to the FRA, except in Little Aden and then only to the British Officers, particularly Gordon Viner, first when he was commanding 1 APL and later as Commander FRA as a Brigadier.

Later McGarell-Groves had three FRA battalions under his command, when he was acting in charge of the Western Area based in Dhala.

I had already made friends with the FRA battalion commanders when in Dhala and soon learned that orders tended to be a matter for discussion and that having decided on an operation the best way to ensure that orders were carried out was to stay right up with the FRA battalion HQ with my own rearward communications with me.

Alan Darcy[54] was an RAF officer who served with the APL in the 1950s, returned to Aden in 1963 and acted as an informal Political Officer in Aulaqi country from 1963 until 1967. He felt, observing the FRA from a new vantage point, that when British Army officers replaced the RAF secondees they failed to

> maintain the same balance between the various tribes that we had strived very hard to achieve. The Aulaqis became particularly dominant and took over most of the prime positions in the Army. That ended, of course, in the famous mutiny of (June) 1967, when the Aulaqis went just that one step longer . . . further on than they should have done.[55]

There is little doubt that both FLOSY and the NLF had their adherents in the FRA/SAA and their influence increased as the time of British withdrawal approached and as the Federal government steadily and perceptively lost credibility as a viable successor regime. Darcy saw it as a gradual process:

> There was within the FRA an infiltration, but I wouldn't call it an infiltration in the sense of something inserted deliberately. It was something that grew up normally, within an ever-awakening political environment – in the same way as servicemen are basically non-political, but are still probably Conservative, Labour . . . or whatever. It's not some matter of a secret approach, it's purely relevant to one's background in the community in which one is living.

Johnny Rickett,[56] as a young acting Captain, was seconded to the 4th Battalion FRA in 1963 and had a second tour with his regiment, the Welsh Guards, in 1965. He hit the headlines in December 1963 when he prevented an Egyptian Air Force Ilyush in transport plane from taking off from Lodar airstrip, after it had landed there by mistake, by blocking the runway with his Landrover.

> The Egyptians later transpired to be highly important intelligence officers on their way to Taiz. They were eventually flown down to Aden and sent back to Egypt; the RAF flew their aircraft to Khormaksar where it was later used for fire fighting

practice. It remained beside the main runway certainly until long after the British army had departed.[57]

At one time Rickett had doubts about some of the more senior officers amongst the Aulaqis: 'There was a strong feeling of unease among the British officers serving in the FRA, particularly those few serving with battalions upcountry, that there could be an Arab mutiny on the lines of the East African Army mutinies in Kenya, Uganda and Tanganyika.' This did not happen, although it was a time when the FRA suffered from poor morale after taking a battering in the early stages of the Radfan campaign. Operation Rustrum in early 1964 had ended with 4 FRA back in camp in Thumeir and under constant sniper and mining attack from rebels in the hills. There was also a command vacuum when the Commander FRA designate, Brigadier McWilliam, did not take up his appointment – according to Rickett because he disagreed strongly that the FRA should try and mount another operation into rebel-controlled country. During this interregnum of command 4 FRA were involved in escorting a court of enquiry including senior Federal officials into the Radfan hinterland. 'This proved to be a fatally flawed business and our leading company was badly ambushed. I remember being ordered by the CO to go forward and extract the company as the Arab company commander had lost complete control and was in a state of panic.' (This is the incident I describe above, in which I was involved, of the FRA Company being eventually able to withdraw under air support.) Although there were surprisingly few casualties Rickett's judgement was

> the dissidents had won – they had seen off 'the Gaysh', they were strongly entrenched and it would take more than our battalion to winkle them out. It was as a result of this that the decision was taken to regain possession of the Radfan, as de facto it had become a 'No-go area'.

And it would need British troops to do it.

Johnny Rickett was surprised about the subsequent very rapid process of 'Arabisation' – moving like an express train. In retrospect, however, I am sure that this was right, as by then each Battalion second-in-command had had more than enough time to learn from his British CO and with the worsening political situation there was in any case no other choice. The proof was in the pudding; [apart from the special case of 20 June 67] there were no mutinies, the Army survived the later traumas of the amalgamation with the FNG to form the SAA, and it remained professional, disciplined and loyal to the Al Ittihad Government almost to the last.

A final comment about the local forces from Field Marshal Sir Roland Gibbs,[58] from 1966–7 Chief of Staff, HQ Middle East Command.

> The local forces were very smart and seemed to like being guards of honour and drill and were very colourful, particularly the mounted camels. And they were very useful for guarding duties, for protection and patrolling. I can't remember them being used on any major operation (except in Radfan in a supporting role). I personally always felt that their loyalty was doubtful, particularly when they had been infiltrated by FLOSY and the NLF. Brigadier Dye (the last Commander of the FRA/SAA) always had confidence in them. But I was always worried for his safety.

Lack of good intelligence is a constant theme in these military reminiscences. Upcountry we Political Officers did what we could but Aden became very bad. Gibbs again:

> We were woefully short of intelligence, particularly after Special Branch agents [had been wiped] out. Although an ex-Hong Kong policeman, who had such success in Malaya, was brought in, he did not have time to establish the infrastructure for sustained intelligence. I was not privy to our agents who were, I imagine, few and far between. Some could have been high grade. I believe [name I have omitted – a senior FRA officer], a member of the NLF, was one. Sadly, I believe he must have been uncovered later and shot. But I would not like to vouch for this.

Micky Tillotson agrees: 'Virtually non-existent in Aden for Crater – our battalion's area of operational responsibility' (especially after the demise of the Special Branch operatives – many of them Somalis according to Tillotson).[59]

In the Radfan and Dhala, we depended on the local Political Officer at Habilayn – a charming Arabist devoted to his flock (Godfrey Meynell), and the local FRA battalion. The only useful intelligence I recall was that given by three NLF would-be saboteurs caught by my company on the road out of Crater.[60] There was nothing particularly baffling about the 'intelligence' received, once one appreciated that all the brown faces were working against us or under duress to do so when required.

Brigadier Sir Louis Hargroves,[61] Aden Brigade Commander from 1964 to 1966, agrees, describing intelligence as 'almost non-existent'.

I asked Frank Edwards, as an intelligence staff officer, G2 (Int) with the FRA, about his assessment of the intelligence and advice he received from other sources such as British political officers like Robin Young, Ralph Daly at HQ and those of us upcountry.

They were conscious of their entrée into the tribal world in which they operated. This led to a tendency to be too dismissive of those working in Aden itself – a very different political environment – and a feeling that the FRA intelligence might be, almost by definition, inaccurate about their particular areas when it varied from their own understanding. There was a consequent impression amongst some of the FRA, British and Arab, that they were at risk of being too much influenced by their own contacts.[62]

By contrast Frank felt that the intelligence he received via the FRA was

(as far as upcountry operations were concerned) both sufficient and accurate enough to allow a sensible and timely deployment of FRA units. [But some caveats:] much was repetitive and a natural exaggeration had to be allowed for. The common danger of all intelligence was to feed off itself. What one reported another took up and re-reported. Then there was the nature of much of the front line skirmishes. I was engaged in two major ones, the Radfan, largely before the British were heavily involved, and another in Mukeiras. One learned, especially during Ramadan, that there were unwritten rules acceptable to both sides. I know that some enemy moves took place unchallenged in turn for untroubled daylight excursions of our own. Not always, but the Arab commanders seemed to know when. At night it was more of a free-for-all, but even then, in most cases a fort was 'shot up' in a way that, unless some uncharacteristic bravado was undertaken, put the occupants at minimum risk, allowing both sides maximum credit for action – and a worthwhile intelligence report to HQ the next day.

Mike Richards served as a Lieutenant, later Captain, with the Air Squadron of the Queen's Dragoon Guards from February 1966 until September 1967. I was curious about what he thought of the politics of the situation and about the wider international context. 'Never thought about it', was the response! And this was true of many of the other service people I have been in touch with. Eric Grounds, for instance: 'I cannot remember a single conversation about the political situation. Our concerns were almost exclusively military.' Colonel Alistair Thorburn again: 'I reckon I didn't think much about government policy! I was too busy looking after my 400 or so Jocks.' Colonel Robin McGarel-Groves wrote of 'a deteriorating scenario of which withdrawal was becoming an inevitable end'. And later down the line: 'I was sad to learn of how many of my FRA friends came to a sticky end after we left and could not get rid of the feeling that we had let them down.'

Others realised that they were on something of a 'Mission Impossible'. Micky Tillotson:

> The CO Roy Birket took great care to explain to all ranks that we were there to support the Federal government until it found its feet. But he and I were old friends from the Malayan Emergency (ten years before) and he knew I would cease to have any confidence after Beswick's visit. We both regarded the Radfan Operation as a means of buying time upcountry before the inevitable evacuation.

George Hutchinson was rather more cynical.

> It appeared that taxpayers' money was being spent to maintain a political system, which was Victorian, to say the least. The people there, i.e. the colonialists, the political officers in

general, these were the guys that tended to be protecting their own positions. Remember without Aden, without the Protectorate, they would have been without a job.

Sir Roland Gibbs also saw it all coming:

I suppose in early days there was some hope that the Federation could work. Perseverance and diplomacy could weld together some sort of government at Al Ittihad. But that all changed when the British government in the mid-1960s decided we would leave Aden and the country. Although we continued with the motions of forming the Federation, nobody was deceived. The rulers (in the country) knew who the winners would be on our departure. And so did Nasser who just had to wait, keep up the nationalist pressure in Aden and in the tribal country and victory would fall into his lap: so there was no alternative but to continue with the charade until the final collapse. In his covering letter to the author Gibbs described this whole episode as 'shameful'. Brigadier Hargroves felt much of the blame lay with political constraints on the military during his time:

The policy of minimum force lost the UK her overseas possessions. Minimum force encouraged the agitators and enabled them to recruit others. The gradual escalation of violence was followed by a gradual increase of UK forces. In other words we had surrendered the initiative.

A different approach might have worked: 'Either get in early with maximum force or get out early.'

As the end approached, some of the comments revealed a deep sense of betrayal – of letting friends down. Colonel Chaplin,[63] a British Officer seconded to serve with the Federal Ministry of Defence, commented after the Beswick visit: 'The fact is that, having encouraged the rulers to take an anti-Nasser line and having made them 'Imperial stooges', hated in the Arab world, we are now about to go back on our word and desert them.'

Not all was bitterness – the last word to Frank Edwards and his wife Marion[64] in reply to my question about a sense of satisfaction arising from the Aden experience:

We both felt that our particular jobs [Marion worked in the Western Aden Protectorate (WAP) office] were well worth doing. It is natural for a soldier to consider, admittedly limited active service as the culmination of his training and his chosen career – but we both felt that the emerging Federation was worth working for. We also have the happiest memories of the wide range of people we worked with and met. All contributed positively to our time there. We, still, feel that it was the time in our lives when we were 'most alive'.

A footnote: the Edwards were to be without a car for their last few weeks at a time when personal transport was increasingly needed. They had accepted an offer for a free flight home for their vehicle.

The day I drove the car to Khormaksar and had a lift back home to our flat in the Ma'ala Strait there was a knock on the door. There stood an FNG officer, Major Abdulla Saleh, with a set of car keys in his hand. He gave them to me, and left his car. His only comment 'I have two.'

CHAPTER SEVEN

ADEN

The 1966 Defence White Paper

John T. Ducker

British officers and Arab leaders in South Arabia alike took seriously the defence commitment entered into by HMG in the treaty which accompanied the creation of the Federation of South Arabia in 1959, reiterated at the time that Cmnd 2114 was issued following the July/August 1964 constitutional conference. Thus the decision by HMG to renounce these defence commitments came as a major shock to all involved. How did this come about?

The Defence White Paper of 1966 was the consequence mainly of a determination to reduce the proportion of government expenditure allocated to defence in favour of domestic expenditure. This fundamental decision forced the British government to consider reductions in commitments around the world. This determination was accompanied by an ideological, almost visceral feeling among some Labour backbenchers and politicians that the day of colonies and military bases was over; that the possession of military bases in the Middle East or 'East of Suez' was a complicating factor in a post-imperial age. The Aden base was closed down in 1967, that in Singapore in 1971.

Anticipating the White Paper, senior Foreign Office officials sought to articulate a position on Aden from the standpoint of HMG's foreign policy. They did this under considerable pressure as is evident in a minute from Sir Paul Gore-Booth, the Permanent Under Secretary, to Sir Roger Allen, Deputy Under Secretary, of 22 July 1965, in which he said:

I am very glad that you are going to have a real go at this immensely difficult question (Aden). We should have done this before, but unfortunately we have been compelled to man temporary trenches on the subject to prevent the Ministry of Defence steam-rollering our foreign policy and this has made it difficult for us to examine our own convictions with the deliberation which we really need.[1]

Unsaid was the reality of a powerful Minister of Defence, Denis Healey, seeking to rationalise Britain's defence commitments, and a not-so-powerful Foreign Secretary, George Brown.

Allen had indicated his concern, in connection with the Defence Review,

that we were in danger of making false assumptions about Aden – that we might have to get out of Aden before 1968 and that we might have to create a substitute in the Gulf – not easy either; that we might find it difficult to leave Aden in 1968 without leaving chaos behind (the trouble with fixing dates in advance); that the knowledge of a British intention to leave Aden before or in 1968 had emboldened Nasser's position in Yemen; that we might therefore end up with two power vacuums, one in Aden and one in the Gulf.

Looking at the situation purely from the Foreign Office angle, the ideal situation

would be for us to sit it out in Aden until either Nasser withdraws or collapses. This would have the considerable added advantage that it would keep Nasser bogged down in the Yemen indefinitely.[2]

The opinion of Sir William Luce, now British Resident in the Persian Gulf, was that it was considerably easier for Britain to stay in Aden than for Nasser to stay in the Yemen, and that it should do so, even if most of the troops were engaged in internal security – which would not apply to the RAF and naval forces anyway. He understood that it might then be necessary for HMG to revert to direct rule of Aden, and even give up the 1968 independence target date accepted by both political parties. If Nasser had left

Yemen before Britain left Aden, however, this would produce a wholly new set of circumstances which would enhance the possibilities of our maintaining a position in the Gulf. In essence, if HMG wanted to stay in the Gulf, they should stay in Aden.[3]

The matter began to emerge into the public domain as soon as August 1965 when an article by Nora Beloff in the Observer was headlined 'Britain's defence chiefs ready to quit Aden base'.[4]

In September 1965, following Cabinet level exchanges on these issues, the Prime Minister directed the Defence and Overseas Policy (Official) Committee (DOP(O)) to draft a paper on Aden. Allen wrote to the Foreign Secretary summarising the conclusions of the paper and commenting on it from the Foreign Office angle.[5] The paper concluded in brief that 'the situation in Aden had deteriorated so far that it was now urgently necessary to make an Order in Council suspending the operative parts of the Aden Constitution and enabling the High Commissioner to exercise direct rule'. Aden and the Federation could not be treated separately (Compare this conclusion with the identical position taken by Lord Lloyd nine years previously.) All the information we had about the control and encouragement by Nasser not only of the terrorist organisations, but also of the Adeni ministers themselves, the penetration and intimidation of the local security forces by NLF agents, confirmed this view. Direct rule would also mean that Makkawi, who was planning to attend the UN Committee on Decolonisation, could not do so as Chief Minister. This would mean that HMG would be severely attacked in the UN and elsewhere, but that would be the case whatever HMG did. The alternative to direct rule might well be that the situation would become untenable and that we would have to withdraw as speedily as possible. The consequences of leaving Aden under duress would be grave for British policy throughout the Middle East, especially for our relations with Saudi Arabia and Iran.

Allen argued that it was therefore essential for the orderly development of British policy in the Middle East that such action be taken now as would keep open for us the options we would need when the Defence Review was finalised. For if Nasser did withdraw from Yemen, it was possible that the future of the Federation might lie in some partnership with the new Yemen. We needed therefore to remain in Aden long enough to see the Egyptians withdraw from Yemen. There was one further point –

George Thomson, Minister of State at the Foreign Office, was about to visit Cairo; Thomson did not feel that this visit should affect the nature or the timing of actions in Aden, but that he would like to be in a position to warn Nasser that the situation in Aden had deteriorated to the point that some difficult decisions may have to be taken. (Note: in the event, HMG resumed direct rule in Aden the day *before* Thomson was due to meet Nasser; the latter therefore refused to receive Thomson – very poor diplomatic management.)

Towards the end of 1965, evidently on the assumption that the Aden base would be reduced to that needed to defend the new state, the Colonial Office submitted a memorandum to the DOP(O) Committee[6] which discussed the reduced British forces which would be necessary to defend the territory and the measures to be taken to strengthen the Federal forces in advance of independence. This paper envisaged the reduction of the Aden Base to a local garrison, plus specialised support for the local forces, with the intention over the medium term to reduce it further. HMG's obligations were couched entirely in terms of the 1959 Treaty with the Federation. No mention was made of obligations incurred under the 1964 White Paper (see p. 29).

On 17 January 1966, talks between HMG and the Federal government were held in London, chaired by Lord Longford, the Secretary of State for the Colonies, to discuss implementation of the proposed new constitution being proposed by Hone/Bell.[7] The Federal delegation said that they had begun to have doubts as to whether HMG was still intending to stand behind the new state and asked for reassurances. Longford said that they had no reason to be concerned, but as they had raised the matter, he would consult with his colleagues and make a formal statement later. The statement he made was as unspecific as it was possible to be.[8] He said that no change was likely in the attitude of HMG to the Federal government. He made no mention of the impending decision to refuse a defence agreement with the new state. The Federal delegation pressed the point, saying that by now senior ministers must know the general outlines of the policy to be adopted in the Defence White Paper. Longford refused to say anything further, though internal discussions continued.

On 16 February 1966, Lord Beswick, informed the Federal Supreme Council that when South Arabia became independent, no later than 1968, the British forces would be withdrawn from the

Aden base, and that, consequently, after independence HMG would not be able to accept any further military commitments in South Arabia.[9] Sultan Saleh, replying on behalf of the Supreme Council, was polite, not to say bland. However, the following day he made a very strong statement describing HMG's intentions as dishonourable, a breach of faith and pressed for re-consideration of the refusal to provide defence support when the base was closed.[10]

On 17 February 1966, Donal McCarthy of the Political Office at MECOM wrote to Frank Brenchley, head of the Arabian Department of the Foreign Office, a five-page letter on the implications of the Defence Review for South Arabia.[11] He referred to an earlier letter sent on this subject on 12 December 1965 on the likely impact, which was, he said, pessimistic enough. The view now was even more pessimistic. He distinguished between the decision to close the base, which was understandable and would have been acceptable to the Federation, the timing of the announcement and the 'gratuitous' announcement of our refusal of a later defence commitment to the Federation, which would make the Egyptians cock-a-hoop, enable them to press their advantage by every means and give them a marked tactical advantage over King Faisal. He referred to the fact that the Arabian Department of the Foreign Office and Sir William Luce, as well as Sir Richard Turnbull had all argued strongly against an announcement now of the intention not to honour our commitment to the Federation, first because it was a breach of our undertakings, second because it would fatally weaken the Federation before it had a chance to increase its military capabilities, and third because of the implications for our ability to honour other commitments in the Gulf.

On the same day, there was an obviously well-informed article in the *Evening Standard* by Tom Stacey, which rehearsed almost exactly the points made by McCarthy.

The Foreign Office eventually withdrew their objection to the proposed closure of the Aden base on being assured that a further battalion of British troops would be based in the Gulf area.[12]

Also on that day, Lord Beswick again met the Federal Supreme Council, which he described as 'deeply and bitterly resentful'.[13] It was not the closure of the base which upset them but our refusal to defend them after independence, which they regarded as being in clear breach of both the 1959 Treaty and the 1964 White

Paper. It was also in breach of public statements made by him, Lord Beswick, in November 1965 and by Mr Denis Healey in January 1966. The chairman of the Federal Supreme Council chose his words with care:

> For many years we have borne the abuse and vilification of most of the Arab world because we believed that the British government was our true friend and that, until we were able to defend ourselves, it would protect us against the consequences of our unwavering support ... we cannot believe it is your wish that we shall be sacrificed just because after many years of repeated promises to the contrary the British government finds that it suits its own self-interest to desert its friends and leave them in the lurch.[14]

On 21 February 1966, two former ministers in the Conservative Government, Duncan Sandys and Christopher Soames, met Lord Longford, to discuss the question of whether HMG intended to honour its commitment to help defend the Federation after independence. The Foreign Office was represented. The Secretary of State said that HMG would not do so – the treaty would be abrogated and not replaced. He did not say, though this was later argued in mitigation, that the defence commitment made in 1964 was conditional on agreements being drawn up between HMG and the Federation, which had been abandoned when the Labour Government came to power. Sandys and Soames said the decision would be a terrible let-down to the Federation, which would not last 12 months without our protection. They also said that even if the base was to be withdrawn, announcing this now would encourage the Egyptians to stay in the Yemen, encourage the Yemen republicans, and would enable Nasser to claim he had won – he had driven us out. They asked what the cost savings would be to Britain, but no answer was forthcoming. Lord Longford said that he hoped that the Americans might be willing to take over from us, to which Sandys responded that they might have done so if we had not already announced the closure of the base.[15]

On the same day, Lord Longford wrote to the Secretary of State for Defence, Denis Healey, to say that by far the most important criticism made by the Federal government to Lord Beswick was the fact that Britain was dishonouring pledges made in the past by the intention to leave the Federation without any continuing defence treaty after independence and the base was closed down. Longford pleaded for sufficient support to enable them to contend with internal dissidence and border forays. If this were not forthcoming, there would be a danger of complete collapse and a difficult withdrawal, and it would be difficult to answer the charge of breach of faith.[16]

The Defence White Paper was presented to the House of Commons on 22 February 1966 and published the following day. This paper made it clear that Britain would accept no obligations in regard to the defence of the Federation of South Arabia after independence. In the exchanges which followed, Duncan Sandys refered to the undertakings given at the end of the constitutional conference in July 1964. Mr Denis Healey, Secretary of State for Defence said, 'A large number of promises were made by the Right Hon. Gentleman when he was Commonwealth and Colonial Secretary, with a government of South Arabia which has now disappeared. There is a completely different government there now'.[17]

On the following day Mr Duncan Sandys made a personal statement in the House of Commons on the subject of the undertakings he had made in 1964.[18] In particular, he reiterated:

(i)   The promise of a defence agreement for the protection of the Federation was made on behalf of the British government at the end of the South Arabian Constitutional conference in July 1964.

(ii)   The undertaking was embodied in a report signed by all the delegates and presented to Parliament in Command paper 2114.

(iii)   The government to which the promise was made was the Government of the Federation of South Arabia, whose constitution is unchanged and whose membership is almost identical to that in 1964.

(iv)   He was concerned that the good faith of Britain might be called into question.

Mr Healey was forced to make a personal statement in response[19] in which he acknowledged the truth of Mr Sandys' statement and apologised for misleading the House the previous day.

On 24 February, Mr Marnham of the Colonial Office wrote to Mr Galsworthy[20] also of that office, giving the background to the defence commitment made to the Federal government in the 1964 White Paper and saying 'I think we owe ministers some explanation as to why we have allowed them to be taken unawares by accusations based on the 1964 White Paper'. This had not been drawn to the attention of ministers engaged in the defence review, and to that extent he felt ministers had been misled. He explained that the decision not to meet these commitments in the Defence Review stemmed from the officials' focus on the Treaties with South Arabia, rather than the White Paper. Since the treaties would become inappropriate at independence, they (the officials) had accepted the change in the defence obligation which went with the termination of the treaties. They had not drawn ministers' attention to the obligations incurred in the 1964 White Paper. He apologised for this error on the part of the officials. Mr Galsworthy, who added his own apologies, forwarded this note to the Permanent Secretary and the Under Secretary. The latter said that officials were in no doubt that the whole policy in regard to South Arabia had been directed at maintaining the base (this was not in fact true – the Colonial Office also had responsibility for bringing South Arabia to independence as a viable state), that this had required a defence commitment to South Arabia and that a decision not to negotiate a defence agreement after independence would be regarded by the Federals as a tremendous let-down.

It may therefore be that HMG's decision to deny a defence commitment at this time to the Federation was at least partly a result of poor staff work by the Colonial Office.

The impact on the Federal government of the Defence White Paper was fatal. In particular, the effect of the decision on the Aden base on the Egyptian government was that they now knew that they had only to sit out the period until the British withdrew from Aden for them to emerge victorious from their struggle to prevent the emergence of a South Arabian state supported by Britain. This is precisely what they did. Nasser abandoned his agreement with King Faisal and limited the Egyptian role in Yemen to the area of most importance – the Sana'a/Taiz/Hodeida triangle. At the very least, the announcement of the Defence White Paper was inept diplomatically. The Egyptians were given encouragement to stay and the Saudis were discouraged from assisting an apparently now doomed new South Arabian state.

The various parties to the independence struggle adjusted to the changed circumstances by seeking to position themselves better for the inevitable struggle for power, though it has to be said that they also continued to attack British officials, forces and institutions. It was particularly dispiriting for those, Arab and British, who had been working for creation of a sound government for the future, often at great personal risk.

When King Faisal visited London in May 1967, just over a year later, he argued strongly that Britain should continue the defence commitment to the Federation after independence. Astonishingly, the Foreign Secretary of the day, George Brown, then announced a new commitment to continue to defend the Federation for a period of six months after independence, an extraordinary reversal of HMG's decision made 15 months earlier to refuse such a commitment. This new commitment was quite specific. It was, however, far too late: the Federation was already unravelling.

At the time of the Six Day War in June 1967, the Egyptians sustained a major military defeat at the hands of the Israelis. They then found it impossible to sustain their commitments in Yemen and, following an agreement with Saudi Arabia at the Khartoum conference that the Saudis would cease their support to the royalists, proceeded to withdraw their troops. Ironically, by that time, the withdrawal of the British forces from Aden was also well under way and the Federation was losing control at various points. By August, the NLF were clearly in control of most of the country. Thus the new commitment made by Britain was unavailing and Britain did not persist with it once the Federal government fell.

All in all, the decision in the Defence White Paper not to defend the Federation after independence, despite the fact that it was largely a British creation, was a shabby renunciation of previous commitments entered into by HMG. It was also diplomatically inept both in regard to Egypt's position in Yemen and in regard to the previous understandings with Saudi Arabia. It doomed any chance the Federation might have had of establishing itself after independence.

CHAPTER EIGHT

BRITISH CIVILIANS REFLECT ON THE END OF EMPIRE IN ADEN

Maria Holt

As I did not arrive in Aden until many years after the British left, I was interested in unearthing clues about a foreign presence that had lasted for 128 years. These were to be found in abundance. What was more elusive was any sense of how it 'felt' for British civilians living in what must have been a very alien environment. The oral history narratives reveal something of the strangeness experienced by the British who ventured to Aden in search of wealth, opportunity, a fresh start or an adventure. The British civilians who lived in Aden varied in almost every respect. While some had very little sense of place or local history, others developed a strong attachment to the area. Many lived the 'ex-pat' life, working and socialising mainly with other Europeans, while a few cultivated local friends, learnt a little Arabic and tried to see something of the country. Almost everyone I met, however, revealed an affection for southern Yemen; they preserved cherished memories.

In this chapter, from the perspective of British civilians who lived or worked in Aden before 1967, I will consider images of the Middle East through the eyes of the colonisers; experiences of everyday life; and how ordinary people coped with the increasing violence from local groups opposed to the British presence in their country.

Although I describe them as 'colonisers', this is not necessarily how they saw themselves. While government officials and soldiers were conscious of representing their country and acting on behalf of Britain, many British civilians had seized the opportunity for lucrative employment or the chance to visit a relatively little known part of the world. Working overseas was an option then as it is now. A man who worked for the Public Works Department from 1954 until 1967 recalled:

> I had been in Aden once, during the war, on a troop ship, and vaguely remembered it. But, after returning from military service and being unable to settle down in the UK in the line of work I wanted or making the progress I wanted, I applied for a job in Kenya and was offered the post there. But I turned it down because the Mau Mau disturbances had arisen and I wasn't prepared to go there and take my wife and two children to what appeared to me to be certain death. I turned the post down and, about 18 months later, applied for a job in Aden and was surprised to receive a little note from the Colonial Office saying an application of mine was already on record and I didn't have to fill in another form. This I took to be the brush off, so I was surprised several months later to receive a letter telling me I'd been appointed.[1]

EVERYDAY LIFE FOR THE BRITISH IN ADEN

According to a woman who went out to Aden with her husband in 1956 and stayed until 1967, her family was told by the Head of the Public Works Department upon their arrival that

> you are going to be very lucky . . . You're going to get a new bungalow. And you can have it painted whatever you like, so long as it's buff! And, of course, we had my little daughter, who was only about three or four months old. It seemed rather strange living in a . . . in a country which was . . . very different. Shopping was . . . rather a shock – you know, going down into the town . . . Crater town, for the first time, because you can smell Crater town long before you get there . . . because it's sort of compounded of leather and spices and all sorts of tropical things. You could go to the *souk*, which you had to do more or less every day because we had no cold storage. The fruit was gorgeous, you know, we got lovely fruit. Meat . . . tended to be very tough and horrible. And they had little chickens which

were even smaller than our bantams. And, one day, I wanted some eggs and I saw this boy going along with a great big bag of eggs . . . big basket of eggs, and so I said to him, give me a dozen, and when I got home, I discovered they were all boiled![2]

A man who arrived in Aden in 1954 to work for the Land and Survey Department talked about family and social life. It continued, he said,

in many ways as normal, if you can call a colonial life normal. There were schools and, when we went to Aden to begin with, my eldest daughter was of school age and went to St Francis Convent School at Steamer Point. She continued there until she passed her 'O' levels. When my middle daughter became of school age, she went to the Isthmus School, which was a private school, built at Khormaksar. Since our working day was virtually confined to the morning, and schools finished at lunchtime, there was always plenty of time in the afternoons and evenings for recreation and social activities. Much of the social activity was taken up with swimming, horse riding, playing squash and badminton, with the girls attending Brownies and Girl Guides. Evenings were . . . we were accused of having a continuous round of cocktail parties, dinner parties and all the rest of it. It *was* fairly hectic, but I don't think we ever went over the top.[3]

A journalist, who was sent to Aden in 1964, recalled the shock of arrival:

I arrived in this blast furnace heat, and was taken to the Rock Hotel, where I was to live for a couple of months before we could find accommodation. And my first impression was, I suppose, the heat and the number of people who were around. It was quite incredible . . . I mean, nowhere near as bad as Hong Kong, but they were right there, in your face almost. I found them very friendly and very helpful, and certainly, when I set out to look for a quarter, or a hiring as it turned out to be, the help I got from the Indian community – and indeed from the Arab community – was tremendous. So those were my first impressions.[4]

In the words of a man who was headmaster of the Isthmus School from 1962 until 1967:

> We left England and it was one of the worst winters that we'd had for years; in fact, they closed the runway at Heathrow just after we left, and the temperature was well below freezing. And when we got to Aden, at the airport, we walked out and the temperature was in the eighties. It was like walking into a hot oven![5]

Aden in the 1950s and early 1960s was considered to be a safe and pleasant place to live and many men took their families. The headmaster, for example, arrived with his pregnant wife. His son 'was actually born in Aden, in the hospital in Crater'.[6] Another narrator described her experiences as a young, newly-married woman:

> To have a first child there was a marvellous experience because . . . there were very few other Brits having babies at the same time – maybe one, maybe two. But when you had your baby, you were the one and the nurses loved to have midwifery experience. So you often gave birth in the presence of about half a dozen midwives, instead of just one. And also, you stayed in hospital for something like a fortnight because nobody wanted you to go home – they all wanted to be dealing with the baby. Whereas now, you know, you're lucky if you're in for 24 hours . . . But you're very cut off from home. You only had letters. The telephone, at the time, we hardly ever used because it was a one-way conversation – you had to stop and let the other person speak to you, and it was very expensive as well.[7]

A man who worked at the BP refinery from 1961 until 1964 said that he 'started out with my wife and two children . . . and by the time we left we had three children and another one on the way'.[8]
A former broadcaster recalled:

> We had three small children and the worry – obviously – of making sure they didn't pick up anything nasty. They all had illnesses, monsoon blisters being the most unpleasant because

some of them were quite huge. But it wasn't long before we were aware that the troubles – which were 'upcountry' – were starting to appear down in Aden itself. And you look back now and you think 'good lord, was it really like that', of saying to your children 'don't pick up anything you see lying around, especially toys'. Some of them had been booby trapped, and to try and say to a four-year old 'don't do it' and he thinks 'why not?' And to see them going off to school in the morning on a bus which was completely screened with . . . well, one assumes sort of blast wiring, and to have an armed guard on the bus – again, a little unusual.[9]

According to most accounts, fresh food was to be had in abundance. In the words of a man and his wife who had lived in Aden in the early 1960s:

Fresh fruit and vegetables were magnificent. They came from Kenya and from upcountry – Abyan . . . Green oranges came from the gardens beyond Shaikh Othman . . . You'd go and sit in one of the gardens up beyond Shaikh Othman and wait for the mangoes to drop off the trees. As the water was so mineral-laden, you just watered sand and things grew. So you could grow tomatoes very quickly. Everything was so cheap at the market – potatoes and onions. We had a garden although we didn't grow vegetables. But once I'd scraped out a pan that I'd used to cook tinned tomatoes and, within three weeks, there were tomato plants growing on this little compost heap – from what had been tinned and cooked! Peaches we used to get as well. I think the only thing that one was really liable to miss was fresh milk. It was all reconstituted stuff, which was not great. And imported wine was impossible. The cows were very thin. But the sheep – they used to bring them over live from Somalia and slaughter them, so that there was fresh lamb available. There was magnificent fish; you soon learned to buy it from fishermen who didn't work in the bay where the refinery effluent went out! We ate shark.[10]

Several narrators remarked on the ever-present sand. According to an army doctor: 'The sand blew most afternoons, around five o'clock, and it was a 'white-out' until about half six, seven o'clock.

You had an inch of sand at the bottom of your soup plate . . . but it added a bit of bulk, you know, a bit of fibre'.[11] Another man reported:

> We learnt to live with sand. The Indian landlord on Khormaksar Beach Road was told 'you must put in fly netting'. So he did. He took the glass out and put the fly netting in, and of course every time the wind blew, it happened to be at our kitchen, my wife had to stand with her back to the window, trying to produce food and get it to the children. She told them to rush into the dining room – because it would get covered in sand'.[12]

The doctor added 'there was this thing called "sand happiness" which, after a while, manifests itself as short-tempered, intolerant of trifling things. But this was just the isolation; we were isolated, there's no question about it'.[13]

A woman musician, who accompanied her husband to Aden in the early 1960s, recalled the thriving cultural scene for British people:

> I was seen to arrive with a baby on one arm and a child hanging on, and a viola strapped to my back. And, the next day, the personnel officer got a phone call that someone they had seen arriving – they thought it was a BP wife – with a musical instrument strapped to her back, and they asked me if I would like to do a broadcast . . . There were quite a lot of quite musical people in the government, and they tended to appoint . . . you know, if they needed a flute for the orchestra, then they would appoint a flautist to a particular post; it was like . . . we need another government secretary but they must play the flute! And one man, who was a government secretary, decided he would produce and conduct *The Mikado*. So I was asked to go and play, which meant motoring into Aden for rehearsals, and we did it for a week, and to packed houses. And then we were asked to put it on the Ark Royal . . . but the captain of the Ark Royal wouldn't bring it right into the harbour because he'd grounded it before, so he was anchored out to sea and quite a lot of the matelots were unloaded and were set, and everything went out by dhows and small boats,

out to sea. They used the lift which was to take the aircraft up on to the flight deck . . . so that became the stage and the orchestra pit was underneath it. It was great! And there were all the P&O liners going past. No publicity or anything, it was just . . . part of life. We did *The Pirates of Penzance* and *The Gondoliers*.[14]

Many British civilians evinced little interest in the growing anti-imperialist movement. Some narrators expressed uncertainty about unfolding events, while others passed their time in Aden in apparent ignorance of nationalist agitation. Most of the people interviewed found life in Aden itself to be relatively pleasant. One man described Aden as 'civilised', 'a perpetual round of drinks parties'.[15] Another, who worked at the BP refinery for eight years, spoke of frequent dances, a tennis club, a restaurant, a library and a snooker table.[16] BP was a self-contained community of ex-pats, situated about 20 miles outside Aden itself. It employed approximately 300 British staff who lived in comfortable air-conditioned accommodation with their families. BP employed local people, as well as Somalis and non-Yemeni Arabs. A man who worked for P&O recalled

there was a place called the Lido, where families used to go to the beach. But they didn't have a shark net in my day, and there was one lady – one of the wives – who was walking, paddling in the water, about a foot of water, and a shark came in and took her foot off while we were there, which was rather dramatic.[17]

A former Aden Airways manager gave a flavour of life for a young, unmarried man at that time:

I went out to parties six nights a week, and the seventh night I entertained at home. It was a wonderful social life! It was mostly meeting people in the company and a few from other commercial firms. Less frequently, it was meeting the military – this was certainly on the dinner party type of thing. Quite frequently, though, I used to go to parties that the General Manager and his wife held – I think bachelors were usually in demand at those sorts of things. They were held at his house down at Ras Boradli, which was a wonderful house for entertaining. Quite frequently, I used to have to go to dinner parties where the AOC and the Admiral – Admiral Le Fanu – I remember he was there quite a lot. And, very occasionally, up at Government House – I think I went there about two or three times. But most of the parties we had were, as I say, among the expatriate community.[18]

For a man living in Aden in the early 1960s with his family:

It was a very good place to work and also to bring up a young family. We worked nominally 12 months in Aden, then two months home leave. I think I would have liked the possibility of spending a little less time on home leave and being able to take local leave, but that wasn't considered to be an option at that time. I think you might have got it if you really fought for it, and it would have been rather nice to go . . . say to Kenya or somewhere like that. But with small children, obviously, you wanted to take a leave somewhere that was tolerably civilised . . . supplies of decent fresh water.[19]

The Aden Airways manager spoke of his interest in meeting people outside the expatriate community:

I suppose I've always been a bit of a rebel on that sort of thing, and I certainly widened my entertaining to bring in local staff that I got to know through the company. I think some of my expatriate friends were slightly scandalised by this – it didn't seem to be the right thing to do.[20]

According to a former BP employee:

There were one or two people who worked closely with the Arabs. One or two developed a liking for their way of life and took what opportunities there were. I think some of the doctors had a wider interest . . . a humanitarian interest, and did a bit more field work on their own account. But I think the majority of us were horribly suburban, and somewhat distant from . . . I mean, I had an awareness of some of the political issues and an involvement with industrial relations because of my job, but 90 per cent of the people working in the refinery had a job to do, that was refining or bunkering – delivering ships' bunkers – and that was their job and they did it. And they went out and enjoyed themselves on their own terms.[21]

Another man recalled: 'I had Arab friends, who were delightful, and who were – I think – possibly – apologetic about what was going on.'[22]

A woman who accompanied her husband, a medical officer, to Aden in the 1950s, recalled her involvement in various social welfare activities:

For the first year or two, I was involved in social work in Aden colony, Steamer Point. I was with the Girl Guides, and was actually the base secretary at that point, which means a lot of communication with headquarters and London. And then I was involved with giving out ghee and food at some of the local clinics, where we saw the need for some of the children who were very undernourished. Later, I was based in Little Aden and the travelling across the causeway, which was then about 20 miles long, was not easy. And I discovered that the children in Little Aden, although they had the facilities that BP could give them, did not have any of the children's clubs. So I spoke to the local padre; he started the Cubs for the boys and I started Brownies for the girls. We had great help from BP; you mentioned what you wanted and they'd give it to you. So we had no hardship whatsoever . . . and so I continued with social work in that area. After [her son] went back to school in the UK, I continued working with the Guides. By now it was quite easy to commute to the other side, and eventually – because I took over from the retiring commissioner, I think in 1962 . . . or '63 thereabouts – it became evident that we were going to have great difficulty if an Arab commissioner was appointed, for this person to go into all the areas, especially the military ones. And then I started negotiation with the UK concerning the splitting up of the districts and the making one for British and foreign folks and the other for local Arabs. This was eventually achieved with the translation of the handbook and the bringing all the tests up to date to suit Arab girls. And, eventually, it went through.[23]

Others had somewhat darker recollections of British-Yemeni relations. A former BP worker, for example, recalled that

we had 'A' class housing, 'B' class housing and 'C' class housing; of course the expatriate British were in 'A', the Indians and other Europeans were in 'B' and the Arabs were in 'C'. And I was always a bit uncomfortable because we were bringing on people to take more senior positions and they did come and join us . . . the senior Arabs joined us in our 'A' class housing, but it generated things like a letter from an Indian who wrote to me about problems he had with educating his 'B' class child. And I thought to be labelled in that way was very demeaning. It was set by the time I arrived there. The refinery had been developed in 1953 and so it had become part of the infrastructure. There was this awful word that was used to describe the 'C' class housing . . . it got Arabised as 'sikelas' . . . and so it got enshrined in the language. Sikelas housing, which the local Arabs had. And that was discriminatory, and it was a difficult thing to administer. I mean, it was accepted because of what was available, but it was not comfortable . . . not comfortable.[24]

A public health inspector described how they attempted to combat diseases:

One of the duties was vaccination against smallpox. We had female vaccinators who went round and vaccinated all the young children – the infants – and, later on, I went round with them. Those children were brought, every so often, to our office and I examined the child and saw that the vaccination had been given, and we issued a vaccination certificate. Very often, that was considered as a birth certificate. They had no birth certificates but they could produce a vaccination certificate, so you knew that the child was born within, perhaps, three weeks or so of the date of their vaccination.

Where there was smallpox, people were hiding it. It was beneath them to admit there was smallpox in their house. So, one time, we got permission from the courts to do a house-to-house search in a street in Steamer Point, and we unearthed 20 cases of smallpox that had been hidden. Our smallpox hospital moved to Shaikh Othman and I had to go there every day to see that the hygiene was being carried out and, on one occasion, I had to send my driver with a van – because we had no ambulance, just a van – to pick up a smallpox case, but the driver wouldn't go; he was afraid – he had a young family and he was afraid he would get the disease. So I had no alternative but to dismiss him, and I had to drive the vehicle, and I took my science inspector with me; both of us lifted the patient in the bed, put him in the van and took him to the hospital at Shaikh Othman. But unfortunately he died. I've seen quite a number of deaths from smallpox in Aden.

Tuberculosis was another thing, but I wasn't closely associated with that. There was trachoma, leprosy . . . one or two cases where I found leprosy cases and tried to get them to go to the hospital, but they wouldn't go. So I contacted our female medical staff who would come down and speak to them and give them medicines. Later on, when I met them, they were thanking me and thanking me because it was surprising the improvement they had. Diphtheria was another thing . . . meningitis, typhoid, pneumonia. There was Bilharzia, which was contracted upcountry, from a snail swimming in the water. And dysentery – 2,700 cases I think it must have been in a year. And influenza. We didn't have cholera, but it was in Iraq at the time and it was on the march.[25]

Anecdotes provide a rich context in which to appreciate everyday life. A former water engineer, for example, related narratives rich in detail:

Upcountry, my work involved acting as an adviser to the sultans and shaikh; and also visiting isolated islands . . . to check on the situation with regard to desalinisation. Some of these small islands had no water supply whatever . . . natural water supplies, and we had to install distillation plant. And it needed attention from time to time, and I used to fly up occasionally, just to check the situation to make sure that the plant was working efficiently. Some of these visits were quite interesting because I used to manage to get a . . . thumb a lift,

possibly with one of Her Majesty's representatives ...
Commissioners for the island; and they would alight from
the plane first because ... being her Majesty's representative. The red carpet would be rolled out, no matter where it
was, whether it was upcountry or on the islands, and when
it was my turn to step off the plane, the carpet was rolled up
just ahead of me![26]

A retired doctor also spoke about the problems of water:

The health in the villages was appalling ... tuberculosis was
rife ... all the diarrhoeal diseases were prevalent. The water
supplies were absolutely ... some of them were appalling.
There was plenty of water in the Protectorates but, in the likes
of Beihan, the wells were 120 foot deep. But the water that
came up was good water. We managed to get – or at least the
Political Service managed to get – pumps put in, to pump the
water up for them. But, in true Arab fashion, they broke
the pump and went back to camels walking round in circles,
or donkeys ... There was one area where they took exception
to our presence and poisoned the well; fortunately they
poisoned it with a stuff that coloured the water blue so we
knew the well had been poisoned. So obviously we couldn't
drink it.[27]

Although a few British civilians seemed to have been unaware
of or uninterested in the environment of escalating nationalist
agitation, most alluded to it, either in passing or as a pressing
concern. A former BP employee spoke of his experiences of labour
relations with local Adenis:

Industrial relations, which was my main role for the five years
I was there, had initially been a straightforward matter of
negotiation between employer and the representative of the
employees. The trade union movement in Aden was under
the leadership of a man called Al-Asnag, who became one
of the well-known political leaders. In the early days, it was
very straightforward ... I had held an industrial relations job
in the UK and the feel of it wasn't terribly different, in the first
phases. But, by 1964, the political situation had deteriorated.
We'd had some of the first attacks on civilian targets, and the

actual procedural conduct of industrial relations itself became highly politicised, such that in late October 1964, I received in my office a list of non-negotiable demands from the union which was in the form of 12 demands, the first of which was a 200 per cent increase in pay and the others were for various improvements of . . . not quite so outstandingly exaggerated but all very difficult to make any concessions on. And it was clear that this was politically motivated. The threat was that, if we didn't concede to these demands immediately, they would take industrial action . . . unspecified. So there was some urgent consultation between the general management of BP locally, with the local . . . the Governor, and also with London, and it was decided that – on this occasion – no attempt would be made to negotiate, being judged that it was political and not industrial. And so we turned down their demands on 1 November, and they started industrial action, which took the form of a go-slow. And clearly – again – there was political influence at work . . . The job was still going on to a certain extent; there wasn't an out and out strike. But it had some comic effects. The . . . sadly comic I suppose . . . the people who worked in the offices – and they were mostly men – either as clerks or typists, or working on the computer input machines of the day, they would lift one finger and press a key and put their hand back in their lap, then lift another press the next key and put their hand back in their lap. And they kept this kind of thing going, very patiently, for weeks on end.[28]

Another man who worked for BP also touched upon labour relations:

The trade unions could be a bit funny. We only had about one substantial strike while I was there . . . but that didn't last very long. But all the expat staff were then sort of assigned jobs which we would do – they would do – if everybody went out, to try and keep the thing going or, at least, if you couldn't keep it going, shut it down safely. On the whole, it wasn't bad.They used to get up to rather odd things, like insisting that a trade union representative decide who was admitted to the company hospital, which was a little odd, and the doctors didn't like that one little bit. They thought that it should be their decision, medically, whether somebody was admitted. I'm not quite sure why the union seized on that one.[29]

Very rapidly, the situation began to deteriorate and incidents of violence became more common. A woman who accompanied her husband to Aden in 1967 recalled feelings of vulnerability after hearing that the home of friends had been attacked:

It was a shock when they were raided . . . a bomb went off . . . it was fixed in the house and it blew up when they were having a party. They found out it was the servant who put it there . . . and halfway through the party he left. But, up until then, I don't think any of us realised how vulnerable we were. After that, even *our* servants were screened because . . . they were natives. Some were friendly, but you didn't know . . . and that was what made us all suspicious. Even myself and my neighbour, we had the same boy who used to come and clean for us. But we were both . . . sort of leery after that. And we both decided that we'd do our own cleaning and not have him, to be on the safe side.[30]

A man who had worked for BP described the first inklings of violence:

Of course, the disturbances started as a result of political pressure, under the influence of Egyptian terrorists coming on the scene. We heard about bombs being thrown. The first bomb awareness that I think any of us had was when the bomb was thrown into the Air Force family quarters and killed the daughter of one of the very senior RAF officers. It was Christmas, and I think she got glass in her jugular. And so it was a double accident in a sense; the bomb itself wouldn't have killed anybody, but the flying glass did.[31]

According to the retired water engineer:

Towards the end, in 1965 and onwards, the situation deteriorated because of terrorist activities, and life became increasingly hazardous . . . There were several incidents where we were involved directly, in some of the riots. There were riots on

occasion, and the police and the military would get involved
with the rioters, and tear gas would be used. Unfortunately,
when you have tear gas in your eyes, you need water to clear
your eyes and, many years before, I had arranged to raise all
the water meters out of the pavements on to the walls outside the buildings – the reason being, of course, that you could
not read meters inside people's houses because of the *purdah*
system. This was all very well until tear gas was being used,
and then many of these – over two thousand meters in one
afternoon – were moved . . . taken off the walls, and there was
water pouring all over the streets. And we had to do something quick about this because we were losing our levels in
the main reservoir, supplying Crater, and I went out with a
number of staff – as we had previously thought this might
happen and we had bought piles of broomstick handles, cut
them into six inch lengths and tapered them – and there we
were going around between the rioters and the police and the
troops, trying to stop the water flowing out of all these pipes.[32]

A former airline pilot recalled:

Certainly, lives were at risk, but just from ordinary casual
terrorists. My wife and I were in . . . a restaurant-cum-nightclub
in Khormaksar, and I had my Volvo parked outside, and there
was a bang, and a policeman came in and said 'is that your
Volvo out there?' I said 'yes', he said 'well somebody's just
thrown a grenade at it!' Fortunately, the grenade just hit the
back window, broke it and bounced off – before it went off. So
it didn't do my car any damage – it made a bit of a mess of a
Mercedes behind me . . . I had a base plug of a grenade come
rattling on to the veranda one night. The grenade went off
just outside. And, of course, there were people killed. A senior
RAF officer lost his daughter. A grenade was thrown into a
children's party – of all things. It killed this poor little girl.[33]

In the words of the broadcaster:

We had riots. Our radio station itself was bazooked and
machine-gunned one night. I'd been reading the news and I'd
just finished and there were three shuddering bangs from

fairly close to where I was – we were on what was known as Clock Tower Hill, that was where the radio/television station was. And I rushed outside and suddenly realised that somebody had fired at us from fairly close to where we were. I reckoned the only place they could be firing at was our station . . . They'd fired three bazooka shells; one had gone through the control room wall, quite close to the studio where the announcer was working. The second one had gone through the General Purposes Studio, where the soldiers who were waiting to go on guard duty were actually doing a bit of relaxation – I think they were playing cards at the time. And the third one – we only discovered the next morning – had actually hit the ground and ricocheted and gone through the library window, the library being on the first floor, had clipped the sill, and our librarian – a woman – was sitting at the desk, catching up with some extra work, and this thing missed her head by about two inches and buried itself in the wall across the room. They also machine-gunned the outside.

We ended up with a machine gun post on the roof which, I think, is the only time in the history of the organisation that we actually had our own machine gun post, with people like the Paras guarding us. They looked upon it as a key point. And of course, you could drive down one side of the road, from the Crescent down to Tarshyne, and there was a little radio station, and you could drive back. So they had two chances of throwing things at us. So, in the end, they put up big wire screens. There were some very very unpleasant – and sad – cases; for instance, a children's birthday party and a 16-year old girl was killed – I think it was *her* birthday when they threw the grenade in.[34]

Others recollected similarly tragic incidents. According to the water engineer: 'Three of my staff were killed; and, when that happens, it shakes everybody, particularly when you have to deal with the widows. In all cases, they were on their way to work, and they were shot at as they were driving.'[35]

The former headmaster remembered that

it came rather abruptly, a sudden change to being completely at risk. You know you took a chance most of the time but it got to a point where you had to be very careful wherever you went, and keep just to the main roads. You couldn't go down the back streets or into Crater or anywhere. Of course, some of the families were beginning to go home by then so the school was getting a bit run down and we knew it was inevitable that we would go. But we were still left behind for several days after the school had actually closed. And we were there when 'Mad Mitch' was attacking Crater; we could see the tracer bullets flying, literally, over our heads.[36]

Dave Johnston, who was teaching at a school in 1967, has described a violent incident at the school in May of that year:

I taught at Khormaksar Boys' Secondary School, which stood on the route between Ma'alla and Crater where the seashore road from Shaikh Othman joined. The school was the Aden government establishment, not the British Forces' school. English was the main language used by teachers in all subjects, except of course Arabic and Muslim religious instruction. Several members of staff came from India and Pakistan, but most were Adenis. I was Head of the English Department, and also in charge of the English language section of the school library. My department consisted of five teachers, T.D., Chris Dodgson, Mike Maguire, all British, and two Adenis, Abdulla Bazara and Mohammed Munasar.

Edward Townend-Dyson-Townend, popularly known as T.D., was in his late fifties, a retired RAF officer and living in Aden with his wife, Mary. Precise in manner, intelligent and articulate, he was always immaculate in his attire and sported a panama hat. He had been teaching at Bayoumi College, near the village of Shaikh Othman, but was withdrawn when security proved a problem and joined Khormaksar Boys' Secondary. Chris had secured a BA in English and was generally interested enough in languages to attempt Arabic. With his dark good looks, Chris had often been mistaken for an Arab, particularly at army roadblocks where only his native Liverpool accent and turn of phrase had saved him. His sense of humour was sufficiently outrageous for him to accept instances of mistaken identity with a nonchalant shrug of the shoulders. Mike was a cheerful, young PE teacher from Derby and newly arrived with his wife, Avril, in January that year. He assisted with English lessons.

The date was 9 May 1967. As was our custom, we four British teachers used the first floor library at break times instead of the main staff room. I was late arriving at the library that morning. My usual place was occupied by Chris. Exercise books waiting to be marked by me were in front of him, so Chris moved to his customary seat. I opened my mark book and searched for a red pen.

I had not even opened the first exercise book when there were two sudden explosions and a small puff of smoke at the doorway. Total silence followed. Then Chris stood up and yelled in disbelief, 'I've been shot!' He clutched his left arm, whirled and fell to the floor. T.D., Mike and I sat stunned for a further second or two; then we scrambled for cover behind the library bookshelves. Half a dozen pupils who were in the room with us rushed out as one. We four teachers waited for more bullets, but none came.

My heart pounding, I waved T.D. and Mike to stay where they were and approached the door cautiously. I peered both ways along the balcony outside the library, then down into the adjoining stairwell. There was no sign of our assailant. I became aware of the pupils in the courtyard below. They were immobile and hushed, staring in bewilderment up at the library. Retreating inside, I overturned a table to shield Chris from view, in case the gunman reappeared in the doorway to attack a second time. T.D. and Mike were reluctant to move Chris, wanting to avoid exacerbating his injuries. They advised him to lie absolutely still. He admitted later that he felt very exposed on the floor. It was probably then that we realised that with all of us unarmed, the terrorist could have entered and killed us easily.

Leaving T.D. and Mike to watch over Chris, I hurried down to the principal's office to report events. The students had recovered from the shock by then and I thought it rather odd at the time, but the students all cheered in a not unkindly fashion when they saw me. I did not discover until later the reason for their attitude. The principal was a young and talented Adeni, Mr Qirshi, who was to become Chancellor of the University of Aden in later years, I believe. He was as nonplussed at the turn of events as we all were. Nothing like this had taken place in an Aden school before. After a brief discussion it was decided that, as the students would not settle to work again that day, the buses should be called in to take them home. An ambulance was sent for, too. There was some doubt as to which hospital Chris should be taken to, but as he was employed by the Aden government, it was decided to take him to the local hospital.

Before the vehicle arrived, I returned to the library where Chris gave me, for safe-keeping, his watch and wallet, then removed his contact lenses. To keep his spirits up I said, 'This'll give you something to talk about when you get home'. He said later that it had felt as though someone had walloped him on the arm with a piece of wood. One of the two bullets had missed, we realised when Mike, searching around, found a fresh hole in the wall opposite the doorway. Two cartridge cases lay on the floor just inside the entrance. I ringed where they had fallen with a piece of chalk, then moved them with a pencil in case any fingerprints could be found.

The Adeni police arrived and surveyed the scene, made notes and took statements. The bullet was dug out of the wall and found to have a cross cut in its nose; a very nasty wound is inflicted by such a bullet. Chris was soon on his way to the Queen Elizabeth Hospital where he was operated upon. Apparently the bullet had hit him above the left elbow, then travelled the length of his arm. As the bullet could not be located, it was assumed that it had ricocheted back up to his arm and exited by the same hole! Three days or so later, when the swelling in his arm had gone down, he could feel a hard lump in the upper part of his arm halfway between his elbow and his wrist and there was the bullet. It was extracted and Chris kept it in his wallet for several years until he lost it.

In discussion with pupils after the incident, it seems that the rumour had spread that Chris was a spy planted by the security forces. How else could his interest in Arabic be explained, and why did he look like an Arab? In addition, Chris had bought some shirts from the Army and Navy Stores before leaving for Aden. These shirts had epaulettes with holes for attaching badges of rank and this reinforced doubts among pupils. Such was the climate of suspicion, totally unwarranted, that prevailed. Whoever the assailant was, he was never identified.

Mr Johnston added that, 'in a letter dated 20th May 1967 from the Ministry of Education, Al-Ittihad, all expatriate teachers were offered terms for release from contracts, following the shooting at Khormaksar Boys' Secondary School'.[37]

A former BP employee described how the situation for the British deteriorated as nationalist agitation, encouraged by Egyptian president, Abd al-Nasser, intensified:

> We got things like school students coming out on strike. I remember one incident when it had been reported that British tanks had been sent to quell a demonstration by Arab school-girls. You can imagine, a whole squadron of these things advancing down the road towards Crater, guns lowered on this mob of small girls. But, a few days after this had been reported, we happened to see the colonel of the tank regiment, and we asked him, 'what have your boys been up to?' and he said, 'well, what *actually* happened was – there were two scout cars down there, no guns, the people in them didn't even have any weapons with them; they had drivers under instruction. They saw a mob of children ahead of them. They went smartly into reverse and came home!' These things tended to get wildly exaggerated. There was an MP who actually produced a rock in the House of Commons and said, 'this was thrown at me by a dissident Arab'. He'd been up to Abyan, wearing a pin stripe suit, and got stoned. We got stoned once. And that was within a mile of Little Aden, in a fishing village; they suddenly decided they didn't like the look of us very much. We should have had a few small coins to chuck to them, I suppose, followed by a volley of very small rocks . . . But that sort of thing can happen anywhere, anytime, in that part of the world.[38]

The retired journalist commented:

> My feeling at the time was that the troubles were controlled from Cairo. The Yemenis were certainly . . . it appeared to me, to be supplied with weapons, grenades . . . I got the impression

there were good Yemenis working in Aden, working in the Port, who were being pressurised by terrorists to carry out terrorist functions. And, if they didn't, then their families back in Yemen would suffer as a result. I believe this was the case of the Yemeni who threw the grenade into the Tarshyne Officers' Club during a function; luckily the grenade just went 'bang' and it wounded a few people, but minor wounds.[39]

His suspicions were echoed by a doctor, who remarked:

There was obviously a propaganda network because Cairo Radio mentioned our CO by name . . . But the propaganda was all wrong because he was supposed, every night, to be annihilating thousands of Arabs; and we know for a fact that he was annihilating a bottle of whiskey at the time.[40]

The end arrived abruptly. In November 1967, Britain finally withdrew from Aden, leaving the south Yemenis to fend for themselves. It was, in the view of many observers, an ignominious, messy departure. According to the retired airline pilot:

Unlike most of the colonies that became independent, there was no . . . for a lot of them it didn't do them much good in the long run – like Uganda and so forth – but nevertheless, there was a proper handover to a proper government. You know – the flag came down and everybody saluted and shook hands all round, and away they went. It didn't happen in Aden, you see. Aden was, as I say, it was an evacuation. You know, they were still shooting each other when we left.[41]

The doctor had mixed feelings:

I wasn't sad to leave Aden. I'd go back to Aden . . . well, I wouldn't really because, obviously, things have changed, and you should never go back to where you've been happy. But I think I was happy because of the people around me, both Arabs and British. Thinking back, I probably had more Arab friends than British friends, because they're really quite friendly people.[42]

A woman, too, recalled: 'There were a few of the Arabs we were friendly with; they invited us into Khormaksar, into Crater. And some of the ones that worked with us, I've often wondered what happened to them, because things weren't right; I knew they weren't right'.[43]

In the words of the water engineer:

> The sad thing was, on the last night we were there, before we flew out . . . I'd left because, in fact, my life had been threatened; I was advised by the security people to move out, and most of the senior people had . . . had their lives threatened. I was due to come on leave and, just before the . . . before we left in 1967, I remember . . . We packed up but, on the night before we left, many of my staff came up at night, under cover of darkness, to say goodbye. It was a very moving experience.[44]

He concluded:

> I feel, generally speaking – taking the overall picture – that we can be proud of what we did there. We may not be able to say the same thing about other places where we've been but . . . I think, in Aden, most of the people that I worked with – Europeans and certainly the local staff – we were all feeling that we had a job to do and we got on with it, despite whatever problems we had. And there was great camaraderie amongst people who were working together. And I think . . . I like to look upon my days in Aden as one of the happiest times of my career, because I was enjoying doing the work and you could see the results of your work, and you could see people appreciating it.[45]

One gets a sense from the British narratives of great variety. While many people cared little for local aspirations and were seeking adventure, career advancement or money, clearly many of those who were in Aden at the end had an interest in the welfare and even the sentiments of Yemenis fighting for independence. Nonetheless, the process of collecting British testimonies was, on the whole, a pleasant experience. Almost everyone seemed pleased to see me and only too happy to share what seemed on the whole to have been enjoyable memories.

CHAPTER NINE

AN ORAL HISTORY OF COLONIALISM AND REVOLUTION IN SOUTHERN YEMEN

Maria Holt

Oral history is built around people. It thrusts life into history itself and it widens its scope. It allows heroes not just from the leaders, but from the unknown majority of the people . . . It brings history into, and out of, the community. It helps the less privileged, and especially the old, towards dignity and self-confidence. It makes for contact – and thence understanding – between social classes and between generations.[1]

When people in Aden heard that I was collecting 'oral history narratives' of the final years of British colonial rule, they would exclaim 'Ah, you're here to talk to the old people.' There are few 'old people' left but even those with only the haziest memory of the British, or no memory at all, are keen to offer their opinions about that period of their history. Yemenis today often remark on Britain's long stay in their country. The British, observe some, were in Yemen for 129 years, yet they achieved nothing. Accusations of mismanagement are frequent. One wonders, however, if such judgements spring from a realistic assessment of history or a deep sense of betrayal in Britain's behaviour at the end.

As we have seen in preceding chapters, the impact of British policies on southern Yemen was somewhat mixed. Although some British individuals, both at official and unofficial levels, claim that Britain brought prosperity and development to this area, others dispute this. Generally absent in this discussion are the voices of the various Yemeni participants in the often painful process of cooperation with the colonial authorities or, in many cases, anti-colonial struggle. The fight for national liberation, which began in the 1950s, intensified from the early 1960s, with episodes of violence and cruelty on both sides. This chapter will consider Yemeni perspectives on the final days of British rule in Aden and the surrounding areas, in terms of nostalgia, anger and hurt. Choice or very often chance led me to the individuals who agreed to participate in the oral history project and the results can by no means be regarded as representative of the population as a whole. For example, I met no one who admitted to having 'thrown the bombs' or 'fired the guns', although several people said they were members or supporters of the two main national liberation groups. Their oppositional activities included demonstrations against British rule and the dissemination of revolutionary material, but all disavowed any involvement in violence. Others said they had little involvement in anti-British agitation. They spoke of trying to do the best they could for themselves and their families in the face of escalating instability. Some actively supported the British administration. This did not mean, however, they were uncritical of Britain's presence.

Bearing in mind the constraints, the following is intended to be a portrait of a particular period of history in the words of some of the people who witnessed it. It is their version of 'truth'. It is clear from other accounts that the final years of British rule was a turbulent and frequently brutal period in which imperialist and nationalist politics clashed and acts of violence were committed by all sides. Memory, however, does not always or exclusively focus on the 'grand events' of history. Individuals often chose to extract smaller, more personal details, perhaps as a way of making sense of the whole, although there was also a tendency to stand back and comment on the larger picture. In my view, the value of the testimonies lies, on the one hand, in their revelation of 'ordinary' life for Yemenis in 1960s Aden and, on the other, in their opinions of and response to events unfolding at the time.

ADEN IN THE FINAL DAYS OF BRITISH RULE

Let us begin by trying to glean a picture of Aden in the early 1960s. It was, by all accounts, a bustling cosmopolitan place, a 'hub' of the British Empire, an exciting environment in which to live. It was also a city with a long and proud history. Many narrators emphasised the multi-cultural character of Aden at that time. According to a former resident:

> Aden is a very very old city; it's about three thousand years old and, being an important trade centre and harbour, the society has always been cosmopolitan. It attracted people from Africa, from India – long before the British came. During the British days again, Aden attracted a lot of nationalities: Indians, Pakistanis, Persians, Italians, Somalis, Ethiopians, and there was also a Jewish community living in Aden . . . and these people lived like a family. I remember, they were treated equally. There was no discrimination against anybody, either by colour, nationality or even religion. The Jewish, Christians and Muslims had their own holy places, their own practices; they used to practice them quite freely.[2]

Said a man who came to Aden as a young boy from the neighbouring Governorate of Lahej:

> Aden was a great city at that time. Life was easy. Things were very cheap because, in 1850, the British had passed a decree making Aden Harbour – Aden Port – the first free port in the world. At that time, Aden Port received about a hundred big ships in a month.[3]

Another man recalled the port area, known as Tawahi or Steamer Point:

> I remember the big number of tourists who were roaming across The Crescent and the front side of the seaside . . . seeing nationalities from all over the world, tourists . . . coming, stopping, buying goods from the tax free shops in Aden . . . There were people from all over the world, passing by. The port was busy and active, the hotels full. I used to be very happy when going to visit my uncle in Tawahi because of seeing the people, seeing the ships arriving.[4]

A woman commented that

Aden was a beautiful country. To live in Aden at that time
. . . it was multi-cultural . . . many different kinds of people
were living there, and there was so much warmth amongst the
people . . . We had Jews, Hindus, British, Somalis, and Arabs
of all kinds . . . Until this day, when I encounter people who
lived in Aden at that time, they said that they roamed the
world but there was no place like Aden.[5]

There was an element of pride in the inclusive nature of Adeni
society. According to one man:

During my studies, we were studying together with Jews and
with Hindus and Somalis . . . and they were really nice days
we spent together . . . we were being taught by Sudanese
teachers. And, during the secondary school, by Jordanians also
and Hindus who were teaching us chemistry and physics.[6]

Many narrators started with an account of their early life. They
recalled childhood, education and their encounters with the
British. According to one man, born in Aden in the mid-1950s,

I was born in the new hospital which was built in Aden at
that time; it was called the Queen Elizabeth hospital in
Khormaksar. And my mother still remembers – vividly – the
kind of professional services which used to be given in that
specialist hospital . . . At that time, Aden was growing so
fast because of the big and vast buildings which were being
built in Khormaksar and in Tawahi and in Ma'alla because
of the changeover of the British air forces . . . they were moved,
I think, because of the troubles in Cyprus, and also perhaps
in Suez . . . My early childhood was spent in Crater . . . and
Crater was, at that time, the commercial centre of the city of
Aden.[7]

One man described his school days in the British educational
system in Aden as 'the golden days'.[8] A woman remarked on the
strangeness of life:

I went to the primary girls' school in Shaikh Othman; it was
1952, I was six then, and my first experience was that I was

asked with the other students to go and meet the Queen [when she visited Aden] . . . that was my first experience of knowing that we were ruled by the British . . . and what astonished me was thinking, 'oh, she is my queen but why is she white and I am not?' You know, because I was six then. So, how come she is not the same colour as me?[9]

A man now living in the Yemeni capital, Sana'a, also mentioned this occasion: 'I still remember the Queen coming in 1953, during the coronation. And we were holding flags. I was at Steamer Point when she passed by. We were at school at the time. And there was a feeling that we are one, we are British'.[10]

One senses a sort of nostalgia on the part of some narrators. Said one man:

I had the happiest times of my life in Aden until 1967. We had the best education in Aden. We had Scottish teachers who were very broad-hearted people. They encouraged us to learn English . . . English was very much liked in the early days and everything – the medium of instruction in schools – was English.[11]

Others echo these feelings of warmth towards the British educational system. A man recalled that,

in 1950, I went to school in Aden where I finished the primary school and intermediate and, in 1957, I took the exam, the competitive exam to go to Aden College, which was – at the time – one of . . . or *the* best secondary school, I would say, in the Arabian Peninsula.[12]

He added:

I spent four years in Aden College until 1961, when I took GCE 'O' Level – University of London – and then two years more to take Advanced Level subjects and, from there, I applied to study medicine. I was accepted at Liverpool University, and I got a scholarship from Aden Municipality at that time.[13]

A man born in the early 1940s in Crater said:

I started my education in the primary school which used, at that time, to be called the Sailors Schools; now it has become a museum. After four years, I moved to the preparatory school and, after three years of preparatory education, I joined Aden College, which led to the GCE; I did my 'O' levels. Unfortunately, I couldn't get a scholarship from the government so my father decided to send me to Cairo. I went to Cairo in 1961 and stayed for two years but, because I didn't have English language as a subject in my GCE certificate, that hindered my joining the School of Medicine at the University of Cairo. So my father decided to send me to the UK in order to pursue my education to become a doctor.[14]

In the words of another man, whose family originally came from India:

During the British occupation, English was a compulsory language. There were two types of education; one was government and the other was national. In the national school, you had a chance to be taught in Gujarati, Urdu, Arabic and English, in primary school. And then, I think the intermediate was English, Gujarati and Arabic. But the secondary was English only. There were some Hindus who built their own school . . . and those who were Muslim Indian used to go there or to an Arabic school. The national schools used to charge fees but the government schools were free; the education was free up to the secondary, even the text books; and they used to give us free milk when we were children – in the government not the national schools.[15]

A man whose father, a pioneering educationalist, founded the Aden Commercial Institute in 1927 recollected

in Aden, we had a number of schools. These were government schools, grant aid schools and private schools. The government schools accepted only those people who were Aden-born and who had birth certificates. And those who were not born in Aden, or who had no birth certificate, the only place to go were the private schools – so that was my father's school, the Aden Commercial Institute; or there was the St Joseph's School, which was called RCM – Roman Catholic Mission School; and we had St Anthony's School, and there was one Indian school, called Gujarati School. There was also a Muslim school.

He added:

There was a great need for education of girls. My father requested my sisters to leave their government teaching posts and join his Institute. He opened a school called Muslim Girls' School in September 1952, and he did all he could to have this school for Muslim girls. And we had, at the beginning, about 120 girls from First Primary up to Fifth Primary. They studied the *Qur'an*, Arabic language, English language, history, geography, domestic science.[16]

His views were echoed by a man who trained as a lawyer during the British period, who observed:

Education was provided for girls up to the intermediate level only. The British at that time always said – or rather gave the excuse – that the local communities were against education in general for their children and particularly for women. But this was not totally true. There would always be certain factions and certain families who would not want their girls to be educated but, at the same time, there were so many others who did want their girls to be educated, and yet this opportunity was not provided.[17]

Although many young people in Aden benefited from British education, and some even received scholarships to study in Britain itself, it could not prevent increasing discontent with the colonial system. Some of the narrators outlined in detail their experiences of discrimination and their frustration with the inadequacies of the system. According to a man who studied accountancy:

They used to consider the local and the expatriate in a different way . . . they tried to give him more or less the same salary with the exception of some allowances – these were for the Europeans . . . like inducements, extra allowances to which locals were not entitled.[18]

The lawyer commented:

> In Aden, a very fair criticism of the British administration
> can be made, which has been admitted by quite a few former
> governors and high commissioners after their retirement,
> which was that the pace of education was very slow indeed. My
> late father was always fighting for more and more education, for
> compulsory education for children in the preparatory school,
> or earlier years of education at least. But even that was not
> provided. In the only secondary school, their admission was
> limited in number, and that was not enough.[19]

Another man noted that, 'even after 128 years of British rule, there
were still no universities'.[20]

According to another man, born in Aden in the 1930s,

> At that time, of course, Aden was flourishing. It was a free port;
> everything was cheap. But, at the same time, we had the
> feeling that the British were here and only a few Adenis – six,
> seven or eight – had the chance to be at the high, top level.
> Otherwise, all other Adenis were employees. At the top level,
> they are either British or Indian or Parsees, and then we come
> after them . . . That's why people started to feel that it is time
> for independence. The other reason was that the British were
> only interested in developing areas which could serve them.
> Even in Aden itself, very few roads were built, a few houses,
> but mainly for British soldiers and their families. It was not for
> Yemenis. Nobody could afford to go and live in that flat or that
> building.[21]

A woman expressed the view that,

> in spite of all the prosperity and all the warmth, there was
> one drawback. In the British time, there was too much
> concentration on Aden – for example, English-speaking
> schools, the port area, the refinery at Little Aden . . . and it
> created a sort of grudge in other governorates, where people
> were illiterate and where they had no schools and no health
> care.[22]

Her husband concurred with this reading of events. People in the hinterlands and the protectorates, he said,

> felt jealous that we benefited from all the schools, the hospitals, the colleges and everything, while they were deprived of that. And I would say that this was the main reason for the extremists taking power. So that is why I say I blamed the British – for handing power to the extremists and not taking care of the protectorates.[23]

Some narrators mentioned the 'discipline' of British rule. According to a member of the one of the former ruling families:

> We were brought up with rules and regulations. Whether you like them or dislike them, you must admit they did a very good job in many areas. Education, for instance, the courts, law and order. It is something you don't inherit, unfortunately, you have to acquire it. After the British left, there was a complete change; there was no rhyme nor reason. The ones who came after the British destroyed the civil service. I wish they had kept the civil service intact but, after independence, it was completely shattered.[24]

In the words of another man: 'There was a lot of discipline. We used to have discipline. The traffic rules, for example, were very good. Now it's become upside down; when they see a "no entry" sign, they go in!'[25] For a third narrator,

> people during the British time were okay. There was law and order and civil institutions. Everything was organised, everything was done through institutions. So if you ask any member of the public, they feel sad and sorry that the British have gone, because things have become not only one thousand and one times worse, it has become a million and one times worse.[26]

The comparison between the so-called 'order' of British rule and the 'chaos' of ensuing events – from the achievement of independence and the socialist regime of the People's Democratic Republic of Yemen to the unification with northern Yemen in 1990

– was a persistent theme and is a clear example of individuals trying to make sense of events most felt were beyond their control. An element of confusion can also be discerned. While most Yemenis recognised the necessity of independence, some still harboured a yearning for the 'law and order' of British times, and this was sometimes experienced as disloyalty.

INCREASING INSTABILITY

The early 1960s was a period of great upheaval in Aden and the surrounding territories as internal and external forces battled for a change in the status quo and ordinary people, on all sides, found themselves caught up in violence. Encouraged by agitation both from nationalist groups within the country and also developments outside, many young people became involved in the struggle for liberation. There were numerous 'terrorist' attacks against British interests and individuals; and, in response, the British adopted harsh and repressive measures. I think it would not be accurate, however, to argue that everyone actively opposed British rule. Some local Yemenis benefited from educational and employment opportunities provided either directly or indirectly by the British. At the same time, there is no doubt that agitation for some form of independence affected the majority of the population. A man who was studying engineering at the time told me that, between 1965 and 1967, 'there were a lot of strikes, and some of the students were threatening to close the classes'.[27] A woman who was born in the late 1940s spoke of the great impact that the national liberation struggle had on her:

> I started to understand what was happening in the world when I was eight years old, in 1956. I saw the labour strikes in the streets of Crater . . . That period was very important to me. I started to recognise that there were things happening in the Arab world. People were asking for their liberation. They were moving towards independence.[28]

Yemenis recollect the period with mixed feelings. A man who had described his school days in Aden as 'really nice', continued:

During that time, I was with Aden Airways and, after marriage, I joined the Aden Trade Union Congress, where we used to fight for our rights for freedom and also for labour's rights. And, in the Aden Trade Union Congress, we used to have a very rough time with the British authorities. I remember . . . going to prison sometimes . . . During the '60s, we . . . had a bit of a rough time because there were a lot of liberation movements, and we used to have explosions . . . shootings everywhere, and the place was really in chaos . . . We used to go out on demonstrations and ask for the liberation of the country.

Yet he acknowledges that, 'under the British in the south, we had the privilege of good hospitals, good schools, good education . . . while, in the north, things were really underdeveloped and they hardly had one paved road in Sana'a'.[29]

What emerges from the interviews with Yemenis is a degree of idealism. A man who was a member of the National Liberation Front (NLF) in 1966 said: 'We were fighting and struggling for our independence; we wanted to implement socialism.' But he also spoke about the complexity of the situation at that time, particularly the struggle between the NLF and the other main national liberation group, the Front for the Liberation of Occupied South Yemen (FLOSY). Instead of a united Yemeni front fighting for independence from the British, he said, they had a war between the NLF and FLOSY.[30]

By the late 1950s, Britain – realising that some sort of change was inevitable – supported the formation of a Federation of Arab Emirates of the south. Its constitution, accepted by the six sultans of the western protectorates, was replaced by a 'Federation of South Arabia' constitution in early 1963 when Aden and five more western protectorates signed on.[31] These and other steps, in Carapico's view, 'were meant to bolster support for British policy, which by then was to hand power over to a constitutional federation comprised of Aden and all the protectorates'.[32] A man from the province of Lahej just outside Aden, described the federation in the following terms:

The feeling of people in Aden was that this was a bad thing, that the federation was not going to work . . . From the time when the NLF raised the slogan of fighting against the British for independence, the federation was over. People felt that the British should not hand independence to these sultanates or to the federation, because they would be puppets; it would not be a free country. One of the accusations made against British policy in Aden was that it dealt only with the sultans, who were not well educated; nor did they take into consideration the opinion of the people.[33]

A man who was in his mid-teens in 1966 spoke of the deteriorating situation:

> We were not allowed to stay in the streets after six o'clock. The riots started; and bombs started. In fact, the strikes and demonstrations started in the streets in 1964. People wanted to have independence from the British. Everybody was demonstrating. Even our teachers used to leave the school to join the demonstrations. I was so young . . . too young. But of course I was asked to leave school and join the demonstrations. And there was no danger really; there was only the tear gas . . . we used to see the British troops coming down the street, but only shooting tear gas.[34]

A woman now living in Sana'a recalled vividly the introduction of curfews in Aden:

> My two sons were born in Aden and, interestingly enough, their births coincided with historical events. My first son was born in the clinic in Crater and, at the moment I was taken to the labour room, I heard the head nurse telling my family, come and see her in the theatre – she has delivered a boy, because – in a few minutes, for the first time in the history of Aden – curfew was enforced. This was due to an assassination of . . . I think it was Sir Charles somebody . . . it was 31 March 1964. And so they imposed a curfew from that time, and it continued for two years and eight months, until the moment my second son was born![35]

Quickly, however, riot control turned more violent. In the words of the one eyewitness: 'I remember, the first killing was in 1964, the first shooting. In those days, the people didn't have any weapons, they didn't have arms; they used to throw stones at the British soldiers.'[36] A woman reported that, by the early 1960s,

> the British army presence was very apparent in the streets – British army lorries and land rovers, with bazookas – fully armed – around the streets. One day, I was returning from my family in Khormaksar. I was driving and, after I passed the roundabout of the cinema in Mansoura in Shaikh Othman, I heard a very big explosion. To my knowledge then, as I saw British army vehicles, I thought it was meant to be for them. So I went back home and just as I entered the house, there was a phone call from the Deputy Attorney General of Aden saying that something serious has happened in Makawi's house. And later we found out that three or four of his children had been killed.[37]

She is referring to the murder, in February 1967, of three of the sons of Abdulqawi Makkawi, a representative of one of the old Aden families, by the NLF. In her view, the British army presence should have protected the Makkawi family. In the months that followed, 'FLOSY and the NLF murdered each other in growing numbers as well as fighting the colonial power whose withdrawal had been announced already'.[38] In the words of the woman narrator:

> They started killing each other, the NLF and FLOSY. There was rivalry between the two fronts, fighting for independence. But, for me, I was furious that the British army was there so how come they couldn't protect an innocent family? Only sons and daughters and the mother of those children, living in their own home. While the politician, Makkawi, was already in exile in Cairo. Why did the British let these things happen? Because they were responsible, they were the ones who colonised Aden; they were the ones who were supposed to look after people. They had the army, they had the intelligence . . . So that was actually the incident that triggered my anger against the British.[39]

Besides anger, many narrators expressed disappointment at Britain's behaviour. In the words of a man who trained at the BBC in London:

> My feeling towards the British is that, although they ruled Aden for 129 years . . . they have done nothing. It's not like Kenya, not like Hong Kong now, not like India. Even the preparation to take over . . . when the British left, we didn't have the experience to run many things, to develop . . . I feel they have deceived us.[40]

He continued:

> Then they tried to form the federation. But it was only stooges being brought in. And a new constitution was under discussion. But, at that time, everything was collapsing and the British government was no longer interested . . . in the Parliament in London, they were discussing how to pull out. And so everything deteriorated. And they just ran away, ran away and left Aden with no government. Nothing prepared for the new government, for the future of the country. They had promised, during the Geneva Conference, to give some financial help to Yemen, but they never did.[41]

A man who had trained as a doctor during the British period noted that there were 'mixed feelings' when the British left.

> The people who took power, who fought the British, they were quite happy that the British left. But for some of the citizens of Aden – of course a lot of business people and foreign people left because the new government started nationalising some of the companies and banks – for some Yemenis in Aden, life became a bit difficult.[42]

In the words of a former government employee, the British 'just left us; they handed over power to people who didn't deserve it'.[43]

Two important events took place that radicalised the population and hastened the end of British rule. Several narrators referred to the fighting in the mountains of Radfan, which began on 14 October 1963, as the start of the revolution in the south.

Historian Paul Dresch describes the events of October 1963 as follows:

> The Qutaybis of Radfan complained of oppression by the Amir of Dali, in whose domain the British always placed them and who, once the Federation was formed, controlled the purse-strings; the accession of Aden in January 1963 made the problem worse. By May 1963 many were going north for weapons, and at the start of October they submitted a petition which shows how British conceits of 'sound administration' had miscarried . . . In October 1963 a patrol was fired on. The Federal Army intervened, killing Rajih Labuzah, a Quteibi sheikh who had been in the North. The British Army, not just local forces, then launched a major campaign in Spring 1964, leading much of the population to flee, and attempts to cut supply routes to the 'dissidents' spread resistance . . . Radfan was subdued by the British, who were soon sinking wells there and encouraging agriculture, but guerrilla action recurred in many places. The fighting was depicted at the time as war again colonialism, and later as class struggle.[44]

A woman who was a member of FLOSY described these incidents thus:

> In 1963, the NLF and FLOSY in the south and the Nasserist front started the revolution from the Radfan mountains. There were girls, women, men of Aden, all of us. And Aden, as a colony, started to understand that a new movement is happening in the life of the whole country.

She added:

> In Radfan, the first strike of tribes took place, that can be called an uprising against British colonisation. Sheikh Rajih Labuzah, the leader of the tribe, was killed by the British. And that uprising came to be seen later as the start of a revolution in the South . . . 14 October. This year we are celebrating the fortieth anniversary of the revolution in the South which, together with the revolution in the North of 26 September [1962] makes the whole Yemeni revolution.[45]

249

The second incident took place in Crater on 20 June 1967. The main reason behind this, according to General Sharif Haider Saleh Al-Habili, was a 'deteriorating political situation and tension in the region'.[46] Dresch says that 'a mass of plots and discontents exploded within the Federal Army when soldiers rioted north of Aden Town'.[47] A woman narrator observed that

> Crater means the face of the volcano, and the people who lived in this area were 'volcanic'. So they started an uprising. This began with labour strikes and mass gatherings in support of [Egyptian president] Abdul Nasir after the nationalisation of the Suez Canal. The period of 1967 witnessed, of course, the failure of the Egyptians in the 1967 war between the Israelis and the Arabs. This, just two weeks later, encouraged the expulsion of British troops from Crater, and Crater then fell into the hands of the Liberation Front. As soon as the revolutionaries took control of Crater, FLOSY and the NLF began negotiations about how to face the rest of the British forces. But unfortunately, as happens in other such cases, the negotiations resulted in civil war between the two factions'.[48]

General Al-Habili, who was Chief of Staff of the South Arabian Army at the time, noted that heavy shooting took place in the morning of 20 June, a British patrol unit was targeted and 15 British soldiers killed.[49] A man who was a teenager at the time, remembered, 'That day some of the British troops were burnt in the street. And a helicopter was shot down on the mountain of Crater. So Crater was free of the British that day; all the British were kicked out.' He continued:

> But it was only four or five days. After that, we used to see the British, during the night, moving in the streets . . . patrols – walking patrols, driving patrols; and I saw them shooting people. They were shooting because it was a curfew and if they saw anybody, they would suspect him and shoot him.[50]

Another man, now retired, recalled that

> during the siege, we stayed in Crater for about three days. And my cousin, who was director of examinations, had the keys of

Figure 9.1 Crater, briefly 'liberated' from the British in 1967, is today an impoverished and rundown area. It retains much of the housing built by the British and remains a lively commercial centre.

the offices where all the London University GCE examination papers were being kept, but he was trapped in Crater! Every morning, they would allow people to pass for one hour, between eight and nine in the morning. So he managed to get to Khormaksar to the office and was able to distribute the papers to the other centres. That was on 22 or 23 June 1967.[51]

Another narrator remembered the curfews imposed by the British in Crater. One day, he said,

a British official was shot dead so they applied a curfew in Crater from six in the evening until six the following morning, and that was where my family's house was. But one evening, I overstayed outside Crater and could not get back. So I went to stay with my brother and some of his friends in Mansoura and the next morning the house was surrounded by police and British troops because, the night before, these people had tried to shoot a British intelligence officer in Ma'ala. They failed but the next morning came to arrest all of us. I spent 11 days in Ras Morbat prison and one month in Mansoura prison. But I kept telling them that I only came for my summer holidays, I am not a member of the National Liberation Front. After they checked this information with the university, they kindly let me out and put me on the plane to go back and continue my studies.[52]

His brother, however, was not so lucky and was forced to remain in prison until Independence Day.

Others told equally harrowing tales. In the words of one:

During the siege, we decided we should leave Crater. The car was with my brother, the family car, but my cousin who was living with us had a friend who had a Morris Minor. So I took all the family and I drove out of Crater during the early hours of the morning, and then we were stopped by the British, and I told my relatives, especially the males, when we get out of the car, they will of course try to search us. You should open your legs wide, or they will hit you. You know, this is a common thing; it happens everywhere – they are military people. So they came and they said, come out of the car. I said, 'okay, we'll come out, but only the males, not the families, not the females.' They agreed. We went out and they tried to search us – nothing; then he said, 'please open the bonnet.' I told him it wasn't my car; we had borrowed it from a friend. I said, 'this is a Morris, it's a British car – if you know, you can come and help us and open the bonnet.' Then he said, 'okay, you just go'.[53]

A man who later became a diplomat recalls turbulent school days in Aden:

In the mid-'60s, by 1965, when I was already ten or 11, I remember there were demonstrations in the streets, and we were taken out of school and the schools have to stop. We used to go out on demonstrations, the young kids, with slogans and shouting in the streets; and then the police would come and they would throw tear gas bombs. It was quite an experience which I will never forget, feeling suffocated by the smoke and tears running out of our eyes.[54]

Another man reported:

> I was compelled to leave school and go to work; I worked in a bank in Crater. One day, during the day, there was an explosion and the British troops came. They brought us downstairs and, as I was the youngest man within the whole group of staff, he accused me of being the culprit. We were detained in the building until the evening and then they said, 'you can leave,' but we said, 'how can we leave, it's curfew – how can we leave? The other patrols will shoot us.' But our houses were near so we went running . . . It was a very difficult time for me as a young man, but I had to work . . . And when you can speak English, it was a problem because they will keep asking, 'whom do you see, what do you notice, why don't you notify us?' We don't see the people who shoot, who throw the bombs . . . we were peaceful people . . . we had no political participation. But it was very dangerous and difficult'.[55]

There were many stories of personal tragedy. A woman whose brother was active with FLOSY spoke of her anguish when he was killed. During April 1967, she said,

> he was assassinated by other partners of the revolution. He was 22 when he was killed . . . And that was the turning point in my life, where I left Aden, direct to Taiz. Of course, in the situation after my brother was killed . . . I was looking towards how to get revenge . . . I was young, I was 16 years old, he was very close to me . . . When I reached Taiz [in northern Yemen], the FLOSY people there tried to calm me down . . . It happens everywhere, in every national movement; it happens that a brother kills a brother. So these things will be forgiven later on; just let us, first of all, finish . . . the liberation movement and have independence and we will come to know who killed your brother . . . That was a very big turn in my life.[56]

There is no doubt that the perceptions and the language of others affected the ways in which many people remembered this period. While all the Yemeni narrators spoke of the strong and legitimate desire, as in other parts of the world, for independence, many outside commentators defined their struggle in terms of terrorism.

British military historian Stephen Harper, for example, in his description of the brief liberation of Crater in June 1967, writes:

> Mobs celebrated the ousting of British authority from Crater by burning down the Legislative Council building, the British Bank of the Middle East and a secondary school. When daylight broke next morning British troops on surrounding ridges looked down on buildings flying NLF flags and armed Arabs walking the streets.[57]

While official records tend to portray British behaviour as restrained and lawful, the actions of those seeking to overthrow British rule are described in terms intended to convey chaos, barbarism and illegality, and this is bound to influence how local people themselves present their versions of that part of their history; some, clearly, were anxious to justify certain actions as unavoidable and to distance themselves from extremes of violence.

As in most liberation struggles, propaganda and outside interference played a key role. As one Yemeni narrator noted: 'We, as young people at the time, were affected by the Egyptian revolution and its proud ideas; we were against British rule. We were asking to have our independence.'[58] Broadcasting, suggests Gavin, 'became one of the principal means by which popular sentiment was galvanized against British rule. As radios poured into Aden in a mounting flood throughout the 1950s and early '60s, the legitimacy of the British presence was steadily sapped away'.[59]

THE END OF BRITISH RULE

When, towards the end of 1967, the British government decided to withdraw altogether from Aden and the Protectorates, the NLF proclaimed victory and there was general rejoicing among the local population. According to one man: 'Oh, we were very glad and we were very happy. On 30 November 1967, we were celebrating ... at that time, we were so young and all the leadership of the NLF was young; they didn't have any experience in ruling the state.'[60] Another narrator echoes his observation:

We were deceived really because, when the British left, there were only a few people who could run the country and unfortunately these people, after three or four months of independence, were discharged because they thought they were more related to the British than the new NLF government.[61]

According to a man who was not even born when the British ruled Aden and is now foreign editor of a local newspaper:

A lot of people had to leave the country after the British left because of the regime changes that happened here in the south and the terrible injustice that followed. So they always remember the period as the 'golden age' in Aden and, even today, when any new development is happening and any new hope for Aden port, any hopeful new programme or new project, people still refer to the old days. Maybe it's going to return again; maybe we're going to live again in that period. But people of my age[62] divide into two groups; one group is resentful about the fact that Britain did not set up a democratic system before it left – and just left it to the socialists to do whatever they want – and the other group who are hopeful for a new partnership – not aid, not pity . . . just development programmes in partnership with the Yemenis.

The withdrawal of the British regime from southern Yemen was not the 'happy ending' that everyone had wished for. The oral history narratives reveal something of the confusion in many people's minds. Although there was a strong feeling amongst the majority of the population that it was time for Britain to go, many people experienced feelings of betrayal or disappointment about the way in which Britain left. It is clear that many of the Yemenis who experienced that period still harbour what might best be described as ambivalence. This is apparent from their accounts, in which one frequently senses a degree of approval for good medical and educational facilities, the prosperity of Aden itself, but this is tinged with criticism, either overt or implicit, about what Britain had failed to do: it did not build an adequate infrastructure; beyond the city of Aden, there was very little development; and it did not put in place the necessary mechanisms for a successor regime. One senses that, at least for some Yemenis, opposition to British rule was a matter for regret. With hindsight, some people even intimate that matters grew considerably worse after 30 November 1967.

CONCLUSIONS

Any analysis of the data described above would, I feel, be superfluous. The sample is too small to draw meaningful conclusions. However, I would like to make three comments in drawing this chapter to a close. First, in almost every case, Yemeni narrators, in their attempts to grapple with the complex legacy of British colonialism, strove to be scrupulously fair. They acknowledged the benefits, in terms of education, health care and economic prosperity, brought through British control of Aden. At the same time, of course, there was widespread criticism of Britain's failure to put in place the political processes necessary for a smooth transition of power. Many were also critical of Britain's failure to provide even the most basic infrastructure, especially in the areas outside Aden.

My second observation concerns the modern relationship between Britain and Yemen. Almost everyone I met expressed a heartfelt desire for closer relations with the former colonial power. While some were of the opinion that Britain had an unmet responsibility to the people of southern Yemen, others were puzzled by British foreign policy towards their country, which has chosen to implicate Yemen as a whole for the actions of a tiny extremist minority. Many of the testimonies emphasised the obligations many people feel is owed to Yemen by the British.

Finally, I would like to commend the Yemeni narrators who took part in this project. While, for a few, the process evoked pleasant memories, for the majority, it generated feelings ranging from distress at long buried yet still raw recollections to fear at the possible repercussions of participation. I believe the experience of oral history transmission presented more risks to Yemeni narrators and, for this reason, I applaud their decision to contribute their memories.

CHAPTER TEN

BRITAIN AND ADEN

A relationship for the twenty-first century

Maria Holt

In September 2003, 36 years after the British left Aden, I visited the Republic of Yemen, the result of the unification in 1990 of the northern Yemen Arab Republic (YAR) and the People's Democratic Republic of Yemen (PDRY) in the south, to meet some of the Yemenis who remembered the British colonial period. My objective was to record 'memories of empire' but also, as a long-time student of Middle East politics, I was fascinated by the former PDRY, an outpost of Marxism and considered something of an anomaly in the Arab world in its day. Not only had it actively supported the efforts of revolutionary groups all over the world – from Palestinians struggling to liberate their land from Israeli occupation to European communist factions seeking to overturn the status quo in their own countries, it had also championed the rights of women in hitherto unprecedented ways.

It was a fruitful and poignant experience which made it abundantly clear that, far from hating the British, most people in Yemen cannot understand why Britain – given its close historical ties with the area – is not playing a much more constructive role both in Yemen and the wider Middle East. Despite the many criticisms of Britain's unseemly departure from Aden in 1967 and also of British participation in the invasion of Iraq in 2003,[1] a surprisingly large number of Yemenis appear to bear little ill will towards the former colonial power. On the contrary, they bewail the fact that the UK apparently takes so little interest in their country's current political and economic woes.

In this final chapter, I would like to highlight three areas that remain high on the agenda of many of the inhabitants of what is today the Republic of Yemen's second city, Aden: first, the aftermath of British rule, specifically the socialist regime of southern Yemen, which lasted from 1967 to 1990; secondly, the idea and reality of Yemeni unification which has, in many ways, been an uncomfortable marriage of unequal partners; and, thirdly, the current crisis for Yemen in terms of militant Islam, international terrorism and poverty. It seems both a paradox and a matter of some regret that Aden, a bustling and cosmopolitan hub of the empire in the early 1960s, has been reduced to an irrelevant, even threatening backwater, and many Yemenis argue that Britain's responsibility did not end with the hasty retreat of November 1967. I would like to reflect on the development of a more positive relationship between our two countries at the beginning of the twenty-first century.

I began my journey in Sana'a, the capital of Yemen, and spent several days interviewing people who had started life under British colonial rule in the south; most had gone on to be successful in their various fields, such as politics, diplomacy and business. I stayed in the magnificent Old City, a UNESCO World Heritage Site, where I quickly discovered just how badly Yemeni tourism has been affected by perceptions of the country as a haven for terrorists and an unsafe place for western visitors. Sitting on the roof of my hotel, enjoying the autumnal warmth, I marvelled at the startling, almost unreal view of the city. Described by a German traveller in 1810 as 'the finest city I have seen in the Orient', parts of Sana'a 'still present the image of an Islamic community of the early phase of development, in which urban culture was in complete harmony with its natural surroundings'.[2] Between interviews, I walked in the streets and through the market and heard of the many hotels and restaurants forced to close in the Old City because there are no longer tourists. Everyone I spoke to was at pains to reassure me that Yemenis are not terrorists and Yemen is not a dangerous place. They demanded: 'why don't they like us?' Their actions spoke even louder; at no point did I – as a foreign woman on my own – feel uncomfortable; rather than menacing me, local residents were helpful and friendly. A shopkeeper near the hotel invited me to sit with him and drink tea. We talked about history, religion and – inevitably –

terrorism. Unlike in other places, he had no ulterior commercial motives but simply wished to make contact.

The few interviews I carried out in Sana'a were productive and also extremely diverse; they took me from a travel agent, who had developed a passion for cricket during his youth in Aden, to the grand residence of a former general. I began to get the first inklings of what gradually became a pattern as I talked to people; on the one hand, they tend to have relatively positive memories of the British who provided an orderly environment and a good standard of education but, on the other, the desire for independence was growing stronger and individuals displayed conflicting emotions about the 'good' and 'bad' sides of British rule. Natural yearnings for independence, they explained, were fanned from outside, specifically by the Arab nationalist regime of Egyptian President Gamal abd al-Nasir.

At the beginning of October, I left Sana'a – regretfully, for the Old City had started to feel familiar; individuals greeted me as I walked through the streets. I needed to go to the south, however, to the heart of the former British colonial project. With a certain amount of reluctance, I abandoned the idea of travelling by bus through the dramatically beautiful Yemeni interior, having been warned that it was 'too dangerous', and instead boarded a plane to fly over the spectacular terrain.

On arrival in Aden, my first impression was of overwhelming heat. It looks and feels very different from the mountainous north and the ancient elegance of Sana'a. The buildings appear run-down, shabby and, at first sight, one feels that it is not a particularly appealing city, dispersed over a wide, sprawling area, with little sense of a single centre. As a result of its 'hot and damp climate' and lack of tourist accommodation, Aden, as Wald remarks, 'will have to work hard if it is to make itself attractive as a tourist desti-nation'.[3] First impressions, however, are sometimes misleading. My first couple of nights were spent in a beach resort; it was the weekend and families were enjoying the seashore with children and picnics; there was a bar selling alcohol, a television in the room. I ate curry and sat on the beach, speculating on how such a radical ideology had been able to seize power.

Soon after arrival, I began the interview process, assisted by helpful friends and contacts. On the one hand, one could say that interviewees revealed little that was startling but, on the other, a wealth of fascinating detail began to emerge. At first, people tended to speak in a lively, natural way, relating frequently colourful anecdotes but, as soon as the microphone was switched on, they often became formal and relatively unforthcoming. I think many people were apprehensive; they did not know who I was or whether I could be trusted, and there was also a suspicion of to whom the information might be passed on. Perhaps it was a mistake to record the interviews but, as I made clear to the interviewees, it was an integral part of the process and their privacy would of course be ensured.

When the British withdrew from southern Arabia in November 1967, the National Liberation Front (NLF), a group inspired by Marxist ideology, took power. In the end, the battle had been between two factions: the NLF and the Front for the Liberation of Southern Yemen (FLOSY). According to some commentators, youthful passion had far outweighed political experience or forward planning. The victors had little idea of how to build a state and, instead, engaged in the politics of vengeance, murdering many erstwhile rivals and forcing others to flee the country. One man, for example, told me how his brother was imprisoned after Independence because he had belonged to a group that was in conflict with the new ruling regime.[4] The end result, whether by accident or design was 'the most radical embodiment of revolutionary transformationist ideology and practice in the Arab world'.[5]

An interviewee in Aden told me that, when the British finally departed, 'We were very happy, we were celebrating. At that time, we were so young and all the leadership of the NLF was young; they didn't have any experience in ruling the state.'[6] In the words of another,

> the first government was good. It consisted of several educated people. But after that, the left wing, in 1969 . . . the collapse started . . . We started copying the Chinese, the Chinese experience, and then the Soviet experience. We were following the socialist regime and it was the worst thing in all the life of the People's Democratic Republic of Yemen.[7]

According to another man,

the people who took power, who fought the British . . . they were quite happy that the British left. Some of the citizens of Aden – a lot of business people and foreign people – left because the new government started nationalising some of the companies and banks and things, so big businesses left, and some of the Adenis left because life became a bit difficult. Salaries were reduced and some of them said plainly they were sorry that the British had left.[8]

Narrators describe pre-independence Aden mostly as a happy prosperous place, a cosmopolitan city which tolerated religious diversity and attracted business. Britain, it seems, was doing a good job in Aden itself; the problem, according to a number of narrators, lay in the outlying areas, which were generally neglected by the British and, therefore, many local people increasingly felt aggrieved. A theme running through some contributions was that the British should not have left; things have become so much worse since independence. Others explained that of course they should have left but they should also have made better preparations for indigenous rule. The leadership that took over in 1967 was 'good at throwing grenades' but unfitted to govern a country.

According to some, the British period was 'paradise', providing the best schools and hospitals in the Middle East, well-built houses, a bustling prosperous environment, a thriving port, shops that stayed open until midnight, beautifully cultivated gardens. But others tell a different story. One man touched on the element of discrimination between British and Yemenis. It aroused in people, he said,

> something against the British and, when the revolution in North Yemen had succeeded in overthrowing the Imam, these people found an outlet for their feelings. They started gathering in Cairo, with Abd al-Nasir, at that time having his radio and propaganda for the Arab world; so there were some of them trained in Cairo, in Egypt . . . And they started building revolutionary committees.[9]

In the words of a man who was in the final stage of his education when the British left, the new government 'looked towards Arab countries and . . . everything changed: the education system, the healthcare system . . . everything was changing, everything was Arabised'.[10] Another observed that 'the state became the owner of everything, all the businesses'.[11]

After unification, the population experienced declining standards of living, as well as rising poverty and corruption and today parts of the city have a sad neglected air, with rubbish piling up everywhere, qualities of 'third world' cities all over the world. The solidly built and presumably once splendid British-built flats and houses have now fallen into disrepair and many have sprouted ugly extensions on top of the existing structures. There is a feeling of desperate existence although this is partly attributable to the relentless heat. In Crater, which is the oldest part of Aden, constructed in the crater of an extinct volcano, we passed the 'Aden Hilton', which comprises rows of beds in the street where migrant workers can sleep cheaply. Walking around Crater, one senses that it must have once been an impressive place, with its broad streets, fine architecture and green spaces. But now much has changed and many regret the disappearance of 'law and order'. In the words of a narrator: 'The law and order . . . we lost the law and order. We lost the welfare. We lost the business. We lost everything.'[12] At the same time, the vast majority of people in Aden are too young to have any recollection of the British period so are not in a position to make comparisons. In addition, when visiting people's homes, one cannot help but be struck by the comfort and hospitality of domestic environments; I was immensely touched by the kindness with which individuals welcomed me into their houses. Despite the poverty and squalor, Crater is far from depressing. Indeed, during the liberation struggle, it was a focus of resistance, and this remains a matter of pride for residents.

I soon discovered that there were very few Adenis prepared to tell me that the British were terrible. Even some former freedom fighters long for the British to return, although I sometimes doubted the veracity of such assertions. I started to feel that there had to be another way of eliciting information. The over-whelming instinct of Yemenis, as with all Arabs, is to make the stranger feel welcome, not to be discourteous or to raise uncomfortable issues. Unfortunately, this does not help the quest for oral historical authenticity. At the same time, of course, inconvenient information sometimes slips out inadvertently. I gleaned through indirect references that education and housing tended to operate in ways that discriminated against local people. While some took this in their stride, others were clearly pained by unwelcome recollections. One could sometimes sense a conflict between the unsatisfactory nature of colonial rule, which the majority of people wished to end, and the shock of the new regime, which failed, in many ways, to do justice to popular aspirations.

A narrator remarked that a lot of people were forced to leave the country after the British withdrew and 'the terrible injustice' that followed in the form of the socialist government. Therefore, he said, 'they always remember the period as the "golden age" in Aden and, even today, when any new development happens or any new hope for Aden port, people still refer to the old days.' He added that people in Aden

> divide into two groups; one group is resentful of the fact that Britain did not set up a democratic system before it left and the other group are hopeful for a new partnership – not aid, not pity, just development programmes in partnership with the Yemenis.[13]

I have sympathy for the British in 1960s Aden on at least one level – the unremitting sweaty heat which, even at the beginning of October, removes all pretence of dignity – must have had a debilitating effect on people unused to it; some of the locals assured me that it was 'unseasonable' and would start to cool down soon. Thinking back to the English ladies, maybe longing for the gentle breezes and soft hills of home, I felt a twinge of empathy. Otherwise, it is very hard to imagine what they thought they were doing; they had 'no policy', in the words of some of my interviewees; others were of the opinion it was self-interest first and foremost but, argued a few, some attempted to create a good environment for the local people, in terms of education, health, law and order. It all seems so long ago, however, and some narrators appeared bewildered at having to cast their minds back to what must now feel like another world.

Adenis appear different from Yemenis in the north. Another distinction I was advised about is that between city Adenis and people who come into the city from surrounding areas; according to one person, they are ignorant and do not understand real Islam; it is these people who are responsible for creating a reputation for terrorism in south Yemen. In October 2000, an armed attack on the USS Cole in Aden Port resulted in the deaths of 17 American sailors, while two years later, the French tanker Limburg was attacked, killing one crewmember. Close links exist between the former Eastern Aden Protectorate and the family of Osama bin Laden, founder of Al-Qaeda.

Several narrators described their feelings of anger and disillusionment after the unification in 1990 of the northern Yemen Arab Republic and the People's Democratic Republic of Yemen in the south. The majority of people all over Yemen had desired it, having expressed the belief that 'we are all Yemenis', but the anticipated improvements have failed to materialise. It was from the start an unequal partnership; the population of the north at that time was around 11 million while the south contained less than three million. The two former Yemens fought a war over the shape of the new state in 1994 and, after that, the Yemeni Socialist Party, the former rulers of the south, refused to participate in elections, further weakening the southern feeling of belonging. Some people admitted that they would now prefer to be separate again as they believe the south would have a better chance of flourishing economically. They point to the enormous potential of the Aden Port. They also allude to feelings of difference.

One discerns a simmering resentment against the north; all the best jobs, according to several narrators, are taken by northerners and people in the south, they claimed, are being treated badly. I was told that South Yemenis perceive themselves to be victims of discrimination. They see themselves as the educated cosmopolitan ones, who went out and established businesses in the Gulf and elsewhere. Northerners are regarded as barbaric and 'tribal'. According to one person, there is a large and growing underground fundamentalist movement here, which is not discouraged by the government. The movement is fuelled by poverty and lack of opportunity and is not helped by the western demonisation of Islam. During the communist era, although religion was not forbidden, it was discouraged. This is very odd in a pious country like Yemen. How, one wonders, does it explain the 'fundamentalist' movement? According to Carapico, 'in the early twentieth century Islamist political thinking was a radical critique of tradition, a modernizing populist movement with an internationalist outlook ... plenty of tribesmen, *Sayyids*, and *ulama* found common ground with their nephews agitating in the streets of Aden for a radical revolution'.[14]

Soon after I arrived, I was interviewed by a local newspaper, *Al-Ayyam*, which resulted in a number of people contacting me to express their interest in the project. A particularly inspiring interview took place with a woman who, in her youth, had been active with FLOSY. She spoke of studying in Algeria, where she met some of the heroines of the revolution against French colonisation. As someone who has struggled for women's rights in her country, she provided fascinating insights into the position of women in post-independence southern Yemen. In her words:

> There were so many changes; women were involved in political parties, in mass organisations, in the Supreme Court and in local councils. All these achievements changed the status of women in the south of Yemen after the success of the revolution. Later, I was elected as General Secretary of the Yemeni Women's Union; we had a lot of work to do, especially in other governorates of the country where illiteracy is a problem'.[15]

In South Yemen, as Carapico notes,

> or at least in the formerly British colonial port city of Aden, where revolutionaries established the Arab world's only Marxist regime ... women enjoyed rights unrivalled in the region. Females represented roughly a third of all Adeni students, teachers, medical personnel, civil servants, and factory workers and a visible minority among lawyers, judges, directors, administrators, middle-level party cadre, and parliamentarians.[16]

Much has changed, however, since unification with the north. The woman in Aden explained that, with the growth of religious fundamentalism,

> there is a kind of violence towards women and the insistence that women should be covered ... Until 1998, I was still uncovered because it was a kind of challenge for me, to show that I am a human being and, as a Yemeni, I have the right to

walk in the street. But there are many kinds of violence, for example violence in the home. And also discrimination; for example, although the election law says that women can stand as candidates in elections, in reality they can be voters but cannot be elected; in the elections of April this year [2003], we aimed to have at least seven candidates in Parliament but unfortunately only one was successful, which means we have one step forward and then ten steps back . . . so the women's struggle has to continue.[17]

Other women with whom I spoke echoed her words. A young lawyer told me that the wearing of the *hijab*, or even total face covering, is now so widespread throughout the country that it would be regarded as an act of rebellion to go outside without it; others admitted they did not wear the veil through choice but out of an unwillingness to challenge prevailing convention.[18]

One day, I visited al-Tawahi (Steamer Point). At the somewhat seedy Crescent Hotel, I had arranged to meet an elderly former sailor, with a view to purchasing old photographs. When the young English Queen Elizabeth visited Aden in 1954, she stayed at the Crescent Hotel. It must have been a grand and entirely appropriate setting for the royal guest but, over 50 years later, its grandeur is hard to imagine. Nonetheless, although it is now run down and almost deserted, it retains mementoes of its glorious past and the manager is only too happy to show visitors the room where the Queen stayed. With the sailor, I walked around the area. He pointed out what had been another once elegant hotel, now a destitute house. There were mounds of rubbish everywhere. My guide informed me that the derelict-looking buildings used to be bars and flourishing shops to service the shiploads of visitors; everything stayed open day and night. I thought if I closed my eyes I could imagine that long ago, altogether more prosperous time. I could not, however; it was just heat, noise, and smells. And I had to question just how prosperous it was for the majority of local citizens and how it was that their longings turned to national independence.

Time was growing short so I decided to give up the wholly efficient and very cheap public transport system and take advantage of the offer of a car and driver. I started to realise that the time I had allotted to this part of the project was inadequate; collecting oral history narratives in Yemen should have been a more leisurely

Figure 10.1 Al-Tawahi, or Steamer Point, was a hub of commercial activity during the British period. However, most of its formerly flourishing stores, which welcomed those arriving by boat at the port of Aden, have now been abandoned.

process, allowing time to get to know people properly, to have more than one meeting with them. Salem, the driver, was from Mukalla but had lived in Aden for many years and so was a mine of fascinating information. I recorded the first interview, with the head of a human rights organisation, in Arabic. He and his colleagues insisted that Britain has a responsibility towards Aden, apart from Yemen as a whole, because it is a special case. Britain thinks it can have an empire, they said, then leave one day and forget about it. Salem showed me fuzzy and fading photographs from the 1960s; one was of a British family outside their flat in Khormaksar in 1966; they looked happy, hopeful about the future. It reminded me of the museum at Raffles Hotel in Singapore, full of faded snapshots of people who do not realise that their lives are about to change forever. Then we drove past the same building.

Once I began to find my way around, I felt comfortable in Aden. I experienced conflict in the sense that, on the one hand, the

Foreign Office in London has issued travel advice warning British citizens not to travel to Yemen because of the dangers of terrorism; yet, on the other hand, I had encountered only friendliness and hospitality; there was no feeling whatsoever of dark and dangerous forces lurking just below the surface. At the same time, as a British person and a westerner, I was in some sense 'the enemy' – a representative of the former colonial power and part of the modern 'crusade' against Islam, and therefore perhaps a target, as had been the group of foreign tourists kidnapped by the Aden-Abyan Islamic Army in December 1998; in the ensuing shoot-out between the kidnappers and Yemeni government forces, four of the tourists, including three Britons, were killed. Having said that, I firmly believe that, on the whole, the people of Aden are well able to distinguish between individuals and government policy.

As I reached the end of my brief sojourn in Aden, I considered my objectives in undertaking this project. The starting point was curiosity rather than trying to prove or disprove something or to engage in a re-telling of history. It is also intense fascination with this small dot on the map and a relatively little known episode of British history. And what do the narrators want to get out of it? They seem to want an 'end result' rather than an abstract process. For some of them, too, it is the dredging up of memory, some of it pleasant but some painful. It is a chance to articulate their version of the truth, the past as they remember it, and to make sense of that past.

It was notable that everyone, almost without exception, did not restrict themselves to talking only of the British period. In a seamless narrative, they usually went on to describe what came next: the socialist era, then unification with north Yemen and the disappointments this has brought. Most of the narrators articulated varying degrees of bitterness about their more recent history, with a few regretting the departure of the British because, after they left, things got far worse. It was not always clear how much of this is true and how much is courtesy to the foreigner.

Towards the end of my stay, I visited Abyan, and went to Ahmad al-Fadhli's farm. We drove east along the coast road, past checkpoints and sand dunes. The farm was situated in the midst of banana and papaya groves. It felt very relaxed, peaceful, even though everyone carried guns. In his caravan, Ahmad showed us old photographs from the 1960s, strengthening the theme of faded images that runs through this project. Then we drove to Zingibar, for lunch with the Fadhli Sheikh Tareq in his somewhat more palatial home. He is an appointed local leader (a member of the *shura*) and authorised to settle disputes. It was a wonderful fish banquet, laid out on the floor. It felt like another, more leisurely era, characterised by seemingly effortless hospitality. I wondered if this too had contributed to the great affection articulated by some of the British narrators towards Yemen and its people.

The last day of my stay in Aden was very busy as I tried to gather as many recordings as I could before departure. With Salem, I travelled to Little Aden, along a long road with water on either side, past Madinat ash-Sha'ab, the 'people's city' (founded as Al-Ittihad, it was the capital of the Protectorate of South Arabia under British rule and became the administrative capital after independence[19]) and past Bin Laden family developments. He showed me where the USS Cole plotters had lived and prepared their suicide mission. On the beach, local families were enjoying their day off, picnicking and swimming.

Memory – recollection – is very interesting. It depends on the circumstances, ideology and kinship of the recaller. It is also located in the present (the time of telling) and the relationship between the narrator and the listener. What message do these tellers of history want to convey? What impression do they wish to make? While some people have thought hard about what to say, others arrive at the meeting completely unprepared. Their different approaches, however, usually have little to do with a sense of responsibility. Rather, it is a question of how best to tell the tale and, in this sense, both spontaneity and careful preparation can be equally effective.

The implications of talking about the past – 'this is how it was' – extend into the present and future. The consistency of the accounts of various narrators suggests a glimmer of 'truth' (as it was perceived by a particular group) or a conspiracy to present a manufactured 'truth' – collective memory, the creation of a myth. One wonders how much it matters to these often quite elderly people to rake over the past, to subject themselves again to the uncertainty of a time when they were young and the world was very different.

There was a certain vagueness about it or a tendency to joke, for example 'the happiest days of our life', 'those were good times', and this helps to blot out individual discomfort. Some narrators, however, talked of the terrible pain – and humiliation – of the British failure to protect them. The pain is usually camouflaged, soothed by the passage of time, into platitudes, but moments of real, felt experience still occasionally broke through the courteous facade in the form of tears or a flash of anger. There is pride too, of having fought for independence because it was the only thing to do; foreign occupation had become unbearable and unaccept-able, and there were pressures from outside to drive out the occupiers. On the other hand, it sometimes sounded like a naive revolution, without any clear idea of what might come next.

I think many of the Yemeni narrators were being polite, trying to protect me from embarrassment. Their easy words of descrip-tion ('the British brought law and order', 'it was a flourishing and cosmopolitan place') veil deeper hurt, disillusion, betrayal, disappointment. The British should have left before, they imply, in the 1950s or early 1960s. They hung on out of greed. Who benefited from this hanging on? I talked to several people who expressed satisfaction with their lives under the British; they had no words of pain or anger against British rule; for example a man in Little Aden who had worked at the refinery. Others were more critical. An elderly former teacher, for example, had wonderfully critical and insightful memories of the British – 'they did nothing; anything they did was just for them' – no sense of responsibility to the place or its people – divide and rule. The Adenis, he said, were treated badly.[20] This seems to be another theme running through the meetings.

I was intrigued by the contrasts I perceived, both in recollections of the British period and today. For example, one man spoke about his parents' memories of British rule. The way they spoke about it, he said, was 'as if they were living in a European society, not in a Middle Eastern society, and that's how they remember it . . . the amount of freedom they had, the social freedoms they had, which do not exist now'.[21]

There was just enough time to take a photograph of the grandiose Indian-style palace of the former Sultan of Lahej. Then off to the airport and to Sana'a on my way back to London. It was sad but also, in a way, a relief to leave Aden. A likeable place in so many ways but also squalid, bitter, somewhat desperate. The beach at Elephant Bay, run-down suite at Crescent Hotel where the Queen had stayed, the tawdry night club at the Aden Hotel, full of foreigners, the man in the market who asked me why I was taking pictures of poverty, people on the bus helping me get back to Ma'ala Decca, the Lebanese bakery, the man who gave me papaya in the street, the man who wanted me to take a picture of him and his car, driving to Abyan in the police car with armed escort.

I am left with memories of my own, for example a sense of powerlessness among many ordinary people, the pretence of power, the desperate clinging to dignity. Dr Yassin Said Noman has returned from years of exile to take up politics again. I met him in a hotel in Aden and, although he was reluctant to be recorded, he spoke at great length about his hopes for the future. For my own part, I wonder if I will ever return. I wonder too what sort of relationship is possible between this faraway impoverished backwater, singled out as a centre of fundamentalism in the 'war on terrorism', and its former ruler, Britain. I met not one single 'terrorist', nor felt at any time that I was in danger; on the contrary, the Yemenis to whom I spoke, both formally and in passing on the street, expressed utter bewilderment at the terrorist label. They would like greater prosperity, less corruption, the return of tourism and more opportunities for people in the south.

Since returning to London, I have kept in contact by telephone and e-mail with some of the people I met in Aden and Sana'a. They are eager to know how the project is progressing, willing to offer more assistance if required. When, they ask, are you coming back to Yemen? It is a tempting prospect. I would like to return some day, not as a researcher or a chronicler of past times, but as a friend of the country and some of its citizens, a representative of a closer, more balanced relationship between Britain and Yemen.

SIR RICHARD TURNBULL REMEMBERS

Synopsis of letter from Sir Richard Turnbull, the former High Commissioner, to Michael Baker, biographer of Admiral Sir Michael Lefanu, written after 1975

The following synopsis seeks to extract the main points contained in Turnbull's letter using his own language wherever possible.

The constitutional background of the South Arabian Protectorates was almost inconceivably complicated, and comprised the Federation of the states of what had been the Western Aden Protectorate, Aden itself (within the Federation but still a Crown Colony) and the three states of the Eastern Aden Protectorate (not part of the Federation and not federated with each other). We did not administer the states and had never done so; we protected them, financed them, directed their foreign policy and by a system of advisers tried to inculcate some notions of probity and common sense amongst them. The Federal states had very little revenue; there was no industry and not much agriculture; nor had the men much to offer in the way of special skills, except those of the fighting man. The states were split by feuds and quarrels at all levels and every one of them was bitterly jealous of its neighbours. Virtually every man went armed; there was not much state loyalty, absolutely no conception of loyalty to the Federation.

Right-wing Conservatives and old-fashioned Arab adulators ('of the white tie and tails school') thought of the rulers of the

States as traditional Arabs *sans peur et sans rapproche*, who could be relied upon to support Britain and maintain a protective screen for the Base against Arab nationalism and incursions from the Yemen. The Labour government on the other hand ('the high tea school') was convinced that they were a bunch of unmitigated blackguards who were holding up the fine democratic march of Southern Arabia towards universal adult suffrage and trade unions for all. Those on the ground, such as Lefanu and myself knew that with a few exceptions they were a futile, useless bunch of self-seeking puppets who had been jockeyed into positions they were wholly unfitted to occupy.

As for the Federation, it was a ramshackle contrivance, crippled by internal dissensions and commanding no confidence anywhere. The Federalis themselves were acutely conscious that as a result of their adherence to Britain they had become the despised and mistrusted men of the Arab world; and they were determined to hang on to the advantages that they had secured from the relationship with us, that is to say British money and British protection, for as long as they possibly could. What constantly amazed one about the Federalis was that in spite of the precariousness of their position, politically, socially, and constitutionally, they refused to do anything to improve their situation and would allow nothing to be done for them. They were split by internal quarrels and jealousies and by a ceaseless rivalry for personal supremacy; it was for this reason that we had to arrange for the chairmanship of the Federal Supreme Council to change once a month on a rota . . .

By contrast, the Adenis were proud of the place and jealous of its democratic institutions, which were indeed well ahead of most other places in the Middle East. They thought of themselves as highly civilised, as indeed they were, and they were damned if they were going to share their wealth with the arrogant, bullying, feudally-governed tribesmen of the Federation. All the same, the Conservative government of 1963 shanghaied them into it. They never forgave us for it.

I ought to interject here that although the Adenis were, I suppose, worthy of sympathy and support, and the Federalis fit to be condemned as wicked barons, yet on the ground it was the latter who gained one's sympathy and not the former. For the Federalis, in spite of all their bad qualities, were brave, handsome and charming whereas the Adenis, when it came to the point were a bunch of smug grocers. It was the old story of the country gentleman versus the man in trade.

Finally, the states of the Eastern Aden Protectorate did not come into the picture very much; such an aura of romance surrounds the Wadi Hadhramaut . . . the states had developed along tolerably peaceful lines; the young men going in for trade instead of raiding and counter-raiding . . . the old men were charming, elegant and cultivated, but so saturated with listlessness and defeat that they would do nothing for themselves and would allow no help to be given to them. A British-financed and commanded force, the Hadhrami Bedouin Legion, helped to secure the peace among the rival parties. Partly as a result of their isolation, their institutions as well as their characters were crumbling away . . . the only positive attitude they ever evinced was to hold themselves aloof from the troubles of the Arab world and to steer clear of any connection with the Federation . . . in spite of what I have said about the dream-like quality of the EAP, by the middle 'sixties the flimsy social structure had started to collapse; in 1966 the 'politically unattached force' murdered their commanding officer and, as the end of our time drew near, the towns of the Wadi Hadhramaut were menaced by rival terrorist groups. . . .

FLOSY was essentially an urban outfit and did not carry much weight outside Aden; it had the wit to lard its bombings and assassinations with pious references to trade unionism and democracy . . . The NLF was quite different . . . rural dissidents who had come up to town . . . their secret weapon was that they were doing what came naturally . . . they had been fighting authority and fighting among themselves since pre-Islamic days; by sheer ruthlessness, they came to dominate the major unions . . . For our part, we were so used to endless internal bickering amongst theArabs that it took us a long time to recognise that there was any prospect of NLF groups from the different states being able to cooperate with one another; the Federal Army and the Federal Guard were deeply penetrated.

Early in 1965 the stage was set for a major South Arabian conference to reform the Federal constitution, surrender British sovereignty in Aden to bring the place into line with the rest of the Federation and grant independence no later than 1968 as a unitary state in treaty relationship with Britain . . . the Adenis did not like the idea; their aim was full independence and accession to a revised Federation in their own time; the Federalis did not like it either; they did not like to face the modern world; they wanted to go on living their feudal way of life at the expense of the British taxpayer. The conference was sabotaged by the Federalis and had to be abandoned.

Meanwhile constitutional experts were studying the possibilities for Aden and the Federation . . . the Adeni government declared the two Commissioners to be prohibited immigrants . . . later in the year we managed to cobble together a conference of some sort, but the acrimony it engendered between Aden and the Federation was so great that we had to abandon it . . . HMG was compelled to suspend the constitution; the High Commissioner, poor wretch, became the government of Aden . . . demonstrations, strikes and civil disturbances were a commonplace; Aden was boycotting the Federal Parliament and its ex-ministers were drumming up an all-out campaign against the constitutional commission; they would settle for nothing less than the destruction of the tribal system and the dismissal of the tribal rulers.

Our own concern was not so much for the rulers as for the general security of the whole area. The Federal Army and the Guard, in spite of the NLF influence, had powerful tribal loyalties, and the disintegration of the Federal government would have left us with a well-armed, highly trained military machine no longer subject to any proper authority.

In February 1966, HMG announced the abandonment of the Base and a firm intention to leave South Arabia without a Defence Agreement. The Federal government were angry and bitter . . . they pointed out once again that their adherence to us had made them an object of hatred and spite in the Arab world; that having robbed them of any possible friendship or support . . . we now proposed to abandon them. They maintained too, with some colour of right, that at a Conference held in July 1964 we had given a specific promise that a Defence Agreement, under which Britain would retain her Base in Aden 'for the defence of the Federation and the fulfillment of her world-wide responsibilities' would be negotiated. Arguments in rebuttal were quite useless; they asserted again and again that the Federation was our creation and that it was up to us to look after it . . . in private conversations, responsible Adenis told us that just as the Federation needed the Base to defend it, so too did Aden need the Base as safe-guard against the feared depredations of the Federal Rulers. Finally, the firm announcement that we were to leave by 1968 caused the Emergency to take a much more violent and intractable form. There was no longer any advantage to be served in sup-porting us . . . the one certainty was that the future government would not be British; everyone therefore – army, police, civil servants, politicos had to look for a new bandwagon. London politicians had been convinced that if we would only make Aden independent it would enable us to come to terms with the parties and heal all existing breaches . . . they could not have been more mistaken.

The only power which could conceivably be enlisted in support of the Federation was Saudi Arabia; and Faisal very sensibly refused to do anything unless the Federation and the EAP could present a united front. The EAP without prior assurance of a rapprochement between the Federation and Aden would not even consider an alliance with the Federation let alone the idea of becoming a member of it; and Aden would sooner become an Egyptian vassal state than resume the position in the Federation that the 1963 agreement had compelled it to accept. As for the Federation, it could not be bothered to do anything to make itself look more respectable in the eyes of the Arab world; nor would it make any attempt to conciliate the Adenis.

In our search for an appropriate constitution, we examined every specifically Arab constitution, a fruitless exercise as the exemplary Arab democracies were all military dictatorships at that time. We tried to curry favour with the United Nations and agreed to accept a mission which would recommend practical steps towards for the establishment of a caretaker government to hold the fort until a constitution could be arrived at and adopted. However, the Adenis were so much under Egyptian direction, their hearts quite plucked out by threats and intimidation from the terrorists, that they could not bring themselves to cooperate with us; they had a pathological distrust of the Federation. The Federalis took refuge in a series of futile conferences in the climatically less disagreeable parts of the Middle East. Whitehall at this time was obsessed with doctrinaire ideas about elections, which they seemed to imagine could be carried out as though Aden was Putney or Hampstead. In the Federation, every man went armed and tribal feuds were endemic. In Aden, even the opposition could not agree on a franchise, indeed the very mention of the subject was apt to lead to civil disturbances. As the magistrates and juries were also intimidated, it was necessary to hold some captured terrorists in detention, as they could not be tried in open court. This is always difficult and brought us much opprobrium.

In March 1967, Whitehall put forward the idea of bringing forward independence by two or three months, calling the Aden nationalist leaders to some neutral territory to seek to work out a modus vivendi, with British protection to be provided for the subsequent few months. George Thomson exercised all his persuasive powers to sell it to the Federation, but they declined to have anything to do with it.

When the UN mission arrived in Aden, it comprised the most bitterly anti-British elements of the UN and had come to South Arabia to make trouble. They were rude, disobliging and quarrelsome. They denied the Federal government had any legal standing; they refused to meet the Ministers. The Adenis also declined to meet the mission or submit any papers to it. The NLF called a strike and the Federal government refused to give the mission airtime to broadcast. The following day they left in a huff.

Although I have spoken so critically, even harshly, of the Arabs, I don't think it can be denied that it was the British government that was chiefly to blame for the South Arabian debacle. We built up the Federation from penniless states (there was no oil in South Arabia) governed by irresponsible men; by causing them to adhere to us, made them the butt of the other Arabian countries. Our purpose was to use their warlike qualities as a protective screen for the Base. As for Aden, it was after all a British Colony and the Adenis British subjects for whom we had more specific responsibilities than we had towards the Federation. We forced Aden into the Federation, partly to secure the Base, and partly to be able to use its wealth in maintaining a Federal government that had no sources of revenue of its own and was entirely dependent on funds provided by the British taxpayer.

The whole thing was made worse of course by the surge of Arab nationalism in the 1960s and by Nasser's determination to avenge Suez. The odd thing was that it was the NLF, not Nasser's men, who won the final victory.

One last thought. Even without Arab nationalism and Nasser, I don't think we should ever have succeeded in bringing about an easy, fruitful partnership between the Adenis and the Federalis; and without such a partnership, the states of the EAP would still have held themselves aloof.

APPENDIX 2

MUKALLA 1960

Matters colonial, consular and curious

John G. R. Harding

In 1959, inspired by the twin thought of public service and adventure, I joined what had by then become known as 'Her Majesty's Overseas Civil Service' and was posted to Aden. I had no idea that the first 15 months of my five-and-a-half years' stint in South Arabia would be as a glorified passport clerk in the Eastern Aden Protectorate.

After three bewildering weeks of induction into the arcane world of colonial administration, in and out of the humid corridors of Aden Colony's government offices, I boarded an Aden Airways DC3 flight in February 1960 to the picturesque port of Mukalla some 300 miles east of Aden. Mukalla was the capital of the largest and most prosperous state in the British Protectorate and the headquarters of the small staff of British Political Officers headed by the Resident Adviser and British Agent (RABA), the senior representative of the Governor of Aden.

At the dusty RAF airstrip, now rejoicing in the name Riyan International Airport, I was met by Lieut-Col Archibald Wilson DSO. Tall, monocled, with greying hair, he cut an impressive if somewhat racy figure in his white safari suit. Archie was a member of an elite group of British Political Officers who had served their country with distinction in the Second World War, and who were now serving out their time in Mukalla. Alastair McIntosh, the RABA, was an Arabic scholar at Oxford; Johnnie Johnson, his deputy (an ex-Chindit); Jock Snell, a former commander of the Hadhrami Bedouin Legion, who had served ten years in India even before the War; and Charles Inge, the Residency's 'Intelligence' Officer. These men combined a scepticism born of age and experience with an enduring affection for the people and barren lands of the Protectorate; and they could laugh without rancour at the somewhat ridiculous business of trying to administer it. Their detachment, however, owed more than a little to the influence of alcohol to which they were prodigiously partial. This would unlock flows of reminiscence fascinating to the ears of a newly-arrived young officer like myself; they spoke of tribal alarums and excursions; of spectacular mud-brick cities hidden in the lunar wastes of the interior; of rock-face inscriptions along ancient incense routes skirting the Empty Quarter; their tales of this timeless world excited my romantic curiosity and I longed to explore it.

Over beer in the tin shed which served as the RAF officer's mess, Archie informed me that I would be taking over from him as Assistant Adviser, Residency (AAR), the central cog in the wheel of the Residency's routine business. With disarming insouciance he evaded my diffident attempts to tie him down to a job description: 'Nothing to it Old Boy; you'll soon pick it up.' And with little more than that by way of handover, he soon vanished from my life.

I quickly discovered that there was in fact everything to it when a procession of red-turbaned peons wheeled into my office a fleet of trolleys piled high with dusty files. These, I found, concerned a raft of outstanding matters which Archie, who had no time for routine administration, had thoughtfully 'brought up' for the new AAR's 'immediate attention'. Many of these touched on consular matters, foreshadowing my most immediate and pressing task, which was to deal with the crowds of Hadhramis who gathered daily within the Residency compound seeking visas to visit Mecca, for it was now the pilgrimage, or Haj season. Supervising the issuance of up to one hundred such visas a day from the scruffy, whitewashed cubicle that passed as Her Britannic Majesty's Passport Office, tested tempers on both sides of the counter. At least the issue of Haj visas was a seasonal phenomenon. More permanent and problematic was the issue and control of British Protected Persons passports.

Before leaving England I had done some homework on the region of South Arabia known as the Hadhramaut, which comprised most of the territory then known as the Eastern Aden Protectorate. I had even called on Harold Ingrams who more than 20 years earlier had helped to bring peace to the areas and been appointed Britain's first Resident Adviser in Mukalla. I knew, therefore, that for centuries Hadhramis, like Scottish clansmen, had ventured overseas to make a living, and that the advent of cheap steamship travel in the nineteenth century and the facilities of the British Empire had greatly boosted the scale of this emigration to India, the Far East and East Africa. This development coincided with a particularly turbulent period of unrest in the Hadhramaut caused by a power struggle between the two major local dynasties – Quaiti and Kathiri, the former owing their rising wealth and influence to service in the largely Arab army of the Nizam of Hydrabad in India. Enterprising young men were able to make fortunes in trade and commerce overseas while still retaining their home links. By the twentieth century, emigration and remittances had become the engines of the Hadhramaut. Ingrams estimated that perhaps a third of the population then lived abroad, sending back their earnings.

In 1960, emigration, travel and trade still under-pinned the Hadhrami economy and was reflected in the 6000 or so applications for travel documents which I processed in 1960 alone, now very often for travel to the Arab oil exporting countries. I sometimes wondered how our tiny passport office, consisting of myself, one clerk and one typist, without an adequate infrastructure of filing cabinets and passport registers could continue to cope with this pressure, especially as consular duties were only part of my remit. Without our energetic clerk, a young Eritrean Christian called Noah Johannes, the ad hoc system we operated would have broken down. Noah himself was an illegal immigrant who was literally picked up off the Mukalla beach; his ambition to become a naturalised British citizen ideally qualified him for his job!

I soon made another perplexing discovery. Whereas Aden had the status of a British Colony, its hinterland was a Protectorate where British Political Officers had no direct executive authority, only an advisory role. Under the protectorate treaties, the states had to accept formal British 'advice' on all matters except religion and the Sharia law. Thus the local states and their rulers retained responsibility for most internal aspects of government, while their British advisers, assisted by various technical experts, sought to improve the quality and scope of their administration and promote economic and social development. However, Britain had responsibility for foreign relations, including the consular function. Yet in the EAP, the Quaiti and Kathiri states both issued their own passports (as they did their own postage stamps). Though this seemed at odds with their protected status, the passports required a British seal and signature before they became valid internationally. The passports, supplied by the Crown Agents, were curious hybrids. They were issued under the authority of the Quaiti Minister to the Sultanate or the Kathiri State Secretary, and contained a three-fold underwritten guarantee of authenticity, incorporating the imprimatur of 'the Resident Adviser and British Agent, on behalf of the Governor of Aden in the name of Her Britannic Majesty'. It fell to me as AAR to sign these documents on behalf of the RABA. Though apparently anomalous, in fact this made practical good sense. Only the states were capable of handling the complexities of logistics and identification. Although few Hadhramis held birth certificates, or any other form of identification, elaborate tribal and family networks generally proved effective means of verification. Applicants had to provide guarantors to meet potential repatriation expenses and the system worked for both home-based and overseas applicants. This pragmatic arrangement brought the states political prestige and useful sources of revenue. The system required close liaison between the AAR and his state counterpart. This brought me into close touch with Quaiti State's Passport officer, 'Isa Musallam. 'Isa's extrovert charm and slight air of dissipation beguiled his limited knowledge of migration and visa regulations; although intelligent, he was no swot and seemed happy to be guided by my advice.

However, a problem which was never satisfactorily settled was the issue of passports to British Protected Persons of the Mahra state. 'State' in this case was a misnomer, for Mahra, a vast chunk of almost waterless terrain in the most easterly region of the Protectorate, and inhabited by fiercely independent tribes, was under the control of neither the British nor its titular ruler, Sultan 'Isa bin Ali Al-Afrar, who lived on the remote and then somewhat inaccessible island of Socotra, some 300 miles south of the Mahra mainland.

Despite this characteristically chaotic state of affairs, when it came to travel documents the Mahra were spoiled for choice.

If you felt affluent, you could get a 'pukka' British Protected Persons passport 'for persons of the Mahra State in the Eastern Aden Protectorate' from me in Mukalla. Alternatively, if you just wanted a return ticket to a single country, I could offer you the cheaper Mahra Identity and Travel Document; or for journeys to Aden or within the Protectorate a free Mahra Travel Pass. Verification of genuine Mahra status was conveniently provided by the Residency's Mahri quartermaster, Abdullah bin Ashoor. Abdulla's family acted as trade and commission agents in Mukalla for Sultan 'Isa and other Mahri personalities and undertook to guarantee all official repatriation expenses without charge. The Sultan refused to take any responsibility for such official documents as they brought him no revenue and he had no means of enforcing guarantees given by his putative mainland subjects. To complicate matters further, the Sultan issued his own travel documents which were cheaper than mine, needed no identifying photograph and so were easily transferable, had an expiry date two years longer than ours and required no guarantee bond. These documents were obtainable directly from the Sultan or alternatively from one of three agents of his on the mainland. Despite their somewhat dubious validity, these documents were acceptable in a number of Arab states, including Saudi Arabia and Kuwait, provided they bore the rubber stamp of the Sultan. They had no international validity and guaranteed neither British protection nor repatriation, but seemed to meet the needs of Mahra seeking work in the Arab countries.

The Sultan's passport issuing enterprise faced competition however from members of the junior, mainland branch of the Al-Afrar dynasty based in Qishn and headed by a kindly patriarch Sultan Khalifa bin Abdulla. Khalifa employed his son-in-law, Ahmed Al-Jidhi as his roving agent in Aden, specialising in sales of virtual facsimiles of Sultan 'Isa's travel document to Arabs of diverse national and ethnic origins who wished to travel to the Gulf. These document were printed in Aden by the thousand, stamped with Sultan Khalifa's seal, and cost 5 shillings less than those issued by Sultan 'Isa. The latter frequently complained to the Residency about Khalifa's thriving business but in my day the British just turned a blind eye.

In a series of reports I tried to explain and disentangle the anomalies and potential problems arising from the system I had inherited. My superiors, however, had better things to do than to meddle with a set-up which had worked tolerably well and which would cost money and resources to rationalise. It was painful to have to admit that Archie Wilson's laissez-faire attitude had been right all along, albeit for the wrong reasons! It was clearly time to move on.

APPENDIX 3

PETER HINCHCLIFFE'S LETTER OF APPOINTMENT

DEPARTMENT OF TECHNICAL CO-OPERATION
Carlton House Terrace, LONDON S.W.1
Telephone: WHItehall 4368

Please address your reply to
THE DIRECTOR-GENERAL
Mark the envelope 'P' in
the top left-hand corner
and quote the following number: BCD/P.22440

1 0 OCT 1961

Sir,

       I am directed by Mr. Secretary Vosper to offer you appointment on
contract to the service of the Government of Aden for one tour of service
as an Assistant Adviser on the terms and conditions contained in this letter
and, where applicable, in the enclosed Statement of Principal Conditions of Service.

       The work of an Assistant Adviser lies in the following spheres:-

    (a) The wilder areas of the Aden Protectorate among scarcely civilised
Baiduin and equally wild but settled tribesmen, where there is no ordered
Government whatever, and where the Assistant Adviser is chiefly engaged in
keeping the peace between the tribes and sections, in providing political and
security information, in supervising the activities of Government security
forces, and in guarding the frontier from foreign intrusion and intrigue.
The conditions of desert life are comfortless and most rigorous.

    (b) The settled states of the Protectorate. Here the Assistant Adviser
is responsible for guiding the states towards stability and the first foundation
of ordered Government. In others there is constant risk of the breakdown of
law and order, and conditions will often be disagreeable and dangerous.

       It will be the first duty of an Assistant Adviser to acquire a really
good knowledge of Arabic.

2.   The salary scale attached to the appointment commences at £1,281
a year (including inducement element) and progresses by annual increments in
the Scale Al - 2, details of which are given in the enclosed Salary Scale
Schedule, to a maximum of £2,409 a year. Under the arrangements for giving
credit for post-war compulsory military service, you would subject to confirmation by the Governor, be allowed to enter the scale at £1,329 a year
(including inducement element). The Governor would also advise you to what
extent your incremental date (which is normally the anniversary of date of
arrival in Aden) would be affected by your compulsory military service.

3.   With reference to paragraph 15 of the Statement of Principal
Conditions of Service, following the recent salaries revision in Aden local leave
has been abolished. However, ten days casual leave may be permitted at the
discretion of Heads of Departments.

4.   Your appointment would take effect from the date of your leaving
this country. Half salary would be paid for the period of the journey to the
territory and full salary from the date of your arrival there.

P.R.M. Hinchcliffe, Esq.

/5.

5.   The appointment is non-pensionable but a gratuity would be payable in accordance with the terms of paragraph 14F of the Statement of Principal Conditions of Service.

6.   A satisfactory medical report has been received from the Consulting Physician by whom you were examined.

7.   Under the terms of this offer of appointment you would not be appointed to membership of Her Majesty's Overseas Civil Service.

8.   Will you please state whether you accept this offer and, if so, indicate the earliest date on which you would be ready to leave for Aden. Your passage would be arranged for the first available opportunity after that date. If you are not prepared to accept, please return the enclosures to this letter.

                  I am, Sir,
                    Your obedient servant,

                  J. A. Chambers
                  (J.A. Chambers (Miss))

APPENDIX 4

AN ORAL HISTORY OF THE BRITISH IN ADEN

Following a brief visit to Aden in 1996, I became intrigued by the ghost of British colonialism; although Britain had left southern Arabia almost 30 years earlier, its presence still hovered in the air. I started to wonder what life must have been like during the British colonial period in that area. As I had already met a number of people, both in Britain and in Yemen, who remembered British rule, it occurred to me that the period and its eyewitnesses could become the subjects of an oral history project. The idea was to glean the recollections of as wide a range of people as possible, both those who were deemed 'important' at the time and the many others whose names are not remembered by history, on both the Yemeni and the British sides. The 'Aden oral history project', which began in earnest at the end of 1999, grew out of a fascination with Aden and its history and was able to reach fruition thanks to the efforts of a disparate array of narrators to bring alive – through their memories and their words – a largely forgotten period of British history.[1]

At first, the process of conducting oral history research seems deceptively simple. All one needs to do, I thought, is to sit someone down, turn on the microphone and invite him or her to talk about the past. But the reality is more complex. The construction of oral history, which is 'a profoundly social practice',[2] involves intrusion, in the sense that one is delving into possibly painful or unresolved areas of an individual's life, the struggle to present a coherent snapshot of the past, and the formation of a relationship between the narrator and the researcher. One should bear in mind that all memories

> are a mixture of facts and opinions, and both are important. The way in which people make sense of their lives is valuable historical evidence in itself. Few of us are good at remembering dates, and we tend to telescope two similar events into a single memory. So when we interview people it is important to get them to tell us about direct personal experiences – eye-witness testimony – rather than things that might have been heard second hand.[3]

It is important to stress the difference between the formal – usually written – records of past events and the memories that individuals carry with them of these events. Oral history has been described as a method of recovering 'neglected or silenced accounts of past experience, and as a way of challenging dominant histories'.[4] But the 'neglected or silenced accounts' are perceived to lie primarily on the Yemeni side and it is they, therefore, who have most to gain from 'challenging dominant histories'. One wonders, too, if many British civilians who worked in Aden in the early 1960s are aware of being the possessors of 'dominant histories'. There is memory but there is also forgetfulness in the recollection of past times.

Written and oral sources may not always correspond, which raises questions of truth and accuracy. Each person has their own version of 'the truth' and this must be accepted as 'the truth of past events as seen by the people, a truth that is often not represented in official literature and records'.[5] What narrators believe, 'is indeed a historical *fact* (that is, the fact that they believe it), as much as what really happened'.[6] In this case, while narrators were being invited to reflect on past events, their reflections were confined to a specific period – the final years of British rule in Aden – and this placed some restrictions on the narrative flow. While British participants usually ended their accounts with the boarding of the plane or the boat to leave Aden, however, Yemenis tended to continue their narratives into the post-colonial era and even, in some cases, the present. 'References to past events', in the words of another oral historian, 'are continual, and judgments about them, explicit as well as assumed, occur in everyday conversation'.[7]

Let us now turn to the role of the interviewer which, in my view, is far from passive; the very word 'interviewer' suggests a degree of interaction, whereas the term 'listener' suggests a less reciprocal relationship. However one describes the person initiating the narrative, he/she must decide what questions to ask, where to place the emphasis, when to interrupt and when to let the conversation flow. On the whole, it is preferable to allow the narrator to speak with as little interference as possible. But this assumes fluency, a degree of self-confidence and an adequate recall of past events. Many narrators lack these skills and require gentle prompting. Questions, verbal reinforcement and sympathetic body language can aid the process. The content of oral sources 'depend largely on what the interviewer puts into it in terms of questions, dialogue, and personal relationship' and the first 'requirement, therefore, is that the researcher "accept" the informant, and give priority to what she or he wishes to tell, rather than what the researcher wants to hear'.[8] Although I may have imagined myself as a neutral, relatively silent listener, handing over all power to the narrators to say what they wished, in reality I sought them out, asked what may have been considered to be probing questions and recorded what they said.

Since the perspective of the interviewer 'cannot help but influence, even subtly, the content of the material',[9] the researcher must acknowledge his or her own 'influence on the shape of the interview'.[10] Although

> we can console ourselves with the knowledge that there is no such thing as 'objective' reporting, we must recognize our own influence in the interview process and make a concerted effort to maintain a balance between what we . . . think is important and what the [individuals] we are interviewing think was important about their own lives.[11]

After all, any interviewing process 'involves multiple roles and several layers of perception. Each person, interviewer and narrator, makes choices in terms of communication, understanding and presentation resulting in the production of different kinds of information'.[12]

The question of 'power' or empowerment is a crucial one in the context of this project and touches on issues of subjectivity, which 'is as much the business of history as are the more visible "facts"'.[13] The problem of how one conceptualises 'Others as subjects in their own right'[14] raises the question of whether one should treat the two sides of the project – the British and the Yemeni – in different ways in order to acknowledge the unbalanced nature of the relationship. Such concerns lead to considerations of how to manipulate oral history as a research tool, which seems to place disproportionate power in the hands of the researcher. In the case of this project, I started with a strong awareness of difference. This needs to be broken down still further to reflect present circumstances. On the one hand, some of the British narrators occupied relatively powerless positions in the colonial order, for example wives and soldiers; and, on the other hand, some of the Yemeni narrators are now influential people, for example diplomats and businessmen, in their society. There is also the element of choice. While some of the British participants felt they had little room for manoeuvre, for example wives and children compelled to accompany male breadwinners, many of the Yemenis interviewed made a deliberate choice to involve themselves in national liberation activities. Therefore, the distinction between power and powerlessness is less straightforward than one might imagine.

While one group, the British administrators, possessed the formal tools of power, in the sense of laws, a bureaucracy and an army, and the other, southern Yemenis living under an increasingly unpopular colonial regime, was struggling against what it regarded as illegitimate control, this must inevitably have had an effect on what people said and how they said it. As a result, there may be a tendency to give more weight to the supposedly 'powerless' tellers of history. As Thompson says,

> by introducing new evidence from the underside, by shifting the focus and opening new areas of inquiry, by challenging some of the assumptions and accepted judgments of historians, by bringing recognition to substantial groups of people who had been ignored, a cumulative process of transformation is set in motion.[15]

Indeed, some of those taking part in the project may have had secondary agendas: for some on the British side, there was a desire to justify what they saw as British shortcomings in southern

Arabia while, for Yemeni narrators, there was a wish – often explicitly stated – to build a new, more egalitarian relationship with the former colonial master.

There is also the question of oral traditions. In some societies, written records are valued above all while, in others – for example, those with a low level of literacy – 'telling stories' is a popular means of communication. Tonkin argues that

> orality is the basic human mode of communication, and although peoples all over the world now use literate means to represent pastness, and written records have existed for many hundreds of years, the business of relating past and present for social ends has for most of the time been done orally; it still is so. The argument is the stronger when one understands how memory and cognition are interconnected in highly literate and non-literate peoples alike.[16]

In the case of both Yemeni and British narrators in this study, most were educated to a relatively high standard and there was little discernible difference between the reactions of the two sides to my invitation to narrate the past. This, I think, has something to do with preparedness and also commitment to the project. Most of the participants had been approached prior to the interview, were aware of what the project entailed and were interested – for a variety of reasons – in taking part and placing their stories 'on the record'.

'Memory' is both a public and a private process. It may be that some people welcome the opportunity to reveal the many personal details of their past lives, while others prefer to present a 'national narrative', to justify communal events and their own part in them. Both are important. In the case of the Aden oral history project, the collection of narratives was based on a short questionnaire designed to establish an individual's background and to encourage the flow of recollection. In some instances, participants had planned in advance about what they wanted to say and needed little prompting, while others felt more comfortable responding to a series of questions. All the interviews were conducted in English which, for the Yemeni side of the project, presented something of a problem. Even the most fluent English speaker – and many of the Yemeni narrators spoke excellent English – were at a disadvantage in the sense that they were not communicating in their native language and, therefore, may have been unable to express fully all that they wished to say. All interviews were recorded and later transcribed. In total, approximately 30 recordings were made on each side; each one is approximately one hour in length. Although the sample is too small to draw sweeping conclusions about the British in Aden, the recordings provide an insight into the activities, thoughts and feelings of groups of people otherwise ignored by history.

Finally, one should bear in mind the constraints of conducting oral history research in places that are unfamiliar. Although I have visited Yemen on several occasions, I do not claim to be an expert either on the country itself or its colonial history; indeed, I was careful not to find out too much information about the British period in case it had an effect, whether intentional or unintentional, on the interviews. The time I was able to spend in Yemen, collecting oral history testimonies, was regrettably far too brief and I was aware that – had I had more time – many more individuals would have come forward and their input no doubt would have enriched the project considerably. I was reliant on other people to put me in touch with suitable narrators, which means I had to trust their judgement; one should also appreciate the degree of bias present in the selection of narrators. These quibbles do not of course invalidate the resulting material which, I believe, is rich and comprehensive.

In the case of Yemen, too, there were a number of problems associated with the process of recollection. There was often a conflict between wanting to 'set the record straight' and pressures against participation. Some narrators were not entirely comfortable about being recorded; they were afraid of getting into trouble, of conveying an inaccurate version of events or of causing offence. As I was able to spend only a short period in Yemen, there was insufficient time to build relationships of trust with individual narrators; they were unable to get to know me and were therefore understandably reluctant to trust me. Some asked who had sent me, whom I was reporting to and what the 'real reasons' for my mission were. Some participants were worried that their words might fall into the hands of the state and that they would be punished for speaking. It was regrettable, I felt, that people feared that even their memories might be politically dangerous. All I could do was to promise anonymity. Some of those interviewed were less than candid. They preferred to speak about everyday things rather than revealing the possibly more interesting information they possess. It means I did not get the full picture. But one cannot ignore political considerations. Some narrators were speaking within a framework of modern political reality; they were constrained by their status. They may have wished to create a certain impression about the current situation. Either they are loyal to the regime or perhaps have an axe to grind.

While the majority of narrators tried hard to present an accurate version of the past, many were unable to recall precise details and a few deliberately falsified their memories of events. When I considered why they might do this and whether it matters, I reached the conclusion that a false account of 'reality' – and we should recognised that 'reality' means different things to different people – may reflect a desire in the mind of the reporters of this reality to tell history as it *should* have been, to render the past respectable or honourable. It is also the case that the importance of oral testimony 'may not lie in its adherence to fact, but rather in its departure from it, as imagination, symbolism and desire emerge. Therefore, there are no 'false' oral sources'.[17] At the same time, I discovered an extraordinary amount of interest in the project. Very many individuals from all walks of life seemed to welcome the opportunity to put into words their deeply felt but perhaps not adequately articulated feelings about British rule and the abrupt decision of Britain to pull out of Aden in 1967.

NOTES

CHAPTER 1

HISTORICAL AND CONSTITUTIONAL BACKGROUND

1 See James Morris, *The Market of Selukia*, Faber & Faber: London, 1957, pp. 198–205.
2 Kennedy Trevaskis, *Shades of Amber*, Hutchinson: London, 1968, p. 112.
3 NA. CAB 21/4357; 103770.
4 NA. CAB 21/4357; 103770.
5 Hansard, 13 June 1956; 919–974.
6 NA. CAB 134/1556.
7 NA. CO 1015/1911; 103770.
8 NA. CO 1015/1911; 103770.
9 NA. CO 1015/1911; 103770.
10 NA. CO 1015/1912; 103770.
11 NA. CAB 134/1558; 113110.
12 NA. CO 1015/1912; 103770.
13 NA. CAB 21/4356; 103770.
14 Kennedy Trevaskis, *Shades of Amber*, see note 2.
15 BL. R/20/D/27. High Commissioner to Secretary of State.
20 October 1963, plus Commission Report.
16 BL. R/20/D/27. High Commissioner to Secretary of State, 6 November 1963.
17 NA. CO 1055/299; 116690.
18 Kennedy Trevaskis, *Shades of Amber*, p 230.
19 NA. CO 1055/136.
20 NA. CO 1055/98. Record of meeting with Kathiri state Council.
21 Hansard, 11 December 1964; 1967–71.
22 NA. CO 1055/282; 107172.

23 Private discussion with Antonin Besse, 2005.
24 NA. FO 371/17861.
25 Unpublished letter from Turnbull to Michael Baker, biographer of Admiral Sir Michael Lefanu, former Commander-in-Chief, Middle East Command.
26 NA. CO 1055/108.
27 BL. R/20/D/106.
28 NA. FO 371/179751.
29 NA. FO 371/179751.
30 Fred Halliday, *Arabia Without Sultans*, Penguin: London.
31 BL. R/20/C/2302.
32 BL. R/20/B/2601; R/20/C/2301.
33 Private correspondence 2004.
34 BL. R/20/B/3097.
35 NA. CO 1015/2489.
36 NA. CO 1015/2307; letter Baillie/Morgan, 29 May 1962.
37 NA. CO 1015/2307.
38 NA. CO 1055/100.
39 NA. CO 1055/74; 105309.
40 NA. CO 1055/98; 107172.
41 NA. CO 1055/107.
42 NA. CO 1056/296.
43 BL. R/20/D/382.
44 BL. R/20/D/382.
45 NA. CO 1056/296.
46 Private discussion, 2005.
47 Private correspondence, 2004.
48 NA. FCO8/169.
49 NA. FCO8/250.
50 NA. PREM 13/1297.
51 NA. PREM 13/1297.
52 NA. PREM 13/1297.
53 NA. PREM 13/1297.

CHAPTER 2

THE INTERNATIONAL CONTEXT OF SOUTH ARABIA AND BRITISH POLICY

1 CO 1055/61. Memorandum dated 17 April 1963 from the Secretary of State for Foreign Affairs to all heads of British missions in the Middle East and the Persian Gulf, setting out HMG's approach to foreign policy in the region.
2 Kennedy Trevaskis, *Shades of Amber*, Hutchinson, 1968.
3 CO 1055/61.
4 FO 371/179863.

4 See for example FO 371/179861; report of a conversation on 12 January 1965 between Leycester Coltman of the British Embassy in Cairo and Ali Abdul Karim (para. 5).

6 FO 371/179863. Letter dated 22 December 1964 from Donal McCarthy, seconded from the Foreign Office to the High Commission in Aden, to Roberts of the Colonial Office.

7 FO 371/179863; Foreign Office telegram of 1 January 1965 to the Jedda embassy, copied to POMEC, Aden.

8 FO 371/179863. Letter of 2 January 1965 from the Beirut Embassy to the Foreign Office.

9 FO 371/179863. Despatch from the Washington Embassy to the Foreign Office dated 5 January 1965.

10 FO 371/179863. Foreign Office telegram to various British representatives in the Middle East.

11 FO 371/179863. Telegram dated 9 January 1965 from the Jedda Embassy to the Foreign Office.

12 FO 371/179863. Telegram from the Jedda Embassy to the Foreign Office dated 6 January 1965.

13 FO 371/179887. Letter of 31 July 1965 from McCarthy to Roberts (Colonial Office).

14 Private letter of April 2004.

15 Private exchanges, 2004/5.

16 FO 371/179863. Letter of 18 February 1965 from McCarthy to the Foreign Office.

17 FO 371/179858. T.F. Brenchley's record of meeting on 20 October 1965.

18 FO 371/179858. Record of meeting between Mr George Thomson and a Yemeni delegation on 25 October 1965.

19 FO 371/179743 George Thomson's record of a discussion with Mr Abdulla al Asnag on 2 August, 1965.

20 FO 371/179743. George Thomson's minute dated 17 September 1965 of his conversation with the Egyptian Ambassador.

21 Extract from Robin Young's diary for 19 April 1966.

22 Private discussion with Mr Frank Brenchley, 2005.

CHAPTER 3

THE POLITICAL OFFICERS IN THE WESTERN ADEN PROTECTORATE (WAP)

1 Political Officer's house in Zingibar: 'Al Geru'.

2 This department was a predecessor of Overseas Development Administration (ODA) and of Department for International Development (DFID) and carried out recruitment for overseas territories.

3 WAP office also had other older, senior men whose arrival from other territories or previous careers predated mine and who were

experienced in the ways of the Protectorates: (Roy Somerset calls them 'willing castaways') Kennedy Trevaskis had been in Rhodesia and with the military in Eritrea. Johnny Johnson was an ex Chindit; George Henderson had been with the Aden Protectorate Levies (APL); Robin Young and Ralph Daly in the Sudan. The Guidance Note was for those who arrived after 1964.

4 Pronounced *Ga*'ar. The South Yemeni 'J' – in the West – is a hard 'G' (Gander not George). Similar to Egyptian colloquial.

5 We were issued with Tide Tables. It was very hard work driving at full tide on soft sand at the top of the beach.

6 This boasted the 'longest hole in the world', 730 yards, followed by the' shortest': 30 yards. The actual holes were made from lemonade powder tins and were slightly larger than the regulation (Royal and Ancient) ones.

7 When my one year contract was (incredibly given the speed of decolonisation) converted into a permanent and pensionable one I was designated a Cadet and put on a year's probation. I believe that on my retirement I was one of the youngest pensioners in the history of Her Majesty's Overseas Civil Service (HMOCS).

8 Godfrey Meynell: Abyan recollections from a paper: *Sultans, Sahibs and a Bounder* sent to the author August 2004.

9 A maktab is a tribal section: a large extended family.

10 His son Aidan has described his father's work in Abyan in *The Zanzibar Chest* (see the section on background reading in the bibliography).

11 Barny Buckton was in Abyan in my time there. A fixture at the Abyan club he apparently lived in great dread of an alien invasion, the imminence of the arrival of which matched the current extent of his alcohol intake. He was a very competent engineer. See also note 60 below.

12 Rex Smith: written response to a questionnaire from the author and exchange of e-mails, 2002–4.

13 Michael Crouch: response to the questionnaire, e-mails and extracts from his book *An Element of Luck* Originally published 1993 (see Bibliography) correspondence spanning 2002–5.

14 Robin Young's diary reveals that he was actually very angry indeed. He certainly nursed a grievance for some months!

15 Roy Somerset: letters to the author, 2003/4.

16 Doreen Ingrams, wife of Harold Ingrams was one of those great British 'Arabian Ladies' in the mould of Freya Stark or Dame Violet Dickson. He husband was famous for 'Ingrams' Peace' in the Hadramaut (see Chapter 4).

17 Taking of hostages was a widespread practice, officially sanctioned. Hostages were often handed over to local government as part of a complicated tribal settlement or as part of an attempt to solve a dispute with the government itself. They were tokens of future good behaviour on part of the offending tribe. I got myself into an awful tangle in 1964

in Radfan trying to explain the niceties of the use of hostages to an incredulous Duncan Sandys, then Colonial Secretary!

18 The Ba Kazim was a particularly obstreperous Aulaqi tribe. Often in dispute with the local authorities and HMG.

19 To 'blacken' someone's face was to bring shame on him or her. To 'whiten' was to convey honour or respect. Direct translation from the Arabic.

20 That is, leading to a blood feud. An eye for an eye was an inescapable element of tribal lore. In my view the JAA was quite right in the local circumstances. The Kazimis had learnt a lesson and there would be no formal repercussions, which would have been inevitable if one of the raiders had died. After Nigeria, however . . .

21 Dissidents rather than rebels or revolutionaries were the usual British official description. The Arabic: '*mufsidin*' literally meaning 'the corrupted ones'.

22 Usually attacks were from long range – the first intimation being rifle or light machine gun shots followed by a bazooka rocket or two. My practice was to go out onto the roof and help to direct counterfire by British troops from their camp using a walkie-talkie. On this occasion I was not alerted by small arms fire and a bazooka was fired first from about 50 yards, hitting the roof parapet, the blast destroying the chair I used as my 'command post' – I dived promptly under the bed (as did my wife Archie) and we remained there until the shooting stopped.

23 The Buffs, a Kentish regiment and the King's Shropshire Light Infantry (KSLI) were flown in from Kenya to help out. The young soldier from the Buffs who was killed must have been one of the last National Servicemen to die in action.

24 The Somersets trace their direct descent from John of Gaunt and the Duke of Beaufort from the time of the Wars of the Roses. Godfrey Meynell remembers another headline 'Plantaganet descendant in Beau Geste Siege'.

25 By the time I arrived in Aden we were on annual leaves. Usually two months leave after ten months in Aden. On top of this we added travelling to and from the UK in order to take our leave. As this was normally by sea it amounted to an extra 24 or so days' holiday.

26 Stephen Day: notes for a lecture and e-mails to the author, 2004.

27 This was a bomb attack in December 1963 at Aden airport on the High Commissioner Kennedy Trevaskis as he was leaving for talks in London. George Henderson tried to shield Trevaskis from the grenade and died later of his injuries. He was awarded a bar to his George Medal.

28 The Bin Lahmar brothers were disaffected Fadhlis who had been recruited by the NLF to kill the British Political Officer.

29 Robin Young records a slightly different version of this incident in his diary. He was delighted that the three Labour politicians had such a

frightening experience; but we should take Stephen's account to be more accurate.

30 Abdulla al Asnag, the leader of the radical People's Socialist Party was the most influential nationalist politician at that time.

31 Captain Godfrey Meynell MC was serving as Adjutant of the Guides, one of the most distinguished of the Indian Army units. He was awarded a posthumous VC to add to his MC for his part in the action, which led to his death in 1935.

32 WAP office moved in 1960 to Hiswa on the Aden-Little Aden road, subsequently named Al Ittihad, the (short lived) Federal Capital, now known as Medinat Ash Sha'ab (People's City).

33 As Colonial Secretary he visited Aden just after the formation of the Federation.

34 Naib means deputy with, in this case, the inference of being the likely successor.

35 The Fadhlis went through Sultans at quite a lick. Abdullah Bin Othman was quietly put out to grass in 1962 to make way for Ahmed. Ahmed then defected to Egypt in 1964 and was in his turn replaced by his brother Nasser.

36 Hugh Walker: various papers sent to the author, 2003/4.

37 An RAF Officer, he had lost an arm after being shot down over Crete. His autobiography: *The Sky and the Desert* (see the memoirs section in the bibliography) describes his ten years in Aden, mostly with WAP office.

38 There is a vivid and well-researched account of this incident in Aidan Hartley's *The Zanzibar Chest* (see note 10 above).

39 Seyyids (or Sayyids) had a special status emanating from an alleged descent from the Prophet. They had a traditional role as peacemakers.

40 There was a distinct attitudinal difference between the 'young lions' in WAP office where Aden was the first job and the later arrivals from other territories. The *esprit de corps* of the first group was, with a few exceptions, exceptionally high and the same went for longer serving members of WAP Office like Robin Young and Ralph Daly who had come in from the Sudan.

41 The issuing of arms and ammunition whether as hardware or via permits to import was handled in WAP office. Individual Political Officers and especially those in the front line stations such as Dhala, Lodar and Beihan had their own stocks but these were replenished on the authority of WAP office. The actual material was kept at Champion Lines, the FG1 HQ. The pros and cons of this practice are discussed in the Robin Young chapter (Chapter 5) but Walker's views as expressed to Eric and to Healey were shared by a number of his colleagues.

42 The General Election of mid-October 1964.

43 James Nash: a letter and a paper (prepared for a government department) 14 July 2004.

44 He attracted a number of oft-repeated stories. For instance: he attended a New Year's Eve party at the (British) Khormaksar Club dressed as an

indigo warrior, covered in woad, with a brief leather skirt and carrying a short stabbing spear. He was removed from the dance floor having covered a number of his partners with woad and having consoled himself in the bar was found next morning asleep in a taxi outside the club! A number of complaints were received by the club committee about allowing 'uncouth tribesmen' into the club. John Ducker tells me that he was at this party when Nash first arrived carrying a 'filthy sack; he sat down in the middle of the dance floor and proceeded to make his coffee.

45 Much of this 'keeni meeni' (see Chapter 5, note 13) is now in the public domain. See Clive Jones, Among Ministers, Mavericks and Mandarins: Britain, Covert Action and the Yemen Civil War, 1962–64. Clive Jones. *Middle Eastern Studies* 40 (1), January 2004. It was later turned into a book. (See the historical section of the bibliography.) A list of covert operations is on pages 106–7. See also the Robin Young chapter (Chapter 5).

46 The Haza Gang. Walker reckoned that they took a lot of money and their successes were purely imaginary. He wrote a 'secret and personal' letter to Robin Young on 15 May 1965, complaining about the futile waste of resources.

47 James' counterterrorist role was taken over by a full-time (if non-career) SIS officer who had his counterparts in the other two frontier posts of Mukeiras and Beihan. They were designated as assistants to the official Assistant Advisers at Dhala, Lodar and Beihan. Some operated under *noms de guerre*.

48 Julian Paxton: paper for author, November 2003, and taped interview with Maria Holt, 29 March 2000.

49 See note 47.

50 A folk hero and legendary freedom fighter but in fact very ineffectual in most of his attacks. He later became Minister of Defence in the PDRY government and was assassinated with three fellow ministers in one of the many coups or counter coups.

51 Translated as *The Voice of the Arabs* broadcasting from Cairo. The most influential Radio station in the Arab World carrying aggressive 'Nasserism' into every home in the Middle East. Everyone had transistor radios and most people believed the message of Arab nationalism and anti-imperialism which it trumpeted. The BBC Arabic Service was also respected at an intellectual level, but was mostly inaudible in Arabia and its somewhat diffident style could not compete with the strident, populist *Sawt*.

52 One of the objects of the Radfan campaign was to restore the Amir's authority over the Radfan tribes – an authority that neither he nor his predecessors had ever effectively exercised.

53 I recorded all this (but sadly missed the pyramid) on 8 mm silent movie film. The film is with the British Commonwealth and Empire Museum in Bristol where much of the material used in this book (and a lot that wasn't) is archived.

54 John Harding: extracts from 'Lahej Recalled: Lahej Mon Amour', December 2004. Only a tiny fraction of a fascinating paper.

55 The tiny state, bordering Aden, whose main income was the rent paid for the Federal capital, Al Ittihad. It returned one member (out of 85) to the Federal Council.

56 Laundry man. One of the many Indian words in common use in Aden.

57 A large urban square or parade ground.

58 The very description aptly used by Robin Young on the role of an Assisant Adviser (see page 79).

59 Bill was the founder and first Chairman of the British Yemeni Society and Stephen Day, the second.

60 He was seconded from the regular army to swell the shrinking ranks of career Assistant Advisers.

61 I have engrossing material from Dr Graham Hunter, a senior medical officer who served in both Protectorates, from Terry Hague who also lived and worked upcountry as an Agricultural Adviser and also from Dr Freeman Grenville, the Federal Educational Adviser, who toured widely. Sadly, there is no room in this chapter for those who were not Political Officers.

CHAPTER 4

THE EASTERN ADEN PROTECTORATE (EAP)

1 BL. R/20/B/3097.

2 BL. R/20/B/3097.

3 Private communication from Stewart Hawkins dated August 2004.

4 Private communication from Stewart Hawkins dated July 2004.

5 See Michael Crouch, *An Element of Luck*, The Radcliffe Press: London, 1993. Several other references to Crouch also come from this book, with the permission of the author.

6 BL. R/20/C/1822.

7 P.S. Allfree, *Hawks of the Hadhramaut*, Robert Hale: London, 1967.

8 *MAN* No. 240 December 1963.

9 *Social and Economic Conditions and the Possibilities for Development of Socotra*, July 1966.

10 BL. R/20/D/382.

11 BL. R/20/D/382.

12 NA CAB 148/78/3605445.

13 BL. R/20/C/1949.

14 BL. R/20/C/1937.

15 BL. R/20/C/1932.

16 BL. R/20/C/1953.

17 NA. FCO8/163.

18 NA. FCO8/163.

19 NA. FCO8/162.

20 Private paper of Sultan Ghalib al Quaiti dated 1972.
21 Private communication from Joanna Ellis, April 2005.
22 PRO. FCO 60/25, UK Mission Geneva to Foreign Office, 1 September 1967.
23 Private paper of Sultan Ghalib al Quaiti dated 1972.
24 Private paper of Sultan Ghalib al Quaiti dated 1972.

CHAPTER 5

ROBIN YOUNG'S DIARIES

1 Two other distinguished ex Sudanis were V.L. Griffiths (educational adviser, based in Oxford) and Dr (Sir) Eric Pridie. He was also based in the UK, had been head of the Sudan Medical Service and made periodic advisory visits to Aden.

2 The only remaining Arabian Oryx left in the wild were rescued by an expedition to EAP in 1962. Michael Crouch was the deputy leader. These Oryx formed the basis of a herd raised in the Phoenix, Arizona, Zoo. They and their descendants have been reintroduced into the wild in Oman and in Jordan. An entertaining account of this expedition is given in *The Flight of the Unicorns* by Anthony Shepherd (Elek Books, London, 1965).

3 Aidan Hartley's Book: *The Zanzibar Chest* has an account of Peter Davey's career in WAP and his death in Dhala.

4 This was Julian Paxton. See Chapter 3 on the Political Officers.

5 Pronounced Zingibar (South Yemeni hard 'g'); the capital of the Fadhli Sultanate and after Lahej the most prosperous and best administered town in WAP at that time.

6 The Wadis Bana and Hassan could flood up to 45,000 acres of cotton growing land in the average rainy season. The Abyan Delta was part of both the Fadhli and Lower Yafa' Sultanates. The cotton (Sudanese Long Staple) growing was managed by the Abyan Board under a British manager and senior expatriate staff and was ginned locally.

7 Sayl was a seasonal flood (or series of floods) arising from heavy rain in the Yafa' mountains. If not properly controlled by a system of channels, banks and flood gates it could cause considerable damage to the irrigation network and make its way wastefully out to sea.

8 A colleague has suggested that Robin may well have been one of those Empire building Britishers who got so used to their own company, and so set in their ways that they were never interested in sharing their lives with anyone else. It's an intriguing question.

9 Not all of Robin's juniors found his management style so sympathetic. One writes: 'my perspective was that he just used his officers like chessmen (me, anyway) and I lost respect for him afterwards.' (The officer in question was sent on a very hairy and abortive flag-waving trip by Robin.) In fairness I think this was a minority view.

10 He labelled people – approvingly or disapprovingly. One colleague was always the 'late Mr so and so'. Another he found annoyingly bumptious and insensitive. These impressions tended to linger, but he would still give them marks for effort when merited.

11 Al Ittihad is the Arabic for 'The Federation'. The Federal Capital's construction started in 1963. In 1967, after the British departure it was renamed 'Medina Al Sha'ab' or The People's City.

12 The senior British government official outside Aden Colony. Before the formation of the Federation the title was 'The Adviser and British Agent'.

13 I believe that this a Swahili phrase meaning, as far as it can precisely be translated, intrigue or political machinations.

14 A charismatic character, formerly Ruler of Lower Yafa', he had intrigued against the British and had fled to the mountains of the Sultanate thoughtfully taking the proceeds of the State Treasury with him. His stronghold at Al Qara was well nigh impregnable. He remained a thorn in the side of the British and the Federation until 1967. On British withdrawal he descended from the hills expecting to be treated as a revolutionary hero. However he was imprisoned and subsequently executed by the NLF as a former reactionary Sultan and a suspected counter-revolutionary.

15 Henderson was posthumously awarded a bar to his previously awarded George Medal for deliberately interposing his body between the grenade and Trevaskis.

16 This autobiography devotes very little attention to the Aden episode, but it is clear from the book that Denis Healey had no faith in the Federation project from the outset, or, at least, a Federation dominated by traditional rulers.

17 As Permanent Secretary, Supreme Council Affairs; Cabinet Secretary would be the UK equivalent.

18 Although it did not look such a success story by this time. Even so, soon after independence, the Sudan was already having major problems with the beginning of the civil war.

19 Robin would have found most people wanting when compared to his hero Kennedy Trevaskis. Turnbull was one of the last great African pro-consuls with a glittering career culminating in bringing Tanganyika to peaceful independence. Aden was not his scene and his previous experience ill-equipped him to take on what was a poisoned chalice. Michael Crouch suggests that the Labour government were so desperate to get rid of Trevaskis that Turnbull was sweet-talked into taking the job – probably against his better judgement.

20 Donal McCarthy, a Foreign Office official, Political Adviser to the High Commission, did, on occasion worry about the loyalty of British people on secondment to the Federal government, or like Robin, civil servants working closely with it.

21 Given Healey's views – see note 16 above – he was almost certainly unmoved by Federal reactions.

22 A branch of the Aulaqi ruling family, which fell out with the reigning Sultan and turned anti-government in the 1950s and with generous assistance from the Imam of the Yemen, proved to be highly effective 'dissidents'.

23 Michael Crouch (see *An Element of Luck*) notes that when Greenwood paid his first visit to Aden as Colonial Secretary in November 1964, the head of the SIS station suggested to him that Asnag could be induced to play ball with the right inducements (i.e. 'money and power').

24 See the revealing article by Spencer Mawby in 'The Clandestine Defence of Empire: British Special Operations in the Yemen 1951–64': *Intelligence and National Security* 17 (3), Autumn 2002, pp. 105–130. And more light is cast on the skulduggery surrounding foreign intervention in the Yemeni war by Clive Jones in *Britain and the Yemen Civil War, 1962–1965*. Sussex Academic Press, Brighton, 2005.

25 A rifle with 'PF' marked on its stock had a local market value of £100. It was otherwise identical to any other Lee Enfield .303. I never found out why!

26 One colleague felt that Robin was a cynical cold-hearted operator. This is not the impression from his diaries, nor my personal recollection.

27 Jack Dye did a remarkable job in keeping the South Arabian army together as a cohesive unit at a time of revolutionary turmoil and dramatic change. Sadly I have not been able to persuade him to tell his story as part of this book.

28 This film, now transferred to video, is available with other Aden material in the archives of the British Commonwealth and Empire Museum, Bristol.

29 That day the Ma'ala Straight was handed over to the control of the South Arabian Army, and later that day Robin Young left Aden for good.

CHAPTER 6

THE MILITARY

1 With a forword by the High Commissioner, Sir Charles Johnston. Price: Ten shillings.

2 Exchange of e-mails with author in 2003.

3 The Navy, Army and Air Force Institute: an organisation established to provide facilities including shops and eating-places for British servicemen at home and overseas. Used mostly by junior members of the services; senior NCOs and Officers had their own messes.

4 Now a local hotel according to the now Rev. Colin Royce, who returned to Aden in 2001 as chaplain to the Anglican Christ Church and to the Missions for Seamen.

5 I can find no trace of this incident. Aden Radio was occasionally shot up by insurgents as being the mouthpiece of the government, but never subjected to a determined and sustained assault.

6 From an account of his time in Aden. Sent to author in 2003.

7 Retired as a Major General, one time Commandant of the Royal Military College, Sandhurst. I am indebted to him for the use of a very full memoir of his time in Aden.

8 The generic term for Scottish soldiers – generally used by officers about 'their' men.

9 As Toyne Sewell puts it: 'an agonising affliction that made life untenable!' Inflamed itchy skin sometimes in inconvenient parts of the body brought on by heat and high humidity. Sleeping in an air-conditioned room was the most effective cure.

10 From a letter to the author, June 2004.

11 From an e-mail to the author in July 2004. I found her contact details on the Aden Veteran's website.

12 Women's Royal Army Corps. Only a handful served in Aden in mostly clerical jobs.

13 The *Aden Veteran's Guest Book* has over 400 entries with comments from servicemen about life in Aden. I contacted a number of contributors via this page (http://pub28.bravenet.com/guestbook) including Brenda Harrigan and David Lawrence whose experiences were e-mailed to me. (See notes on sources of contributions.)

14 From a series of e-mails to the author in response to a questionnaire.

15 Correspondence with the author.

16 He asked if I was the Political Officer at that time. I wasn't but he believes James Nash (see later) attended the incident but was not the local Assistant Adviser.

17 From an article in the PWO's Regimental Magazine sent to the author.

18 Taped interview with Maria Holt on 10 February 2002.

19 This comes from a tape interview (10 February 2002) conducted by Maria Holt. As with all the interviews the transcription has been faithfully adhered to with no attempt at any grammatical or other corrections.

20 This does seem to indicate inaccurate briefing or simple misunderstanding. Very few APL (FRA) soldiers came from the Yemen as defined before the independence of Aden. Nearly all were from the Western Aden Protectorate with a handful of Adenis in mostly clerical positions. Defections to the Yemen, however, were not rare and the Yemen authorities both in the days of the Imam and subsequently offered generous inducements to tempt soldiers to desert.

21 In response to a written questionnaire from the author, June 2004. Additional material from his book *With the Prince of Wales' Own* Michael Russell, Norwich 1995.

22 Tillotson retired as a Major General. His *With the Prince of Wales' Own* is the official history of the regiment from 1958 when it was

formed as an amalgamation of the East and West Yorkshire Regiments. I had a short service commission with the West Yorkshire from 1955–7. Had I chosen to remain a soldier, rather than go to university, I may well have served in Aden in the military and not as a Political Officer!

23 'Pantomime' maybe but dangerous. Major Tillotson was awarded an MBE for his work in Aden, specifically for the dangerous practice of inviting grenade attacks when 'coat trailing' in Sheikh Othman.

24 A Bazooka, which fired a 3.5 inch rocket: an anti-tank weapon it could penetrate several inches into masonry and punched holes through breezeblock. Tillotson described it as the most effective weapon in the dissident's arsenal.

25 This 'intelligence' probably came from one of my (usually unreliable) informants. According to my diary entry the dissidents were a party of 40.

26 Britain's Small Wars website. I am indebted to the Webmaster for permission to reproduce some of Trooper Lynch's entry.

27 As for note 11 above.

28 This was a unit which operated, often behind enemy lines, in the North African campaign, 1941/2.

29 These were canvas water bags attached to the front of vehicles, which kept the liquid cool through movement of the car and evaporation.

30 A cavalry regiment.

31 The Khoreiba Pass – between the Radfan area and Dhala. The scene of many ambushes and mining incidents.

32 More likely to be *Qat (Catha Edulis)*. Widely chewed throughout the Yemen. It has a narcotic effect. One tribesman told me that after a Qat session he felt he could pluck aeroplanes out of the sky!

33 Too prominent as time went on for both domestic and international public opinion. Critical UN scrutiny of our Aden policies and growing unease amongst the political left in Britain ensured that air action, especially the punitive use of bombing, was less frequently authorised by the British authorities in Aden.

34 Taped interview with Maria Holt on 22 March 2003.

35 British-led campaign against rebels fighting the Sultan of Oman. Sharjah (then one of Trucial States) housed a small British base. It is now one of the seven states making up the United Arab Emirates.

36 Mohamed Aidrus features elsewhere in this book.

37 See note 33. Retaliation became increasingly difficult to authorise in the case of cross border incidents. I believe it was I (acting for Robin Young (on leave) in June 1967) who authorised the last RAF air strike before our withdrawal. This was, however, within Federal territory on a government building (!) flying the NLF flag near Mukeiras on the upper Audhali plateau.

38 There are a number of books, which describe the Radfan campaign. The most recent and benefiting from many eye-witnesses' accounts is *Aden Insurgency: The Savage War in South Arabia, 1962–67* by

Jonathan Walker. The best of the rest are (a) *The Gaysh: A history of the APL/FRA* by Frank Edwards who served as a staff officer with the FRA throughout the campaign; (b) *Last Sunset* by Stephen Harper, a Daily Express reporter covered the fighting and was an eyewitness to a number of engagements; (c) *Last Post Aden, 1964–67* by Julian Paget, who as a Lt.Col, ran the High Commissioner's Security Service and is an expert on counter-insurgency; and (d) *South Arabia: Arena of Conflict* by Tom Little, a journalist with wide Middle East experience. Perhaps the most vivid of all, much of it an oral history, covering the entire Aden military experience but with considerable material on Radfan is *Return to Aden* by Peter Richards, which is self-published and printed in Canada; 2004 (see bibliography).

39 From a letter to the author in response to a questionnaire, 10 November 2003.

40 Here again *The Gaysh* is recommended reading. In the absence of any personal accounts of operations by Arab soldiers in Federal units it is an excellent account of the Radfan and other campaigns from a FRA perspective.

41 Mostly taken from a letter, dated 4 April 2004, to Frank Edwards (author of *The Gaysh* – see note 38 above) commenting on my questionnaire.

42 The Mark II was the most effective of the anti-tank mines formerly used by the British Army. Even an armour-plated Landrover would suffer severe damage and there was a good chance of death for the occupants despite the protection. After the arrival of Egyptian forces in the Yemen in 1962 the number of mines in rebel hands dramatically increased.

43 I deal with concerns over Arab forces' 'loyalty' later in this chapter. Fortunately the number of incidents of targeting British servicemen in local units were rare. The relationship between British secondees and their Arab hosts was generally very good.

44 Taped interview with Chris Morton, 8 March 2002.

45 Letter to the author, 26 October 2002.

46 Woad in fact. Indigo in colour. Good camouflage and (like the ancient Britons) gave some protection against the elements.

47 A well-loved and colourful character known, because of his name, as the Chinese Admiral. His biography *Dry Ginger* by Richard Baker (W. H. Allen, London, 1977) is well worth reading.

48 This epithet became widespread amongst British soldiers even if it was not used as aggressively as in the unit I have in mind.

49 Memorandum dated 15 July 1964 to Lord Shawcross, Attorney General in the Labour government of 1964. Mr Besse had close contacts with politicians of both main parties through his high level commercial enterprises.

50 Who wrote *The Gaysh* (notes 38 and 40 above), in a paper for the author, April 2004.

51 Taped interview with Maria Holt, 10 March 2003 and conversation with author.

52 Woad-covered.

53 Response to questionnaire and correspondence with the author, 200/2004.

54 Taped interview with Maria Holt and correspondence with author.

55 The appointment of a long-serving senior Aulaqi officer, Colonel Nasser Bureik, as Commander Designate of the South Arabian Army (SAA) was a significant factor leading to the mutiny on 20 June 1967.

56 Letter to the author in response to a questionnaire on 20 September 2004. He retired as a Brigadier having commanded the 1 Battalion, the Welsh Guards in the Falkland campaign.

57 Robin Young confirmed that some very valuable documents, in terms of intelligence, were found on the plane. The presence of this Egyptian aircraft at Lodar proved to be embarrassing for the Federal government as local nationalists took the opportunity to hold pro-Nasser demonstrations and anti-Federal ones.

58 Letter to author in response to a letter in August 2003.

59 See *With the Prince of Wales' Own* (note 13 above) p. 29.

60 Ibid.: pp. 34 and 39.

61 Letter to author in response to a questionnaire on 8 February 2003.

62 I discuss the role played by Political Officers in gathering intelligence in Chapter 3, but I was always conscious that what I got in places like Dhala or Radfan was mostly inaccurate from low-grade sources.

63 Comment recorded by the author at that time.

64 Appended to her husband's paper.

CHAPTER 7

ADEN: THE 1966 DEFENCE WHITE PAPER

1 NA. FO 371/179751. Minute of 22 July 1965 from Sir Paul Gore-Booth to Sir Roger Allen.

2 NA. FO 371/179751. Sir Roger Allen to Permanent Under Secretary, FCO dated 22 July, 1965.

3 NA. FO 371/179751. Record of meeting on 26 July 1965 between Sir William Luce and Mr T. F. Brenchley.

4 *Observer*, 1 August 1965.

5 NA. FO 371/179751. Minute dated 23 September 1965 from Sir Roger Allen to the Secretary of State for Foreign Affairs outlining the content of a paper on Aden prepared for the Defence and Overseas Policy (Official) Committee.

6 NA. FO 371/179751.

7 NA. CO 1055/299/116690. Minutes of meeting with Federal government representatives chaired by Lord Longford.

8 NA. CO 1055/299. Statement by Lord Longford, Secretary of State for the Colonies.

9 NA. CO 1055/307. Statement by Lord Beswick to Federal Supreme Council

10 NA. CO 1055/307. Translation of statement by the Chairman of the Federal Supreme Council.

11 NA. CO 1055/299/102944.

12 Private discussion with Mr Frank Brenchley.

13 NA. CO 1055/299/102944.

14 NA CO 1055/307.

15 NA. CO 1055/299/102944.

16 NA. CO 1055/299/102944.

17 NA. CO 1055/299/102944.

18 NA. CO 1055/299/102944.

19 NA. CO/1055/299/102944.

20 NA. CO 1055/299/102944.

CHAPTER 8

BRITISH CIVILIANS REFLECT ON THE END OF EMPIRE IN ADEN

1 Interview, Motherwell, May 2000.

2 Interview, Dorset, December 1999.

3 Interview, Motherwell, May 2000.

4 Interview, Hampshire, April 2000.

5 Interview, Chelmsford, March 2000.

6 Interview, Chelmsford, March 2000.

7 Interview, 4 February 2000.

8 Interview, Surrey, November 1999.

9 Interview, Hampshire, April 2000.

10 Interview, Surrey, November 1999.

11 Interview, Perthshire, May 2000.

12 Interview, Hampshire, April 2000.

13 Interview, Perthshire, May 2000.

14 Interview, Surrey, November 1999.

15 Interview, 2 February 2000.

16 Interview, 4 February 2000.

17 Interview, Essex, 2000.

18 Interview Surrey, 1 March 2000.

19 Interview, Surrey, November 1999.

20 Interview, Surrey, March 2000.

21 Interview, London, January 2000.

22 Interview, Hampshire, April 2000.

23 Interview, Motherwell, May 2000.

24 Interview, London, January 2000.

25 Interview, Motherwell, May 2000.
26 Interview, Dorset, December 1999.
27 Interview, Perthshire, May 2000.
28 Interview, London, January 2000.
29 Interview, Surrey, November 1999.
30 Interview, Sussex, September 2003.
31 Interview, London, January 2000.
32 Interview, Dorset, December 1999.
33 Interview, Bedfordshire, March 2000.
34 Interview, Hampshire, April 2000.
35 Interview, Dorset, December 1999.
36 Interview, Essex, March 2000.
37 Dave Johnston, written account of the shooting at Khormaksar Boys Secondary School.
38 Interview, Surrey, November 1999.
39 Interview, Hampshire, April 2000.
40 Interview, Perthshire, May 2000.
41 Interview, Bedfordshire, March 2000.
42 Interview, Perthshire, May 2000.
43 Interview, Sussex, September 2003.
44 Interview, Dorset, December 1999.
45 Interview, Dorset, December 1999.

CHAPTER 9

AN ORAL HISTORY OF COLONIALISM AND REVOLUTION IN SOUTHERN YEMEN

1 Thompson, Paul, 'The voice of the past: Oral history', in Perks, Robert and Thomson, Alistair (eds), *The Oral History Reader*, London & New York: Routledge, 1998, p. 28.
2 Interview, Sana'a, 30 September 2003.
3 Interview, Aden, 8 October 2003.
4 Interview, Sana'a. 1 October 2003.
5 Interview, Sana'a, 1 October 2003.
6 Interview, Aden, 10 October 2003.
7 Interview, Sana'a, 1 October 2003.
8 Interview, Aden, 6 October 2003.
9 Interview, Aden, 10 October 2003.
10 Interview, Sana'a, 1 October 2003.
11 Interview, Aden, 5 October 2003.
12 Interview, Sana'a, 30 September 2003.
13 Interview, Sana'a, 30 September 2003.
14 Interview, Aden, 10 October 2003.
15 Interview, Aden, 4 October 2003.
16 Interview, Aden, 5 October 2003.

17 Interview, Aden, 4 October 2003.
18 Interview, Aden, 4 October 2003.
19 Interview, Aden, 4 October 2003.
20 Interview, Aden, 10 October 2003.
21 Interview, Aden, 10 October 2003.
22 Interview, Sana'a, 1 October 2003.
23 Interview, Sana'a, 1 October 2003.
24 Interview, Aden, 5 October 2003.
25 Interview, Aden, 6 October 2003.
26 Interview, Aden, 3 October 2003.
27 Interview, Aden, 10 October 2003.
28 Interview, Aden, 5 October 2003.
29 Interview, Sana'a, 1 October 2003.
30 Interview, Aden, 10 October 2003.
31 Carapico, Sheila, *Civil Society in Yemen: The Political Economy of Activism in Modern Arabia*, Cambridge: Cambridge University Press, 1998, p. 86.
32 Carapico, *Civil Society in Yemen*, p. 86.
33 Interview, Aden, 8 October 2003.
34 Interview, Aden, 6 October 2003.
35 Interview, Sana'a, 1 October 2003.
36 Interview, Aden, 6 October 2003.
37 Interview, Aden, 10 October 2003.
38 Dresch, Paul, *A History of Modern Yemen*, Cambridge: Cambridge University Press, 2000, p. 111.
39 Interview, Aden, 10 October 2003.
40 Interview, Aden, 10 October 2003.
41 Interview, Aden, 10 October 2003.
42 Interview, Sana'a, 30 September 2003.
43 Interview, Aden, 6 October 2003.
44 Dresch, Paul, *A History of Modern Yemen*, Cambridge: Cambridge University Press, 2000, p. 97.
45 Interview, Aden, 5 October 2003.
46 General Sharif Haider Saleh Al-Habili, interview with BBC, 2004.
47 Dresch, *A History of Modern Yemen*, p. 113.
48 Interview, Aden, 5 October 2003.
49 General Sharif Haider Saleh Al-Habili, 'The Incidents of Saturday 20 June 1967 in Aden', 2004, pers. comm.
50 Interview, Aden, 6 October 2003.
51 Interview, Aden, 10 October 2003.
52 Interview, Sana'a, 30 September 2003.
53 Interview, Aden, 10 October 2003.
54 Interview, Sana'a, 1 October 2003.
55 Interview, Aden, 6 October 2003.
56 Interview, Aden, 5 October 2003.
57 Harper, Stephen, 'South Arabia and Aden, 1964–1967: Tribesmen and Terrorists', in Thompson, Julian, editor, *The Imperial War Museum*

Book of Modern Warfare: British and Commonwealth Forces at War 1945–2000, London: Pan Books, in association with the Imperial War Museum, 2003, p. 239.

58 Interview, Aden, 7 October 2003.
59 Gavin, RJ, *Aden under British rule 1839–1967*, London: Hurst & Company, first published 1975, second impression 1996, p. 334.
60 Interview, Aden, 7 October 2003.
61 Interview, Aden, 10 October 2003.
62 He was 31 years old at the time of the interview.

CHAPTER 10

BRITAIN AND ADEN: A RELATIONSHIP FOR THE TWENTY-FIRST CENTURY

1 In March 2003, a military coalition, initiated and led by the United States, invaded and occupied Iraq in order to overthrow the Ba'athist regime of Saddam Hussein.
2 Wald, Peter (translated by Sebastian Wormell), *Yemen*, London: Pallas, 1996, p. 73.
3 Wald, *Yemen*, p. 246.
4 Interview, Sana'a, 30 September 2003.
5 Hudson, Michael, *Arab Politics: The Search for Legitimacy*, New Haven: Yale University Press, 1977, p. 352.
6 Interview, Al-Tawahi, Aden, 7 October 2003.
7 Interview, Aden, 7 October 2003.
8 Interview, Sana'a, 30 September 2003.
9 Interview, Aden, 10 October 2003.
10 Interview, Al-Mansurah, Aden, 6 October 2003.
11 Interview, Al-Tawahi, Aden, 7 October 2003.
12 Interview, Aden, October 2003.
13 Interview, Aden, 4 October 2003.
14 Carapico, Sheila, *Civil Society in Yemen: The Political Economy of Activism in Modern Arabia*, Cambridge: Cambridge University Press, 1998, p. 106.
15 Interview, Aden, 5 October 2003.
16 Carapico, Sheila, 'The Dialectics of Fashion: Gender and Politics in Yemen', in Joseph, Suad, and Slyomovics, Susan, editors, *Women and Power in the Middle East*, Philadelphia: University of Pennsylvania Press, 2001, p. 184.
17 Interview, Aden, 5 October 2003.
18 Meeting with group of women, Aden, October 2003.
19 *Encyclopaedia Britannica* Online.
20 Interview, Aden, 10 October 2003.
21 Interview, Aden, 4 October 2003.

APPENDIX 4

AN ORAL HISTORY OF THE BRITISH IN ADEN

1   The British side of the Aden oral history project was conducted by Maria Holt and Chris Morton in 1999–2000, under the auspices of the Council for the Advancement of Arab-British Understanding. Additional interviews were carried out by Helen Balkwill-Clark in 2003. Maria Holt visited Yemen in September–October 2003 and recorded interviews with Yemenis.

2   Tonkin, Elizabeth, *Narrating Our Pasts: The Social Construction of Oral History*, Cambridge: Cambridge University Press, 1992, p. 12.

3   Oral History Society, *Getting Started*, www.oralhistory.org.uk

4   Perks, Robert and Thomson, Alistair, 'Advocacy and Empowerment: Introduction', in Perks, Robert and Thomson, Alistair (eds), *The Oral History Reader*, London and New York: Routledge, 1998, p. 183.

5   Howarth, Ken, *Oral History*, Stroud, Glos: Sutton, 1998, p. 127.

6   Portelli, Alessandro, 'What makes oral history different', in Perks and Thomson, *The Oral History Reader*, p. 67.

7   Tonkin, *Narrating our Pasts*, p. 2.

8   Portelli, 'What makes oral history different', p. 70.

9   Gluck, Sherna, 'What's So Special About Women?' in Dunaway, David K. and Baum, Willa K. (eds) *Oral History: An Interdisciplinary Anthology*, Walnut Creek, California: Alatmira Press (a division of Sage Publications), 1996, p. 219.

10 Sangster, Joan, 'Telling Our Stories: Feminist Debates and the Use of Oral History', in Perks and Thomson, *The Oral History Reader*, p. 92.

11 Gluck, 'What's So Special About Women?', p. 219.

12 Fleischmann, 'Crossing the Boundaries of History: Exploring Oral History in Researching Palestinian Women in the Mandate Period', *Women's History Review* 5(3), October 1996, p. 361.

13 Portelli, 'What makes oral history different', p. 67.

14 Raissiguier, Catherine, 'The Construction of Marginal Identities: Working-class Girls of Algerian Descent in a French School'. In Hesse-Biber, Sharlene, Gilmartin, Christina and Lydenberg, Robin (eds) *Feminist Approaches to Theory and Methodology: An Interdisciplinary Reader*, New York & Oxford: Oxford University Press, 1999, p. 139.

15 Thompson, Paul, 'The Voice of the Past: Oral History', in Perks and Thomson, *The Oral History Reader*, p. 26.

16 Tonkin, *Narrating our Pasts*, p. 3.

17 Portelli, Alessandro, 'What makes oral history different', in Perks and Thomson, *The Oral History Reader*, p. 68.

BIBLIOGRAPHY

PRIMARILY MILITARY

Edwards, Frank (2004) *The Gaysh: A History of the Aden Protectorate Levies 1927–61 and the Federal Regular Army of South Arabia 1961–67.* Helion: Solihull. The author was an officer seconded to the FRA and this book should be seen as a companion volume to Lord and Birtles 2002.

Lord, Cliff and Birtles, David (2002) *Armed Forces of Aden, 1839–1967.* Helion: Solihull. A comprehensive account of all militias, military formations, police forces and other uniformed units raised and deployed from the establishment of Aden Colony until the British withdrawal.

Lunt, James (1966) *The Barren Rocks of Aden. Herbert Jenkins: London.* Brigadier Lunt commanded the Federal Regular Army from 1961–64. A collection of essays rather than a pure military history. Atmospheric.

Paget, Julian (1969) *Last Post Aden 1964–67.* Faber and Faber: London. Good coverage of Radfan and counter-insurgency in Aden up to the final withdrawal.

Richards, Peter (2004) *Return to Aden.* G.F. Murray: Vancouver. Memoirs of an RAF NCO stationed in Aden, 1964–65. Vivid and chatty account of a serviceman's life in Aden and the Federation at that time. Many anecdotal contributions from other people, mostly in the services. Quite good historical survey. Much on the Radfan campaign.

Tillotson, H.M. (1995) *With the Prince of Wales's Own: The Story of a Yorkshire Regiment, 1958–1994.* Michael Russell: Wilby, Norwich. The author served with the PWO in Aden in 1959 and then 1965/6. Entertaining account by a company commander.

Walker, Jonathan (2005) *Aden Insurgency: The Savage War in South Arabia, 1962–67*. Spellmount. Staplehurst: Very readable and with more detail than Julian Paget. Incorporates 'oral history' material from a number of people who served in Aden.

HISTORICAL (GENERAL)

Balfour-Paul, Glen (1991) *End of Empire in the Middle East: Britain's Relinquishment of Power in Her Last Three Arab Dependencies.* Cambridge University Press: Cambridge. A classic well-written work by a former British diplomat. The chapter on Aden is concise and authoritative. One of the best short studies.

Bidwell, Robin (1983) *The Two Yemens.* Longman westview Press: Harlow. The days of the Federation are concisely but accurately described as part of a larger history. The story is brought up to 1981.The author was a political officer in WAP from 1955–59.

Dresch, Paul (1993) *Tribes, Government and History in Yemen.* Clarendon Paperbacks: Oxford.Social and anthropological study which is very useful for understanding tribal society.

Dresch, Paul (2000) *A History of the Modern Yemen.* Cambridge University Press: Cambridge. One of the better scholarly historical studies of all Yemen. Interesting and accessible coverage of the 1960–67 period in Aden and the Federation. Some good Arabic sources mainly ignored by most other recent historians.

Gavin, R.J. (1975) *Aden under British Rule, 1839–1967.* Hurst: London. The 'definitive' history of Aden. Scholarly and well researched but comparatively 'thin' on the last ten years: 30 pages out of 350.

Halliday, Fred (1974) *Arabia without Sultans.* Penguin: London. Professor Halliday in his Marxist youth! Similar approach to Helen Lackner, but scholarly and readable.

Harper, Stephen (1978) *Last Sunset: What Happened in Aden.* Collins: London. Covers Aden's history from 1839 but is predominantly focused on the last seven years. The author worked for the Daily Express.

Holden, David *Farewell to Arabia.* Faber and Faber: London. Covers the Gulf but has interesting if gloomy coverage on the Federation up to early 1966.

Jones, Clive (2004) *Britain and the Yemen Civil War, 1962–65.* Sussex Academic Press: Brighton. Fascinating account of British (and some other governments') covert action in the Yemen in support of the royalists after the overthrow of the monarchy and the intervention of the Egyptians.

Kostiner, J. (1984) *The Struggle for South Yemen.* Croom Helm: London. Marxist interpretation of the last years of the British Empire. Heavy-going but reflects a number of nationalist sources.

Lackner, Helen (1985) *PDR Yemen: Outpost of Socialist Development in Arabia.* Ithaca Press: London. Positive account of the PDRY by a strongly socialist viewpoint. One chapter covers the 'colonial period' from a mainly nationalistic perspective.

Lapping, Brian (1985) *End of Empire.* St Martin's Press: New York. Book of Grenada TV programme in 1985. The chapter on Aden is easy reading and gives a fair if somewhat superficial account of the last years of British rule.

Little, Tom (1968) *South Arabia: Arena of Conflict.* Pall Mall Press: London. Another journalistic account (the author worked for the *Observer* and the *Economist*). Concise account of the rise and fall of the Federation. As an 'instant' book it is short on source material but readable.

Mawby, Spencer (2005) *British Policy in Aden and the Protectorates, 1955–57. Last outpost of a Middle East Empire.* Routledge: Abingdon. A very new scholarly work. Well researched and comprehensive. Written with a determinedly 'anti-colonial' bias but readable and an important contribution to scholarship on this topic.

Naumkin, Vitaly V. *Red Wolves of Yemen. The Struggle for Independence.* Oleander Press: Cambridge. By a Soviet scholar who had very close links to the NLF and lived in post-independence Aden. Mainly reliant on radical nationalistic material.

Waterfield, Gordon (2002) *Sultans of Aden.* Republished by Stacey International: London. The book originally published in 1968 describes the capture of Aden in the 1830s, but the new edition has an interesting Envoi by Stephen Day, a former political officer (see Chapter 3) covering the last years of the Federation.

MEMOIRS: SENIOR OFFICIALS AND POLITICIANS

Bell, Sir Gawain (1989) *An Imperial Twilight.* Lester Crook Academic Publishing: London. Bell was a member of the two-man constitutional commission in South Arabia in 1965 and this second volume of his memoirs covers this period.

Boustead, Sir Hugh (1971) *The Wind of Morning.* Chatto and Windus: London. Sir Hugh, a remarkable and highly eccentric colonial official/soldier/mountaineer/athlete was Resident Adviser in Mukalla in the early 1950s. A legendary colonial official's atmospheric account of life in Mukalla at a time of increasing British involvement in the Eastern Aden Protectorate.

Healey, Denis (1989) *The Time of my Life*. Michael Joseph: London. The author was Defence Secretary in the Labour Government of 1964. Surprisingly scant coverage of Aden. He never had any faith in the Federal project and it shows!

Hickinbotham, Sir Tom (1958) *Aden*. Constable: London. A good introduction to the time covered by our book. Sir Tom was Governor of Aden in the early 1950s.

Reilly, Sir Bernard (1960) *Aden and the Yemen*. HMSO: London. Sir Bernard was the Governor before Tom Hickinbotham. Good background to our period by a respected colonial servant.

Johnston, Charles (1964) *The View from Steamer Point: Three Crucial Years in South Arabia*. Collins. London. Sir Charles Johnston was Governor, later High Commissioner, Aden, from 1960–63. Light but authoritative account of his stewardship by a senior diplomat on secondment from the FCO.

Trevaskis, Kennedy (1968) *Shades of Amber*. Hutchinson: London. Sir K. Trevaskis succeeded Charles Johnston as High Commissioner in 1963. Previously he had been British Agent for the Western Aden Protectorate. Well written and more revealing than most other similar works.

Trevelyan, Humphrey (1970) *The Middle East in Revolution*. Macmillan: London.The chapter on Aden is a terse but penetrating account of his time as the last High Commissioner from May until November 1967. Solid defence of British policy of withdrawal as the least damaging of all possible options.

MEMOIRS: POLITICAL OFFICERS

Allfree, P.S. (1967) *Hawks of the Hadhramaut*. Robert Hale: London. Interesting personal memoir by a regular soldier working as a political officer in the EAP. It contains a unique description of the establishment of a British presence in the Mahra State in 1963.

Crouch, Michael (2000) *An Element of Luck: To South Arabia and Return*. Rawlhouse Publishing: West Perth, West Australia. 2nd edition (1st edition, Radcliffe Press: London, 1993). Entertaining and readable. Michael Crouch served in both protectorates and in Aden itself. He has made a major contribution to Chapter 3. Good illustrations.

Folkard, Lionel (1985) *The Sky and the Desert*. United Writers: Penzance. A former RAF squadron leader who served from 1949 until 1965. First as a RAF officer in Aden, then in WAP as a political officer and finally in WAP office at Al Ittihad. Atmospheric with a wealth of anecdotes.

Foster, Donald (1969) *Landscape with Arabs*. Clifton Books: Brighton and London. An elegant memoir by one who spent 14 years in South Arabia up to 1966. He mostly worked in WAP office.

BACKGROUND AND FUN READING

Two classics by Lord Belhaven who was the first regular political officer in WAP in the 1930s: *The Uneven Road* and the *Kingdom of Melchior*. John Murray, London, 1949 and 1955 respectively. Vivid writing about work upcountry in areas rarely penetrated by officials. *Sheba Revealed* by Nigel Groom. A political officer in Beihan just after the Second World War. Beautifully written and evocative of a period when Britain was cautiously embarking on a 'forward policy' in South Arabia. London Centre for Arabic Studies. 2002. Also well written is *The Zanzibar Chest* by Aidan Hartley. His father was a very distinguished Director of Agriculture in WAP in the early 1950s and although the book is mainly about Africa in his father's time the *leit motif* is the story of Peter Davey, a political officer who was killed in Dhala as mentioned in Chapter 2. HarperCollins, London, 2003. *Arabian Sands* is a classic travel adventure by Wilfred Thesiger. He crossed parts of the Empty Quarter in the 1940s. Some of these journeys were partly in the EAP with companions from that area. Longmans, 1946. *Arabia and the Isles* is another classic, by Harold Ingrams, who travelled in both Protectorates in the 1930s. It is particularly interesting about the Hadhramaut where 'Ingrams Peace' is still remembered. John Murray, London, 1942. And a great read by one of Arabia's most accomplished travel writers: *A Winter in Arabia* by Freya Stark. A travel diary mostly about the Hadhramaut in 1937/38, John Murray, London, 1941. *In the High Yemen* by Hugh Scott is wonderfully descriptive of Dhala, other parts of WAP and the Yemen of 1937/8. Written following a British Museum Natural History Expedition to southwest Arabia. Lavishly illustrated, John Murray, London, 1942. Another classic of travel writing is *Aden to the Hadhramaut* by Van der Meulen. He travelled through both protectorates in 1931 and again in 1939, John Murray, London, 1949. *Qataban and Sheba* is Wendell Phillips's account of an American archaeological expedition to the Beihan/Harib area in 1950. Interesting on the ancient kingdom of Qataban and on the old spice routes. Victor Gollancz, London, 1955. *The Flight of the Unicorns* by Anthony Shepherd is a memoir of the expedition which captured the few remaining Oryx in the EAP to start a breeding programme in captivity. Elek Books, London, 1965. *Island of the Dragon's Blood* by Douglas Botting is about another expedition, this time to Socotra in the 1950s. Hodder and Stoughton, London, 1958. *From Aden to the*

Gulf: Personal Diaries, 1956–1966 by Lady Margaret Luce, the wife of Sir William Luce, Governor of Aden, 1956–60. Good on life in Aden as a senior official's spouse at a time of significant political change. Michael Russell, Salisbury, 1987. More journalistic in style and with a light touch is *The Sultans Came to Tea* by June Knox-Mawer, the young wife of the chief magistrate in Aden in the late 1950s, who hobnobbed with the Lahej Ruling family. Gentle and gossipy. Buck and Tanner, Frome and London, 1961. *Yemen Travels in Dictionary Land* by Tim Mackintosh-Smith is an insider's travel book mostly about the northern Yemen but also about the former Federation and the old EAP. Witty. Historical coverage of the pre-independence period is too reliant on nationalist sources to be an objective or accurate record.

ORAL HISTORY PROJECT

Carapico, Sheila, *Civil Society in Yemen: The Political Economy of Activism in Modern Arabia*, Cambridge: Cambridge University Press, 1998.

Carapico, Sheila, 'The Dialectics of Fashion: Gender and Politics in Yemen', in Joseph, Suad, and Slycomovics, Susan, editors, *Women and Power in the Middle East*, Philadelphia: University of Pennsylvania Press, 2001.

Fleischmann, 'Crossing the Boundaries of History: Exploring Oral History in Researching Palestinian Women in the Mandate Period', *Women's History Review* 5/3, October 1996.

Gluck, Sherna, 'What's So Special About Women?' in Dunaway, David K., and Baum, Willa K., editors, *Oral History: An Interdisciplinary Anthology*, Walnut Creek, California: Alatmira Press (a division of Sage Publications), 1996.

Harper, Stephen, 'South Arabia and Aden, 1964–1967: Tribesmen and Terrorists', in Thompson, Julian, editor, *The Imperial War Museum Book of Modern Warfare: British and Commonwealth Forces at War 1945–2000*, London: Pan Books, in association with the Imperial War Museum, 2003.

Howarth, Ken, *Oral History*, Stroud, Glos.: Sutton, 1998.

Hudson, Michael, *Arab Politics: The Search for Legitimacy*, New Haven: Yale University Press, 1977.

Oral History Society, *Getting Started*, www.oralhistory.org.uk

Perks, Robert, and Thomson, Alistair, 'Advocacy and Empowerment: Introduction', in Perks, Robert, and Thomson, Alistair, editors, *The Oral History Reader*, London and New York: Routledge, 1998.

Portelli, Alessandro, 'What makes oral history different', in Perks, Robert, and Thomson, Alistair, editors, *The Oral History Reader*, London and New York: Routledge, 1998.

Raissiguier, Catherine, 'The Construction of Marginal Identities: Working-class Girls of Algerian Descent in a French School', in Hesse-Biber, Sharlene, Gilmartin, Christina, and Lydenberg, Robin, editors, *Feminist Approaches to Theory and Methodology: An Interdisciplinary Reader*, New York and Oxford: Oxford University Press, 1999.

Sangster, Joan, 'Telling Our Stories: Feminist Debates and the Use of Oral History', in Perks and Thomson, editors, *The Oral History Reader*, London and New York: Routledge, 1998.

Thompson, Paul, 'The Voice of the Past: Oral History', in Perks and Thomson, editors, *The Oral History Reader*, London and New York: Routledge, 1998.

Tonkin, Elizabeth, *Narrating our pasts: the Social Construction of Oral History*, Cambridge: Cambridge University Press, 1992.

Wald, Peter (translated by Sebastian Wormell), *Yemen*, London: Pallas, 1996.

INDEX